MORE PRAISE FOR *BRANDS THAT ROCK*

From the first time I saw the phrase "band loyalty" I knew this wasn't a typical, dry marketing tome. Leave it to Roger and Tina to find pure marketing wisdom in a perfectly logical, yet entirely overlooked (and unappreciated) place–rock music! But it works. Open your mind and open *Brands That Rock* to kick-start your marketing creative juices.

> Phil Urban, CEO
> Grange Insurance

Brands That Rock strikes a pleasing chord, whether you're a Fortune 500 CEO, a first-year MBA student, or simply a musician at heart. The authors remind us that our love affair with music can translate into lucrative rewards if strategically linked to a progressive marketing approach.

> Lloyd Trotter, President and CEO
> General Electric Industrial Company

Blackwell scores! A fascinating read that connects you emotionally to the hidden brand strategies in rock's legendary bands. A fresh approach to creating profitable and successful brands in a dynamic marketplace, *Brands That Rock* provides a rockin' road map to successful brand creation and dominance.

> J. E. Issler, President and COO
> H.H. Brown Shoe Company, Inc.,
> a subsidiary of Berkshire Hathaway, Inc.

Not only do Roger and Tina analyze branding and marketing strategies from the world of rock and roll, they show you how some of the world's great companies have implemented similar strategies to capture market share and customer loyalty.

> Walden O'Dell, CEO
> Diebold

Once our parents worried about the influence rock musicians would have on us. In *Brands That Rock,* Roger Blackwell and Tina Stephan convince us that it's a *must* to learn from the rock jocks. The lessons of rock-and-roll branding apply to companies universally.

> Don Peppers and Martha Rogers, Founders
> Peppers and Rogers Group
> Coauthors, *One-to-One* book series

Roger Blackwell 'rocks' audiences when he speaks to groups around the world. Now the passion and energy audiences have seen in person are translated to the pages of *Brands That Rock*—in which he and Tina show how that same passion helps energize great brands.

> Jose Silibi Neto,
> Partner and Cofounder
> HSM Group

A guitar has been part of our brand for many years and *Brands That Rock* shows why and how music makes such a strong emotional connection with customers. We were so impressed with this book that we intend to make it mandatory reading for our marketing and advertising staff.

> Rhett C. Ricart, President and CEO
> Ricart Automotive, Inc.

By examining how bands that evolve become brands that endure, Stephan and Blackwell show enterprises of any kind how to create more fans and capture more revenue.

> R. Brad Martin, Chairman and CEO
> Saks Incorporated

Roger and Tina always bring fresh thinking to marketing topics. This time, lessons from the world of rock and roll. It's unique, insightful . . . and fun reading.

> Tom Moser, Vice Chairman, Consumer & Industrial Businesses
> KPMG LLP

A fun read filled with new ideas and out-of-the-box analogies, *Brands That Rock* makes an emotional connection with the reader and gives strategic guidance to anyone interested in creating brands that last.

Howard D. Putnam, speaker and author
Former CEO, Southwest Airlines

Roger has tread where the consumers are fickle, loyalty lasts through one turn of the platter, and few brands survive. *Brands That Rock* explores new territory in how brands evolve and stay current with their consumer base. In today's fragmented marketing world, this is a great new source of ideas.

Jim Oates, former President
Leo Burnett Company

In a time when brands are looking for new ways to connect with customers, great companies are stepping outside the business arena to examine how other industries create fans. In *Brands That Rock,* Tina and Roger help you take a fun, bold leap.

David Chu, Vice Chairman and Chief Creative Officer
Nautica Enterprises

Roger and Tina have shown us all how the sweetest music ever sung can sweeten companies' bottom lines and entertain others.

Jack Kahl, Founder and former CEO
Manco, Inc.

I've been fortunate to have helped develop strong brands like Barbie, Hot Wheels, Sega, Sonic the Hedgehog, and Leapfrog, to name a few. Music was strongly identified with the Barbie and Sega brands and very important to building their popularity. The Sega Scream even became part of rock concert culture. Yet the strong analogy between what it takes to be an enduring rock-an-roll band and building a strong brand had never occurred to me. Roger Blackwell and Tina Stephan make it crystal clear. . . . Who would have guessed that Sam Walton, Wal-Mart, Gene Simmons, and KISS have a lot in common?

Tom Kalinske, Chairman
LeapFrog
Former CEO, Sega and Mattel Inc.

Whether your brands are consumer packaged goods or business-to-business, *Brands That Rock* provides a fresh, stimulating perspective on how to connect with your consumers and customers. Rock 'n' read on!

John Hayek. Senior Vice President of Marketing–
Office Products Group
MeadWestvaco Consumer & Office Products

I really enjoyed *Brands That Rock* and read some chapters twice. Your use of the bands as a source of information to communicate about brands is very useful.

Michael O'Neal, President and CEO
Gemini Industries Inc.

I always thought of branding as being on stage, as being entertainment. *Brands That Rock* proves that brands can sing, play guitar, wear huge amounts of makeup, and trash hotel rooms. Just like any good brand should.

Nick Graham, Founder and Chief Underpants Officer,
Joe Boxer

Brands That Rock is a fascinating and insightful journey of how to make customers of ordinary brands into raving fans by learning from what music legends such as the Rolling Stones, Elvis Presley, and Aerosmith do to arouse strong emotional bonds in their audiences on a global basis. I particularly enjoyed reading the brand making of Elton John!

If you are into branding, this book is a must read!

Jagdish N. Sheth, Charles H. Kellstadt
Professor of Marketing
Goizueta Business School
Emory University

BRANDS THAT ROCK

What Business Leaders Can Learn
from the World of Rock and Roll

BRANDS
THAT
ROCK

ROGER BLACKWELL
TINA STEPHAN

WILEY

John Wiley & Sons, Inc.

Copyright © 2004 by Roger Blackwell and Tina Stephan. All rights reserved.

Published by John Wiley & Sons, Inc., Hoboken, New Jersey.
Published simultaneously in Canada.

Limit of Liability/Disclaimer of Warranty: While the publisher and author have used their best efforts in preparing this book, they make no representations or warranties with respect to the accuracy or completeness of the contents of this book and specifically disclaim any implied warranties of merchantability or fitness for a particular purpose. No warranty may be created or extended by sales representatives or written sales materials. The advice and strategies contained herein may not be suitable for your situation. The publisher is not engaged in rendering professional services, and you should consult a professional where appropriate. Neither the publisher nor author shall be liable for any loss of profit or any other commercial damages, including but not limited to special, incidental, consequential, or other damages.

Designations used by companies to distinguish their products are often claimed as trademarks. In all instances where John Wiley & Sons, Inc. is aware of a claim, the product names appear in initial capital or all capital letters. Readers however, should contact the appropriate companies for more complete information regarding trademarks and registration.

For general information on our other products and services please contact our Customer Care Department within the United States at (800) 762-2974, outside the United States at (317) 572-3993 or fax (317) 572-4002.

Wiley also publishes its books in a variety of electronic formats. Some content that appears in print may not be available in electronic books. For more information about Wiley products, visit our web site at www.Wiley.com.

Library of Congress Catloging-in-Publication Datat

Blackwell, Roger D.
    Brands that rock : what the music industry can teach marketers about customer loyalty / Roger Blackwell and Tina Stephan.
        p. cm.
    Includes index.
    ISBN 0-471-45517-2 (cloth)
        1. Music trade.   2. Musicans—Marketing.   3. Popular music—Economic aspects.
    I. Stephan, Tina.   II. Title.
    ML3790.B6   2003
    658.8'23—dc22   2003017894

Printed in the United States of America

10 9 8 7 6 5 4 3 2 1

CONTENTS

ACKNOWLEDGMENTS

What can business leaders learn from rock and roll? It's a question that appears simple, yet it proved to be extraordinarily complex. The answer started as one that was entertaining (to us, and we hope to you), yet it yielded highly educational principles. The topic was conceptually intriguing, yet verbally challenging. These polarities of a seemingly contradictory paradigm excited us as we began talking to friends, professors, and business leaders ranging from frontline salespeople to CEOs about the *Brands That Rock* concept. Most nodded with gestures of increasing understanding as they began to grasp the power of the paradigm, with many adding the question, "But where did you get the idea for the book?"

It happened during a five-mile run on a hot summer afternoon in 2001. A DJ from a local rock station announced, with surprise in his voice, that the Aerosmith *Just Push Play* concert scheduled for a local amphitheater later that summer had sold out. His comments focused on why a group of fifty-something guys, who had been playing together almost 30 years, could not only continue to fill venues but continue to produce hit rock songs that appealed to young consumers as much as to aging baby boomers like themselves.

The DJ's question was intriguing, and we took it a few steps further to make it our absorbing hypotheses for research. Why do some bands and musicians stand the test of time, producing hits decade after decade, while others are doomed to one-hit-wonder infamy? What does it take to become a part of fans' life soundtracks and a part of American culture? What are the parallels in business?

It wasn't long before we began to develop a model that could help firms win fans for their products and improve profits for their stakeholders. We saw the process as one of customers migrating to become loyal customers and eventually to become fans, producing brand equity, a topic we had addressed together while writing an op-ed piece for the annual report of Wendy's several years earlier. Together, we had also written a case study for Wendy's, identifying the role of Wendy Thomas and her father, Dave, in building a brand that could compete very successfully against much larger firms. The research for that case helped us clarify the roles of functional attributes of products, but it also focused the spotlight on the role of a personality like Dave Thomas and his passion for "the best burgers in the business."

What can Gene Simmons of KISS and Sam Walton, founder of the world's largest corporation, have in common? That was a question asked by some of our more skeptical colleagues. Remember when Sam Walton donned a grass skirt and danced the hula on Wall Street? The makeup on the members of KISS and a grass skirt on Mr. Sam are not that different—they both create an emotional connection, whether the fans are rock and rollers or Wall Street analysts. And that's just a beginning to the insights we found when we built on decades of research about consumer behavior and branding and added the secrets of why some rock bands and performers last for decades.

Our goal in writing this book is to show how those principles apply to the marketing of companies, products, services, nonprofit organizations, and people themselves. Hence, *Brands That Rock*—a book we hope you'll enjoy and learn from whether you are a business enthusiast, a rock-and-roll fan, or both.

In a project such as this one, heartfelt thanks abound. First and foremost, we would like to thank Laureen Rowland, agent extraordinaire, who's been a part of our last three books. During the course of this project, however, she departed the David Black Agency, leaving us in the capable hands of Joy Tutela, whose guidance was invaluable. So was the direction of Airié Stuart, our editor at Wiley. Her excitement for this book never wavered; in fact it fueled us, even during moments of weariness. Many thanks also go to Michelle Patterson, Jesica Church, and Emily Conway, all part of the Wiley team.

Brands That Rock resulted from more than consultation with editors and agents, however. It resulted from hundreds of conversations with industry leaders, performers, business executives, friends, and students, all of whom cannot possibly be listed. Yet, special thanks go to the following people who provided great insight, reviewed chapters, challenged us, and encouraged us: Scott Semerar, Jim Oates, Jim Miller, Brian McCarthy, John Collins, Dan Morris, Phil Urban, Rhett Ricart, Christopher Connor, Angela Haslett, Jack Kahl, Jack Shewmaker, Ohio Secreetary of State Ken Blackwell, Cheryl Weeks, Nathan Ebert, Rebecca Cummings, Michael O'Neal, Neeli Bendapudi, Dave Robbins, Xen Riggs, Ian Smith, Josie Natori, Jose Carranza, Jim Issler, Jay Pauley, Sean Dunn, Mike Loparo, Henry Juszkiewicz, Carmine Appice, Dwayne Johnson, Rita Carroll, Bob Coppedge, Craig Deep, David Fisher, Dennis M. Fisher, Joe Mallin, Cynthia and Gary Kinman, Tom Ham, Ric Dillon, Nick Chilton, Dan Hill, Kris Carter, Kathy Gornik, Paul Lambert, Jorge Donoso, Roberto Abramson, Bonnie Brannigan, David Pugh, Michelle Manning, Kim Solomon, Matthew Goldstein, Kelly Mooney, John Mariotti, Jim Wyland, Jim Haring, Susan Lapetina, Michael Lynch, Raj Bhavsar, Tim Miller, Tom Thon, Sheri Spelman, Jonathon Easley, Mazen El-Khatib, Steven Burgess, Mike Henry, Stuart Burgdoerfer, Brian O'Leary, and Zachary Meade.

The Rock and Roll Hall of Fame was also supportive during the preparation of this manuscript. Terry Stewart, executive director of the hall, gave willingly of his time and knowledge about the music industry, and his insights are reflected on several pages in this book. Jim Henke, curator extraordinaire, was also a great resource.

The Fisher College of Business also played an instrumental role in creating the final version of *Brands That Rock*, especially Roger's MBA students who volunteered to read, review, and comment on many of the concepts and strategies contained in this book. Comments from the technology management MBA students at the University of Washington were also helpful, especially the careful editing of key chapters by Dave Sampson. Of particular assistance during this process was Farzen Bharucha, who was exceptionally effective as Roger's teaching assistant at the Fisher College of Business, and we thank all of the faculty members in the marketing and logistics department, who inspired us to look for new research topics. The musical preferences and reactions of Roger's undergraduate students forced us to see things through the eyes of today's generation and tomorrow's consumers. One of the joys of teaching in a comprehensive, diverse, leadership university such as The Ohio State University is the opportunity to see tomorrow before it happens.

Special thanks are warmly expressed to Dr. Joseph Alutto, dean of the Fisher College of Business, for his encouragement to transcend the walls of the university, glean lessons from the business community, and impact the world of commerce. We also thank him for his patience and support in times of adversity. And we express appreciation to Dr. Karen Holbrook, president of The Ohio State University, who we know enjoys Paul McCartney concerts!

Special friends and colleagues take writing a book from possible to pleasurable. Thank you to Kelley Hughes, who kept the Roger Blackwell Associates office running during yet another writing hiatus, and to Mary Hiser for helping with research, preparing the manuscript for final submission, and coordinating contacts with the many organizations involved in this book.

Finally, we would like to thank the most important people in our lives—our families. Roger would like to thank his parents, Dale, who at 88 years of age scoured the Internet for up-to-date music information, and Rheva, who baked cookies and showed her love in many ways. Special thanks to Becca Blackwell, who always provides much-needed comic relief, and Christian and Frances Blackwell, whose emotional support will always be remembered, as will the hugs and laughter of Josette and Lindsey. Tina would like to thank her parents, Trudy and Al, for their extraordinary love and unwavering support during this process; it will always be cherished, perhaps more than they will ever know. Gavin Cadwallader's insights into popular music and Anna Cadwallader's unending energy and hugs are deeply appreciated as well. Special thanks also to Tina's "research associates"— Karen Kasich, Christine Demos, Dara Pizzuti, Holly Hollingsworth, and Susan Meeder—for their true friendship and to "The Quartet" for their newfound friendship and support. Finally, Tina gives special thanks to God for His unending wonders, especially the gift of sunshine, which brightens every day and reminds her of the difference between existing and living.

After collaborating on eight books together in 12 years, we realize that we've taken a few steps toward the "legendary band" category of the business book world. For us, a great rock concert is somewhat reflective of writing a book. Our written concerts begin with an idea that sparks our curiosity, fuels research and deep discussions, and ignites the passion and energy required to complete a manuscript. And they end with a toast to the final word. As for the *Brands That Rock* concert, the house lights are now on—a revealing time in which we get to observe people's reactions to our thoughts. It is also a time of self-reflection during which we think back on the process, smile at the outcome, and thank each other for our dedication to the project and our support of each other.

So, put on your favorite CD or MP3 tracks, open the following pages, and *rock on*.

FROM BAND LOYALTY TO BRAND LOYALTY

Music washes away from the soul the dust of everyday life.
—JOHANN SEBASTIAN BACH

Your first kiss. Your first car. The day you said "I do." Chances are the most memorable moments of your life are connected by a soundtrack of music—songs that heighten your senses and evoke emotions that help you experience those memories all over again.

Perhaps that soundtrack includes Wagner's triumphal "Bridal March" from *Lohengrin,* sparking an overwhelming sense of joy and expectation, or Sarah McLachlan's "I Will Remember You," recalling the painful breakup of a love not meant to be. Or perhaps it's a pulsating refrain from Aerosmith's classic rock song "Love in an Elevator," reminding you of—well, you get the idea. Regardless of the style of music included in your soundtrack, the magic lies in the ability of music and the bands that create it to connect with people at an emotional level.

Think of what happens when U2, the Rolling Stones, Janet Jackson, or Pink Floyd enters the stage in front of a crowd of 50,000. People scream as a band member walks toward their side of the arena, they cheer at the opening riffs of their favorite tunes, they belt out the words to most of the songs, and they dance, jump, and rock for hours. These are not just "crazy" teenagers; they are people with families, good jobs, college or graduate degrees—in fact, we may even be describing you. And while you probably don't walk around your office building or community screaming, singing, and dancing, you become swept away by the concert experience—letting yourself behave like every other fan in the house.

The power of music is undeniable; the loyalty showered upon those who create it, unmatched; and the lessons for corporate America, boundless.

It is difficult to think of any product or industry that evokes more emotional intensity from its followers than rock and roll. Their attitudes and behavior shatter the traditional measures of customer loyalty in terms of reach, quantity, and degree to define outright fanaticism—the ultimate level of devotion a firm can hope to receive from its customers.

What is it about music and rock stars that transform people's emotions, behavior, and lives? Enlightened marketers have asked the question, but few have ever bothered to look for the answers. Yet corporate executives sit day after day scratching their heads, looking for insight as to how their brands might inspire even a fraction of such emotional response, loyalty, and commitment. They benchmark the success of others; analyze what promotional and design strategies have worked in the past; and review their advertising and promotional campaigns. And while marketers have been proficient in analyzing how to create successful brands and satisfy customers, most of their strategies mirror those that other businesses have already implemented.

But what of the companies looking to go one better than what other businesses have been able to accomplish in the battle for customer loyalty? Creating such a breakthrough often requires a bold leap out of one's comfort zone and into the unknown. Only then can marketers identify the processes and strategies that, when applied to the business world, can provide a leg up on their competitors.

Few look beyond the world of commerce for answers. Why, after performing for over 30 years, do the Rolling Stones continue to sell out venues around the world? How has Elton John been able to have a top-10 hit each year for 30 consecutive years? And how is Neil Diamond able to sell out concerts with minimal PR and advertising expenditures night after night? The answer is *band loyalty*—the fanatical devotion and propensity to spend that rock-and-roll followers have to a specific performer or band.

How bands create loyalty and devotion in their fans is the focus of this book. The book is designed to help unlock the secrets of how to build emotional connections between your brand or company and your customers similar to those associated with legendary rock-and-roll acts and their fans. It will take you behind the music and reveal branding and marketing lessons that can boost creative thinking, increase market share, enhance the longevity and success of a brand, and create a brand that becomes a cultural icon.

The artists, however, are the first to admit that some of their successes were not necessarily by design. In retrospect, the process of examining why some bands have increased in popularity, remained commercially successful, and increased their fan bases for several decades yields tactics that marketers might use to boost their brand loyalty.

Analyzing the phenomenon of band loyalty is not for the close-minded. It requires marketers and managers to abandon the language and corporate-based thinking they probably engage in day in, day out at work and escape into the wild, fun, larger-than-life world of music and entertainment. Marketers must look beyond the values of bands that they may not personally endorse and open their minds to the ideas and creative processes used in the entertainment arena to cultivate long-term, die-hard fans. Only then can they understand band loyalty and the lessons they can apply to enhance their own *brand* loyalty.

BEYOND CUSTOMER LOYALTY: CREATING SINGING, SCREAMING, MONEY-SPENDING FANS

In today's competitive arena, the battle to attract and retain customers is intense. Firms of all sizes continue revamping their product and service offerings, honing their customer service skills, and revising their loyalty programs. Yet few achieve an emotional connection with their customers.

Ask the most successful music acts of the past three decades about customer loyalty, and they'll tell you it's all about creating *fans*—people willing to stand in line for hours to buy the latest albums of their favorite bands or plunk down hundreds of dollars to buy concert tickets. Although this category of customer is not exclusive to the world of rock and roll, fans are far more prevalent and the lessons are more profuse than in the world of commerce.

Why? Because the music world is fan-oriented; in fact the word *customer* is rarely used. *Customer* implies that a person walks into a store wanting to buy a CD and decides, after scanning the thousands of albums available, which one to snatch up. A *fan* walks into the store with the intent of buying the latest Alanis Morissette CD; the person made the decision long before he or she entered the store, because the fan's desire is not just to buy the latest music but to create a further connection with a particular band or performer. Often the need is even more innate—helping people deal with emotions and express what they are feeling, achieving what Hallmark does in written communication and human emotion.

Although all firms in business today have customers, only the most successful have *fans*. Why all the interest in creating fans? Because of the effect attitudes and buying behavior have on long-term sales and profit levels. In short, *customers* buy from a variety of retailers and choose many brands, often influenced by temporary price breaks or other promotions. Firms spend more promotional dollars securing purchases from cherry-pickers (whose tendency to buy a specific brand can be described as sporadic at best) than they do capturing more sales from loyal or frequent customers. *Friends* (loyal customers) tend to buy certain brands and shop specific stores more often than others—often because of good past experiences. Loyalty programs have helped retailers and consumer product companies foster relationships with consumers and modify their cherry-picking behavior.

Fans, however, take loyalty to the next level, seeking out specific brands, shopping only certain retailers, and closing their minds to other alternatives, as seen in Figure 1.1. Fans invest time, attention, energy, emotion, and money into building and maintaining a relationship to a brand, and these strong emotional attachments between company and customer are difficult, if not impossible, for others to break. And fans are vocal—they not only tell others about their favorite brands, they recruit others to buy what they buy and shop where they shop. Customers and devotees can be described more in terms of their frequency of behavior, while fans are described more in terms of the emotionality and intensity of their behavior. Fans don't drink coffee, they crave Starbucks. Fans don't drive a car or ride a motorcycle, they pilot a Saturn or a Harley-Davidson.

FIGURE 1.1   Customers versus Friends versus Fans

Customers	Friends (Repeat Customers)	Fans
Are price-driven	Are value-driven	Are experience-driven
Shop opportunistically	Shop purposefully	Shop for pleasure
Want you to sell them products	Want products and good service	Want personalized advice and solutions
Need a reason to buy from you	Prefer to buy from you	Are devoted to you and are yours to lose
Are surprised by good service	Have a history of good experiences with you	Automatically assume you will delight them
Drop you if they're disappointed	Tell you if they're disappointed and give you a chance to respond	Tell you if they're disappointed, want you to fix it, and are anxious to forgive and forget
Are indifferent to your company	Feel a connection with you, rationally and/or emotionally	Actively invest in their relationship with you—time, emotion, attention, money
Don't think or talk about your firm	Recommend your firm casually	Evangelize about your firm

In that category is Target, or "Tar-zhay," as so many of its devoted fans like to call it. A mass retailer to the casual observer, Target has bridged the gap between discount store and department store by combining the best of both worlds, offering value-oriented prices to customers who don't want to sacrifice quality, aesthetics, and style. Its affordable, up-to-date clothing, hip accessories, and design-forward home fashions have made Target a cool place to shop and branded the people who buy there as shopping-savvy. No longer categorized as merely a department store's stepchild, Target has moved discount retailing from outcast to star status, with more than half of its customers having college degrees and incomes over $50,000. In the past, many consumers were reluctant to give someone a gift from a discount retailer, afraid of the negative connotation. Today, a gift from Target is not only accepted, it's often requested—with the help of Target's national gift registry program.

Have branding and fans made a difference to Target? You bet. Similar to bands that evolve from warm-up acts for their better-known counterparts to top headliners, Target's image, supported by its operations systems, became the retailer of choice rather than retailer by default for millions of loyal buyers. This translated into $44 billion in sales in 2002, after a decade of growth and profitability based on the strength of a brand that gave consumers a reason to drive past Kmart or other competitors to get to Target. Just as the Dave Matthews Band evolved from opening for Big Head Todd and the Monsters to headlining and selling out stadiums (Big Head Todd still delights its loyal following at smaller, more intimate venues), Target's brand, image, and strategies were more successful than that of its parent, Dayton Hudson. Soon, the parent changed its family name to Target, capitalizing on the company's strong fan base and brand presence to create a stock market darling in the late 1990s and early 2000s.

But even a superstar such as Target can face problems and fall from its fans' graces. Diana Ross discovered during her 2000 tour that one surefire way to alienate fans is to create high expectations and fall short at the execution stage. Billed as a glitz and glamour concert extravaganza, with ticket prices to evoke high expectations, Ross missed cues and forgot the words to many of her songs. Critical disdain and fan backlash forced her to cancel the rest of the tour.

Cher also created high expectations for her farewell tour—but unlike Ross, Cher delivered.

"Cher's entire concert tour sold out because of how she communicates and connects with her legions of fans," explains Scott Shannon, program director of New York's legendary FM station, WPLJ. "Critics can't stand her; radio certainly doesn't love her; but her fans are among the most loyal in the business. While Diana Ross fell flat and didn't connect with her audiences, Cher wowed her fans night after night with a string of high-voltage concerts that left fans dancing in the aisles and screaming for more."

One of the risks Target faces in terms of its branding strategy is creating expectations through its advertising that might not be met when customers shop its stores. The images and expectations that slick, design-oriented ad campaigns conjure up must be congruent with the experiences inside the store or else retailers risk customer dissatisfaction and fan backlash. Although a fate similar to that of Ross seems harsh, success similar to Cher's seems unlikely for retailers who fall short of customers' expectations.

Creating and strengthening relationships with customers has been on corporate America's radar screen for quite some time—with the need for intimacy creating the largest blip. In recent years, marketers have implemented customer relationship management (CRM) programs and strategies to guide their relationships with customers. Much progress has been made in terms of creating customer databases that track everything from individuals' product choices and buying patterns to their birthdays and anniversaries. These data help marketers forecast sales of specific items, narrow customers' product choices to those they are most likely to buy, and even remind customers it is time to buy a birthday gift.

Even the best CRM software, however, can't transform customers into fans—that requires an in-depth, from-the-gut understanding of and respect for human nature and behavior. The devotion of long-term fans to their favorite performers and bands, from Tony Bennett to the Kinks or 50 Cent, illustrates that it takes a connection at a deeper level to develop brands that people will not only buy, but incorporate into their lives and daily vernacular. And that is a primary goal of brand strategies—determining how strong those emotional connections are and how they can be reinforced or altered to develop loyalty to the brand among a target group of customers.

Rock-and-roll bands are notorious for writing lyrics, creating music and rhythms, and putting on shows that mirror what people are doing and what they fantasize about doing—the right mix of which entices certain fans to embrace certain bands. Once a performer makes that connection with a fan, it takes song after song, album after album, and concert after concert to cement the relationship. If a performer veers too far away from what has made a connection with a fan in the past, the connection may be jeopardized. But a song that makes an emotional connection remains in a fan's personal greatest hits collection; the loyalty and emotional connection is only strengthened with each song that is added to the list.

Jock Bartley experienced much success in the 1970s when his band, Firefall, topped the charts with a string of hits including "That's a Strange Way" and "Just Remember I Love You." But it was "You Are the Woman" that made the biggest connection with fans. "Every female between the ages of 18 and 24 wanted to be the woman portrayed in that song, and that caused their boyfriends and spouses to call radio stations and subsequently flood the airwaves with dedications of the song and the sentiment," explains Bartley. "The message was simple and sincere, and the song was easy to sing. It was like our fans let us be a singing version of the Hallmark card that said what they weren't quite sure how to express."

After 25 years, chances are you'll hear this song in office buildings or elevators. "I remember, not too long ago, sitting in my dentist's chair and hearing 'You Are the Woman.' And that's when it hit me how ingrained the song had become. The mistake we made was not to associate the Firefall brand with our songs enough." Bartley adds, "When you mention Firefall, a lot of people tip their heads in recognition of the name, but it's not until you sing a few words of a song that the light of recognition really turns on."

As Bartley points out, a brand promotion that doesn't tie the product and brand closely together doesn't create as much long-term equity for the brand as one that makes the connection clear and reinforces it over time.

Emil Brolick, CEO of Taco Bell, agrees. Faced with the tough job of taking over the company after several years of declining sales—and, yes, axing the famous Chihuahua—Brolick made some important strategic decisions. The first was shifting the direction of the advertising campaign to focus on Taco Bell's products and brand. "While the Chihuahua got a lot of attention, the campaign was all about the dog. It needed to be about Taco Bell—our food, our stores, our strengths," says Brolick. "For direction and insight, we turned to our customers."

Through a series of focus groups, Brolick learned firsthand about the current state of the Taco Bell brand. "While our heavy users told us about some problems they thought we had, I was amazed by the passion they had for the brand. In essence, they wanted Taco Bell to pull itself up by its socks and deliver in the marketplace so they could support the brand of their choice—they wanted to be proud of the brand that they supported," he says. With a smile, he adds, "I really sensed an emotional connection between our fans and our brand. In a way, our customers identified with the brand that they saw as 'one beat off center' and they wanted us to fare well in what others might categorize a burger world."

Marketers take note: You have to get under your customers' skin, inside their minds and souls, and figure out what makes them tick if you want to create an emotional connection. Why do they laugh or cry, and when do they think it's appropriate to do either? What makes them angry, and how do they deal with their emotions? How do they define success, fulfillment, and living happily ever after? Understanding your customers, over time, at an emotional level and communicating with them accordingly is an important part of brand-building and brand-loyalty strategies.

THE VALUE OF A BRAND

Building brands is a key management skill for any firm. It doesn't matter whether you are a surgeon or a store, a manufacturer or a wholesaler, an Intel or an Amazon.com, a nonprofit organization, a for-profit corporation, or the Rolling Stones. Some brands, such as Wal-Mart and Victoria's Secret, are highly successful. Some were once stellar in consumer acceptance, but turned disastrous—Montgomery Ward and Kmart come to mind—and others simply were put out to pasture, like Borden's famous mascot Elsie the Cow. But regardless of how good, how bad, or how poorly designed and nebulous, every firm, every institution, and every person is a brand. Even government leaders are brands—consider how the brands of Presidents Clinton and Bush and Mayor Giuliani evolved during their terms of office.

A brand is perhaps the greatest asset of any company not to appear on its balance sheet. Because accountant types find the concept of *brand* difficult to quantify, it is often thought of as a fuzzy marketing concept, which involves a logo, a tagline, and large expenditures. But a brand is much more than that. It is a product or product line with an identifiable set of benefits, wrapped in a recognizable personality, carrying with it a connection between product and customers. It is the difference between a watch and a Rolex, a car and a Mercedes, a cup of coffee and a Starbucks latte. It is the difference between the Eagles and A Flock of Seagulls or a host of other rock-and-roll wannabes. In the language of business, music stars are brands. Some are the Cokes and IBMs of music; others are the Shasta colas and Digital (DEC) computers.

A powerful brand creates an image and an identity for a product or a company; it is a promise to consumers, telling them what they can expect when they and their cash or plastic are separated. If the brand promise is kept, customers end up saving time because less time is spent deciding between various brands. But when the promise is not fulfilled, consumers switch to another brand more likely to deliver on the promise, as rapidly as one number-one hit record replaces another.

Contrary to the prevailing belief among the financial ranks, branding is not just a marketer's problem. It affects the marketability and financial well-being of the entire company, and when executed properly, it sends a unified image and message throughout the firm and throughout the marketplace. The price-to-earnings (P/E) ratio and market capitalization of a firm are often dramatically higher if it has a powerful brand, or a particularly strong portfolio of brands, in the marketplace. The difference in profitability between firms with powerful brands and those with weak brands is known as *brand equity*—the difference in value created by a brand less the cost of creating the brand. It may be measured as the difference between market capital-ization and book value, but when brands rock, they create investor value that lasts for decades.

As the legendary rock bands exhibit throughout this book, creating brand equity is not a static concept or merely a marketing goal. Rather, it is a dynamic process that requires that brands be engaged in con-versation with customers. This type of two-way relationship implies mutual transfer of information, from the brand to the customer and from the customer to the brand. But the relationship between brand and fan goes beyond information flow to become emotion flow. For example, Krispy Kreme evokes such intense emotions among its doughnut fans that even the most time-pressed consumers will stand in line to satisfy their physical and emotional cravings. But police offi-cers aren't the only ones drooling at the sight of the now-famous green-and-white polka-dot box. Many financial analysts missed the ground floor of stocks of companies like Krispy Kreme, Starbucks, and Wal-Mart because they underestimated the impact of emotional con-nections between brands and customers and failed to see the relation-ship between these brands and the culture.

After a stint of insanity during the dot-com heyday, the business world has again turned to more realistic views of corporate value, for the most part. Warren Buffett and like-minded investors, whose focus was always on return on investment, earnings per share (EPS), earn-ings growth, dividends, and similar measures, can exhale—financial analysts have put renewed faith in the old-time religion that equates the salvation of a firm with its profits, not its prophets. In this reborn truth lies the fundamental role of the brand: It is a mechanism to boost a firm's sales and profits higher than those of its competitors'.

LEGENDARY BANDS, LEGENDARY BRANDS

Only a few brands last so long that they might be called legendary. One of those is Wedgwood china, cited by brand historian Nancy Koehn in her book *Brand New* (Harvard Business School Press, 2001). Dating back to the 1700s, this brand still leads the market in terms of closet share among the rich and famous, and tops the wish lists of brides-to-be around the globe. By no means exclusive to the world of products and commerce, legends abound in the music world. From Bach, Beethoven, and Brahms (whose music has transcended the centuries) to Al Jolson, Glenn Miller, and Louis "Satchmo" Armstrong (who crossed racial barriers and defined an era of music), artists have connected deeply with people and helped to shape culture.

And then there's Elvis—proving that even though an artist may die, a legendary brand lives on and continues to sell, sell, sell. The Elvis brand, like those of Frank Sinatra and Tony Bennett, has remained a favorite among all sorts of people for decades. Such long-term market presence is amazing, especially when you remember how fickle people can be; what's hot one day isn't the next. Staying ahead of changing tastes and preferences is difficult. The question is how to create a brand strong enough to remain popular with customers over time—especially in the wake of a constant onslaught of new competitors armed with new promotional and communication campaigns designed to steal attention and loyalty. An intense look at the music industry sheds some light.

For every band like the Beatles, there are tens of thousands of Sassy Peppers (Never heard of them? Our point precisely!) and thousands of Men Without Hats (anyone into popular 1980s music knows "Safety Dance," this band's one and only hit). Most rock-and-roll artists spend more time clawing their way up the music ladder and sliding dramatically back down it than they spend perched at the top of the charts. For many, their 15 minutes of fame is exactly that—15 short minutes. Actually, they provide great lessons on how *not* to create long-lasting brands; however, we are most intrigued by the living legends that have kept their fans over the years, continue to create new ones, and, as a result, sell millions of dollars of product. Some of these legendary bands are truly talented in their musical ability—mavericks and visionaries in their art form—yet others are not. And for every rock-and-roll legend, there are thousands of others who may be just as talented musically, often with better voices or more musical training, who never even make it into the recording studio, let alone to the top of the lists in *Billboard* or *Variety*.

Sound familiar? The world of commerce is filled with a myriad of products and companies in similar predicaments. A great idea is only that, unless it is executed well in the marketplace—but few ever are. In fact, they frequently fail to leave the space of their inventors' brains. Just because a product may be technologically better than an existing one doesn't mean it will automatically squash its competitors. The same holds true for the role of talent in the formula for creating music megastars.

Stephen Swid, founder of *Spin* magazine and chairman of SESAC, Inc., explains, "Sure, the core of what you produce has to be at an acceptable level, let's say at least a seven in terms of music sound and quality. But, after that, it's what happens in the areas of image (design, visuals, marketing) and delivery (performance experience) that makes one band a phenomenon and the other a flop." He adds, "In competitive arenas, which the music business definitely is, not everyone that is successful can be the best, but each has to be good enough to deserve a spot on the field. If everyone were the best, then there would only be one brand of everything—from toothpaste to rock star—and that would make for a boring world."

It takes more than quality for a product or a company to succeed in the marketplace, just as it requires more than musical talent for a band to reach megastar status. Some call it passion; some call it fire-in-the-belly enthusiasm. Ron Wood of the Rolling Stones describes it as a force that just takes over. At the opening for a collection of his paintings held at the Rock and Roll Hall of Fame, he explained his passion for art—in this instance painting rather than music. "When I'm really grabbed by it, there's nothing I can do. I just have to drop everything. Sometimes in the middle of the night, I have to get up and start painting." Wood's words ring true for entrepreneurs who have dedicated their lives to the conception, care, and feeding of their business babies.

The difference between the megastars of music and the millions of wannabes is a strategic gap that should intrigue every entrepreneur who wants to create a megabrand. It should also concern executives of major, successful firms who hope to stay at the top of their industries. Some of those would-be competitors will become megastars, poised to revolutionize an industry, much as Elvis and the Beatles shook up the music industry, and ultimately affected the social mores and values of our nation.

If you find yourself starting to think about some of your

favorite bands and hypothesizing what has made them successful, congratulations—you get it. But if you are pondering the relevance of rock and roll to your firm's performance, remember that businesses and rock-and-roll bands share several goals, including:

♪ Breaking through the clutter and creating awareness among consumers otherwise inundated with messages and advertising about competitive products and companies

♪ Creating and maintaining loyalty or devotion among customers

♪ Identifying mechanisms for remaining current and relevant in the minds of existing customers and attracting new customers

♪ Creating lasting brands that are accepted by a culture

♪ Becoming long-term industry leaders

♪ Attracting and keeping talented people who make up and market the brand

♪ Identifying one or more market segments and crafting products that appeal to them

♪ Creating a brand image and promise that will maintain its appeal from one year to the next

♪ Generating profits

Although many of the issues faced by bands and businesses are the same, and many of the solutions are similar, the approach to finding the solutions and implementing them are often quite different.

The process of innovation and creative thinking is a vital step in company evolution, whether it pertains to the development of a new product, service, packaging concept, operational design, or marketing campaign. Although not all ideas make it past the brainstorming process inherent to innovative thinking, let alone make it to market, the value to the organization lies in the creative process as well as in what it can lead to. The process allows a firm's most talented people to remain challenged and involved in the future direction of the company, giving them a heightened interest in the performance of the company and hopefully increasing their desire to stay with the firm.

SHATTERING THE CREATIVE STATUS QUO

If you want to do something different from what your competitors have tried in the marketplace, look to rock and roll's living legends for creative inspiration and ideas. Then, apply these lessons to your organization's marketing, branding, and customer-related strategies. Challenge yourself to let your hair down and open your mind to new analogies and tactics for addressing traditional business issues.

We believe many marketers will experience the big "Aha!" as they allow themselves to dive into the world of rock and roll and emerge with a better understanding of band loyalty and fan creation in the music industry. We believe that retailers, manufacturers, wholesalers, and service providers alike need to examine how the most successful rock bands have achieved long-term success and devise ways to incorporate those unorthodox forms of creative thinking to affect innovation within their own companies. At risk is the ability of well-established firms to remain fresh in the marketplace when compared with younger, hungrier, and more innovative competitors.

Our analysis focuses primarily on bands that have had an impact in the marketplace for 20 years or more. They have proven their ability to attract fans, connect with them emotionally, and keep them engaged over the years. Some of you will like their music and others will not—frankly, it doesn't matter. The lessons their stories offer are not about music preference; they are about long-term brand dominance in a fickle marketplace. The following is an introduction to the bands that are featured in this book.

ELTON JOHN

Ask most baby boomers about the special moments in their lives, and they are likely to tie an Elton John song to several of them. Some boomers may think of his 1970 breakthrough hit, "Your

Song," while some of their children may think of "Can You Feel the Love Tonight," from Disney's 1994 megahit, *The Lion King.* Though known for his Liberacesque costumes and style and his 30-year string of top-10 hits, Sir Elton's career has roots in classical piano. John studied at the Royal Academy of Music as a teenager but left the world of classical music for the world of rock and roll to reach larger audiences and make the most of his talents and passion. He partnered with lyricist Bernie Taupin to create a string of hits spanning three decades.

Elton John is the very definition of how to blend music and marketing, providing stellar lessons on how to grow profits with segmentation, driving marketing and brand-development strategies one segment at a time. Taupin and John's musical creations serve as a blueprint of consumer behavior—the science of understanding why people buy and motivating them to buy from you with appeals to consumers' lifestyles and most basic motivations. John also serves as a classic example of balancing the functional and emotional elements of a brand to delight customers, a strategy flying high at the airline JetBlue. Like JetBlue, John knows how to turn brand equity into sales, whether he is promoting his latest CD, concert, Broadway show, or commercial endorsement. He went beyond appearing in Coca-Cola ads by placing the product on his piano during his concerts, pumping up sales in grocery stores.

KISS

Who can forget KISS—four makeup-clad men who strutted around stage in tight costumes and 6-inch platform shoes, setting off fireworks and smashing guitars? If your memory needs a refresher, KISS was the scary-looking rock band that played during the closing ceremonies of the 2002 Olympic Games. The bandmates admittedly are not the best musicians to enter the world of rock and roll, but their success was not dumb luck—it was the result of strategic planning and marketing at its finest. The more KISS frightened parents and other "normal" people with its appearance and antics, the bigger its fan base became, and the more its fans adopted the band into their lifestyles.

But KISS found itself in a dilemma early on in its career—on one hand, it would sell out midsized arenas and venues, but on the other, it couldn't sell records. In quasi–focus group fashion, fans told the band that they loved the experience of a KISS concert. They paid to experience the ultimate escape, not to sit idly and listen to KISS music. In an effort to package the KISS experience, the band decided to record and release a double live album, which many producers thought to be the kiss of death at the time. Breaking the record industry's traditional mind-set, the band decided to forgo high sound quality and go for concert-quality sound, which included pyrotechnics and fireworks. Chapter 4 discusses the strategies KISS used to amass fans and satisfy them, which are uncannily similar to those that have made Wal-Mart the world's largest corporation and allowed home improvement retailer Lowe's to take on and beat Home Depot's urban store strategy. Gene Simmons and Sam Walton—birds of a feather? In some ways, yes—and some of those ways have led to sales of over 75 million albums to date for KISS and revenue of a quarter-trillion dollars for Wal-Mart.

THE ROLLING STONES

Amid the British invasion of rock and roll in the 1960s, the Rolling Stones hit the United States with a vengeance. Armed with Keith Richard's legendary guitar riffs and Mick Jagger's unconventional sex appeal and throaty voice, the Stones took their place in American pop culture and haven't relinquished it yet. In fact, "Satisfaction" has become the unofficial anthem for baby boomers, with dozens of other Stones songs comprising stereotypical baby-boomer life soundtracks. At 60, Jagger released a solo album, *Goddess in the Doorway,* to keep his creative juices flowing and to stay relevant among younger audiences by pairing up with contemporary rock talents, from Rob Thomas of Matchbox 20 to Lenny Kravitz.

Jagger is at his best, however, when piloting the Rolling Stones, with Richards flying right seat. The band's 2002–2003 *Forty Licks* world tour is prototypical of what any firm seeking to keep a 40-year-old brand dominant in the marketplace should do. From pricing, cobranding, and promotional strategies to enhancing emotional connections, Chapter 5 shows how the band imposes its corporate goals and measures to manage a wildly creative process and create a unique experience that people will pay big bucks to see. With a reported net worth of over $500 million, Jagger is at the top of his game, both as rock star and "chairman of the board" of the corporation called the Rolling Stones.

AEROSMITH

If American rock and roll had a poster child, it would most likely be Aerosmith. Perhaps best known for the hit "Walk This Way," named as the fifth-best rock song of all time by MTV in 2000, Aerosmith hit rock bottom and broke up in the early 1980s. Years of drugs, alcohol, and excess had taken their toll. Aerosmith's comeback would require a complete reinvention of the band and its image. Aerosmith surprised the music world when it collaborated with the rappers of Run-DMC on their "Walk This Way" remake. Not only would the song and the video help rap music cross from the urban market into the mainstream, it would be the first rap song to break into the *Billboard* Top 10 chart. It would also launch Aerosmith's rebirth—armed with a fresh image and new group of fans.

Led by the consummate front man Steven Tyler, Aerosmith has redefined age, vitality, and sexiness in an industry in which good-looking twenty-somethings are the norm. The band embodies energy and passion to connect with young music fans, capturing the Best Rock Song category for "Jaded" at the 2001 Teen Music Awards. In Chapter 6, you'll learn how Aerosmith shows marketers the way to cultivate *angel* fans, how to involve them in building a brand, and how to transform a dying brand into one stronger than its predecessor.

MADONNA

Since she slithered onto the music scene in 1983 with her hit single "Holiday," Madonna has proven that sex certainly does sell. Never afraid to offend the masses, Madonna understands shock value and rebellion, but most important, she understands her fans, to whom her antics and convictions are not offensive but expected and accepted. Her sexually charged (and often explicit) lyrics and videos don't turn off her female fans because Madonna is not about using sex to degrade women; her goal is to empower them by breaking down barriers and touting equality, spawning as many Madonna wannabes as male fans. She makes a conscious effort not to promote a particular lifestyle, but to present different ones in an open—albeit revealing—light and let people choose for themselves.

Throughout her career, Madonna has remained true to one of her greatest strengths—a chameleon-like ability to change and stay one step ahead of the times. Madonna is a better "product" now than she was when she started, continually improving her voice, dancing, and stage productions and imposing quality control whenever and wherever possible. Firms such as Abercrombie & Fitch, Calvin Klein, and other fashion brands use similar appeals in their communication and marketing strategies, but few do it better than Victoria's Secret, as you'll see in Chapter 7.

NEIL DIAMOND

Neil Diamond is the anti-Madonna. Remembered for the rhinestone-studded jumpsuits that defined entertainers of the 1970s, Diamond sells out concert venues in cities as large as Chicago and as small as Dayton, Ohio, without much publicity. Dancing, swaying, and singing to classics such as "Sweet Caroline," you might feel more like you're in a geriatric aerobics class than at a rock concert. The fans, nonetheless, are as avid as those attending any Pearl Jam concert.

Diamond, who suffers to some degree from Barry Manilow syndrome, remains extremely popular outside his traditional fan base as well, even though these younger fans may not admit that they actually enjoy and listen to his music. For people who like the familiar and look for constants in their lives, Diamond is the answer, as you'll also discover in Chapter 7. His music and concerts play to people's unending hunger for nostalgia, appealing to their desire for security and memories of the good old days, shedding light on how to keep a mature product or brand popular in a changing consumer market. Neil is a diamond that still shines brightly, demonstrating how to be sexy more than sexual by maintaining rather than abandoning culturally relevant values.

BRANDING IN AN ERA OF IMPATIENCE

The formula for what it takes to get on the shelves of leading retailers has changed over the years to reflect more closely what it took for legendary bands to make it in the music business.

Charley Lake, a promotions director for Infinity Broadcasting, has spent over 35 years in marketing and promotions in the music business, observing firsthand what it takes to build long-term band loyalty. "In the 1960s and 1970s, the cream seemed to rise to the top more readily because of musical talent, performance ability, great song writing, and audience reaction." Bands like the Eagles, Bon Jovi, and Aerosmith toured for years before selling a significant number of records, which not only let them develop their talent and build fan bases, but also let them build a repertoire of material and evolve their brand personalities.

"By the time these artists got their first record deal, they'd often had six or seven years to write songs and try them out on audiences," he adds. "They knew which ones would sell based on audience reactions at concerts—revenue-generating test marketing at its finest. This then led to more touring and the release of a follow-up album."

The process today is similar, but the timeline, hype, and formula have changed to reflect corporate America's stifling focus on profits, continuous growth, and larger-than-life expectations. In the past, bands and record labels were more patient in selling records— cultivating fans rather than fabricating them with a lot of glitz. They were also more patient regarding sales growth and velocity, just as product companies were about product, brand, and innovation acceptance timelines. Now, if the follow-up record doesn't meet lofty sales goals, today's golden child and star brand is not only forgotten but quickly flushed.

Hootie & The Blowfish was arguably *the* band of the mid-1990s, selling 15 million copies of its first hit album, *Cracked Rear View*. For several years you couldn't turn on the radio without hearing the deep, emotion-filled voice of front man Darius Rucker singing feel-good tunes that people couldn't help but sing along to. With overnight success came over-the-top expectations of record executives for the band's next album. When sales of *Fairweather Johnson* fell short of inflated expectations (selling only a few million copies), the band fell out of favor with Atlantic Records, which moved it from the "hot" to the "not" list. By previous standards, Hootie was still successful, even though the band suffered the marketing faux pas of brand overexposure and unrealistic sales expectations.

The band fell victim to what Robert Summer, chairman of World Theater, Inc., and former executive vice president of Sony Music Entertainment, describes as the changing economics of the music industry. "The heightened pressure to make more money in less time has affected the view of longevity in the business," he says. "The ability to invest the time and the funds required to nurture artists, help them mature, and build careers over time is eroded by the fact that the industry is owned by conglomerates with near-term financial pressures. That pressure can also be distorting to the artist and the artistic process." This results in an industry laden with overnight success stories that are overmarketed in the short term and underdeveloped for the long term.

Part of the problem is that some marketers fail to identify which products or brands are flash-in-the-pan successes and which may start slowly but are likely to be adopted by a culture in the long run. In a market driven by quarterly results, long-term growth, marketing, and branding strategies that require intensive capital, labor, and resource investments have in many instances been sacrificed for short-term strategies that quickly impact the numbers.

FROM MARKETING CAMPAIGN TO BRAND EQUITY

Today's music world has become so marketing-driven and image-focused that the formula for success almost mirrors an algebraic equation into which various artists can be inserted to represent the unknown variables. The formula seems heavy on PR, standout clothing, eye appeal, and dance talent, and short on songwriting and singing ability, which has changed the type of artists that have recently racked up commercially successful hits.

"Today, the music industry is very song-driven," says Lake. "People may connect with a particular song, but they often don't know who sings it, let alone the names of the front men of the group, which is different from bands of the past." Rather than focus on which bands have the talent to impact the music world in the long run and build large fan bases into the future, the industry focuses on the songs that can hit number one today. If the artist behind the song can release several hits over a few years, that's icing on the proverbial cake.

What is missing from the formula is a focus on *emotional connection* and the long-term goal of *cultural adoption*. Since marketers hold tight rein on who will actually break into the music industry, they often market artists who fit the mold rather than break it. As a result, seemingly less than stellar artists achieve success, albeit contrived and most likely short-lived. In an effort to find the next hit and to sell the most records this year, music marketers sacrifice the long-term investment in music brands that generate long-term revenue and profits, as has been the case for Elton John, U2, Dave Matthews, and Billy Joel. If today's rock-and-roll darlings have disappointing sales on their second go-rounds, marketing and PR dollars disappear, new stars are created, and the process repeats itself. And after a decade of hits by flash-in-the-pan artists, *who* sang *what* becomes a blur—band loyalty as known in previous decades is rare, and so is the sense of relationship of music to personal life events.

On the other hand, once bands and their music are adopted as part of a culture, the role of advertising, promotion, and other branding activities take on different dimensions and goals. Rather than selling the band or creating awareness, branding activities can focus on evolving the band to maintain its emotional and cognitive connections to the culture. For example, the Rolling Stones and Neil Diamond know that when they announce a tour, they can count on a large proportion of their fans to buy tickets and concert garb. And many of their fans are of the generation that still buys music, opting to pay for CDs rather than invest the time to learn how to download music and then actually do it.

As long as the band remains relevant, it can count on a certain level of support from the culture that adopted it—much as Crest can count on a certain level of sales because it is the brand consumers grew up with and have little reason to abandon. Compare that to a band that has had a few hit songs but has cycled in and out of popularity and relevance to its audience. With each appearance or new release, not only does the message need to promote the event, it needs to remind people of the band's identity and why they should attend the concert or buy the album. Without an emotional connection to fans, the baseline levels of sales and support are unknown and unpredictable. That is the value of creating brand equity in the market.

LESSONS FROM ROCK-AND-ROLL MARKETING

The rock-and-roll bands featured in this book have spent their careers generating their own versions of tried-and-true branding strategies, from the brilliant to the bizarre. At times they needed to bolster recognition among would-be fans; at other times, a complete reinvention or repositioning of the band was required after years of absence from the music scene. GM's Cadillac division—a cultural icon of the 1950s and 1960s—could certainly learn from the brand-reinvention strategies of Aerosmith, while Swiss Army knife maker Victorinox might very well benefit from the transgenerational marketing strategies of Elton John. Entrepreneurs looking to get onto retailers' shelves can learn from fledgling icons, such as Madonna, while existing brands can learn about maintaining shelf space from the Rolling Stones.

All of the bands and performers highlighted in *Brands That Rock* have stuck closely to their core sounds and strengths over the years, but they have evolved to stay fresh and viable in a dynamic marketplace. They have mastered the art of evolving at a rate that doesn't alienate their current customers and attracts new fans. Rock artists understand the role that repetition, accessibility, entertainment, and emotion have in creating band loyalty. They use all of these strategies and a host of others to keep bonds with their fans strong. Among these lessons are:

1. Create an emotional connection with your customers; nurture it over time.

2. Build brand loyalty, one fan group at a time.

3. Stay fresh in the market but true to your core sound or strength.

4. Evolve at a rate that doesn't alienate current customers.

5. Focus on the entire brand experience, not just the core product.

6. Develop talent continuously; package it well; relate it through multiple mediums.

7. Create realistic expectations that you can meet.

8. Match your message with your mission and your audience.

9. Exude energy and passion—they command respect and engage the audience.

10. Define the brand by more than just the product; include the functional and emotional attributes of the brand.

11. Monitor brand adoption and customer behavior to drive brand adaptation.

12. Play for cultural adoption by focusing on relevance to, reflection of, and influence on the culture.

13. Resist the temptation of overexposure.

14. Empower your fans to help your brand become and stay successful in the market.

These strategies, employed by the most successful rock-and-roll bands in music history, can boost a brand's acceptance, sales, and relevance in the market and achieve the ultimate goal of every significant brand—adoption by a culture, the focus of Chapter 2. In the words of Steven Tyler, Aerosmith's flamboyant front man, the goal of his band is "to kick ass and leave a footprint"—to have a long-lasting effect on people's emotions, experiences, and lives.

Rock and roll has done just that. It has become the global tongue—the common language now spoken throughout the world. As time goes on and rock and roll grows even deeper roots in society, it is beginning to write history, portraying in song what is happening in the world and also affecting history with its global reach. In fact, the adoption of rock and roll by modern culture is worth studying in and of itself, along with the acceptance of specific bands.

It is our hope that you will read this book and be fascinated by the music, the stars, and their stories. But our goal is to be more than a fun read about the fascinating sounds and strategies of the music industry. By the time you have finished reading this book, you should gain a sound understanding of how to implement branding strategies to achieve the position in consumers' minds that will lead to customer loyalty and market dominance. *Brands That Rock* looks at the concepts and principles that show firms how to build, maintain, and reinvigorate brands, ultimately helping their organizations survive, thrive, and rock on for many decades.

2

CREATING CULTURALLY RELEVANT BRANDS

Rock's sheer pervasiveness makes it the most profound value-shaper in existence today. Unless you are deaf, it is virtually guaranteed that rock music has affected your view of the world.
—*NATIONAL REVIEW*, FEBRUARY 24, 1989

Brands, like bands, can generate significant profits when everyone from salespeople to CEOs are focused on turning customers into fans and nurturing a robust fan base. This first, vital, step promotes cultural adoption of a brand, which can translate into brand loyalty and sales even during an economic slowdown.

EMOTIONAL BRANDING

Examine closely the rock-and-roll stars that span generations and an important principle of longevity emerges. The long-lasting successes of the Rolling Stones, Neil Diamond, U2, and other legendary bands are achieved through special relationships and connections with their fans, not just their own talent and competency. The lyrics, rhythms, and delivery of their music reverberate with the realities, desires, and aspirations of their listeners. It's the total music experience that impresses fans, and, in most cases, the lifestyles and personalities of the musicians as well. The response equals more than the sum of the individual attributes to create an extrasensory connection between band and fan.

The reason for this emotional bond may not be apparent to the casual observer or completely understood by the bands and their fans, but it exists. Analyzed from a consumer behavior perspective, the reasons for the emotional connection are apparent. First, bands and songs *evoke emotions* in people. Just as the B-52s' monster hit "Love Shack" might make you bop around in your seat, Whitney Houston's "I Will Always Love You" may reduce you to tears. Second, people often *associate the specific emotions evoked by life events* (both good and bad) with the soundtracks of their lives. Whether it's Led Zeppelin's "Stairway to Heaven" (your first make-out song) or Gloria Gaynor's "I Will Survive" (your first breakup song), these anthems become attached to strong emotions, which resurface when the songs are heard later.

Emotional connections are not exclusive to the world of music. Some of the most profitable brands also create an extrasensory connection with consumers, evoking emotions just as powerful as those associated with music. Remember the loyal Coca-Cola fans who rioted and filed lawsuits demanding a return to the original formula when the company made the executive decision to discontinue Classic Coke and replace it with New Coke? Beyond preferring the taste of Classic Coke, fans saw this as an attempt to eliminate an old and trusted friend (brand) that had for decades been a part of their lives. And what about Harley-Davidson loyalists and weekend warriors who shed their corporate and professional titles on weekends to tour the country in leather-clad packs? Harley fans have been so vocal and influential that foreign governments have changed their environmental laws to allow the importation of "hogs".

When an emotional connection with a brand occurs across a large group of people, it becomes adopted by a culture, emblazoned in the minds and lifestyles of those consumers. That is what happened to rock and roll with the help of Elvis Presley. Though he made a real connection with Americans in his own right lasting into the twenty-first Century, perhaps his greatest impact was being the conduit for the adoption of rock and roll by American culture.

Legendary rock-and-roll bands are often conduits to the changing culture of markets. Bob Dylan, for example, is considered by many to be the voice of the baby-boomer generation. Elvis embodies the late 1950s and the end of an era of innocence; Bruce Springsteen represents the working people of America. These types of characterizations, from representing a generation or group of people to defining an era or time in history, are informal measures of the cultural adoption and long-term success of a band, sometimes recognized on a more formal basis by induction into the Rock and Roll Hall of Fame.

ARE YOU IN THE HALL OF FAME?

Marketers should ask themselves, "If there were a Hall of Fame for brands, would we be in it?" And if so, "Would our customers swoon with the same excitement and fervor as the fans of the music legends inducted into the Rock and Roll Hall of Fame?" Perhaps you are nodding in affirmation, or maybe you're hanging your head in shame. Or, perhaps, you're wondering, "Does it really matter?"

Especially in today's competitive environment, where best-of-breed retailers and manufacturers have slashed operating expenses with leaner inventories and efficient logistics systems, branding is about seizing the increased profits that accompany greater *share*—from market share and closet share to share of wallet, time, and attention. Ultimately, it can also be viewed as share of *heart*, signifying the emotional connection between brand and fan that permits a premium price. Today, gaining share depends on more than just having a superior product. Contrary to popular belief, it also depends on more than marketing and advertising budgets that support short-lived promotions or ad blitzes. Increasingly, it is the firm's brand and its fans that helps the organization through tough times, carrying it into higher profitability during good times.

BECOMING PART OF THE FABRIC OF AMERICA

When evaluating the cultural adoption of a brand, the brands that last, marketers should ask, "If we were painting a picture of American life, would our brand be a part of it?" For example, a portrait of a typical American shopping scene would likely include a Wal-Mart greeter, while a holiday shopping scene would feature bustling shoppers toting Bloomingdale's iconic big brown bags in New York or visiting Marshall Field's at Christmas in Chicago. An outdoor cookout scene would likely include a Weber grill, bottles of Heinz ketchup, Oscar Mayer hot dogs and French's mustard (who, during the Iraq War, quickly explained that, "Our name may be French, but we're not yellow"). Successful brands, like legendary bands, try to hear the "background music" that accompanies these scenes to determine whether they are part of the soundtrack of consumers' lifestyles.

How do your brands fare? How prevalent are they in the snapshots that define your customers' lives and fit their consumption patterns? Your brand helps establish a relationship—an emotional connection—with consumers and society for your product or organization.

One of the valuable lessons rock and roll offers people involved in marketing and branding is how it evolved from its ethnic roots to become part of mainstream America, spotlighting what it takes for innovations, products, and brands to become accepted by an entire culture. Analyzing this process in the most successful legendary bands discloses that to achieve cultural adoption, a band (or brand) should *have relevance to people in a culture, represent a culture,* and *have influence on a culture.*

IT'S ONLY ROCK AND ROLL BUT I LIKE IT

If you think rock and roll burst onto the scene with the introduction of Bill Haley and the Comets, you are a few decades late and a few shades too white. Rock and roll evolved from what was known during the 1940s and 1950s as *rhythm and blues* (R&B). It had roots up and down the Mississippi River, starting from New Orleans and Memphis, traveling north to Chicago, and fanning out in both directions to clubs in cities such as Kansas City and Detroit. R&B was ingrained in the African-American culture, with songs reflecting the lifestyles and blues culture of that community.

What was often described as "race music" by the predominantly white, mainstream musical culture of the 1950s eventually became *rock and roll,* a well-understood slang term in the black culture for making love or simply having sex. Although Trixie Smith, a famous blues singer, had recorded the song "My Man Rocks Me (With One Steady Roll)" years earlier, the meaning of *rock and roll* remained relatively unknown in the majority culture, except among a few progressive white disc jockeys (DJs) and music fans. In an era when radio stations still received albums from record companies with such tracks as "Makin' Whoopee" marked "Not for air play," it was probably better to keep the sexual meaning of the name from traditionalists— namely parents, advertisers, and station managers.

Nonetheless, some artists, such as Chuck Berry, Bo Diddley, Little Richard, and Fats Domino, began attracting more and more white consumers as fans. Among them were small groups of DJs (today referred to as "on-air personalities") who spun Patti Page, Frank Sinatra, and Pat Boone records in the daytime, but fiddled with their AM receivers at night, listening to music from WLAC and other Southern stations. Though they couldn't yet broadcast this music, they understood the impact its sound and messages would have on American culture. They became fans who would play an important role in the eventual migration of ethnic music to the mainstream culture, because at that time DJs were gatekeepers of the music world.

As music styles began to blend, so did audiences. Although most country and bluegrass music enthusiasts were white, there were plenty of black listeners who didn't have access to the few black-oriented stations in large cities. Some listened to *Grand Ole Opry* from Nashville and responded when black performers Chuck Berry and Bo Diddley incorporated a little bit of country or rockabilly into their songs. Likewise, many white GIs listened and danced to R&B and blues in the slightly more integrated environment of World War II. By the 1950s, many key market segments (mainly young people, often living in Southern or Midwestern regions) had developed—the appeal of the music was too universal to remain in the minority culture. In his speech at the 2003 Rock and Roll Hall of Fame induction ceremonies, Elton John acknowledged the contributions of these early R&B performers. He said, "Every person owes their musical heritage to their influence; we owe our heritage to black artists because that was the best music to listen to," adding sentiments about the influence they had on his career.

Young people embraced rock and roll, but older Americans hesitated to accept the music; they saw it as a threat to the white-bread culture of the early 1950s. There was an all-too-familiar dissention among the generations about things that affect culture—appearance, sex, language, music, and other contributors to the overall makeup of values and morals. But these 1950s teenagers, like most teens, rebelled and broke the rules. The music, the message, and eventually the lifestyle of rock and roll began to transcend racial, ethnic, and cultural lines, moving from the minority culture toward a mass market. The primary conduit for this transition would be none other than Elvis Presley.

AMERICAN CULTURE—B.E. AND A.E.

Elvis was born in 1936 in Tupelo, Mississippi, where he grew up in a modest, predominantly black neighborhood. He was raised in a religious home and loved attending church from the time he was a young boy. Though he belonged to a Pentecostal church in Tupelo, he reportedly sneaked out frequently to the African-American church around the corner, where he absorbed the sounds of gospel choirs and singers. Gospel music became his first love as he sang with his black friends and their families, learning the rhythms and sounds of their music.

Elvis went on to cut his first record in 1952, motivated primarily by his desire to make a recording for his mother. But the executives at Sun Records knew they were hearing—and watching—something special. The way he sang his particular style of rock and roll was unique; the way he moved was edgy; his looks were movie-star quality; and his connection with people who watched was intense.

Elvis crossed many established lines. Just as Microsoft would dominate the computer industry decades later by combining the best practices and innovations of other industry pioneers, Elvis rolled R&B, gospel, and country into a new form of music that would go on to rock the world for the rest of the century. He also pushed the envelope of what society considered sexually appropriate. And finally, Elvis himself broke the race barrier by being white and singing black. Soul singer James Brown said it well: "Elvis taught white people how to get down."

Not everyone was ready for Elvis and his provocative style; he encountered resistance from many traditional, suburban, middle-income, family-oriented people. Appearing on Ed Sullivan's *Toast of the Town* took Elvis from the fringe of society to the mainstream. Sullivan's show dominated television ratings at that time, reflecting and influencing American culture with each act it presented. Initially rebuffed as unsuitable for a family show, Elvis was later booked by Sullivan for three appearances, despite protests from segregationist leaders and parents concerned that his type of music would corrupt American youth. His hip, leg, and arm movements, many of which he adapted from what he had seen in black churches and in the performances of the Statesmen Quartet, the Blackwood Brothers, and other gospel groups, were so controversial that Sullivan decreed that Elvis was not to be shown below the waist. Elvis was also told not to perform gospel songs on the air, a directive he defied with his rendition of "Peace in the Valley," reportedly because it was his mother's favorite.

Several significant things happened that night. Elvis touched the collective nerve of the nation with his voice, beauty, and stage presence, transcending traditional age and race divisions within the American culture of the 1950s. Audiences applauded his voice and singing talent, but they screamed for the way Elvis performed. He didn't just sing a song on stage, he entertained people—gyrating, swaying, and flashing his little-boy smile. To many of his female fans, the songs he sang were secondary to his personality and the way he performed them, evoking an emotional response that made the girls swoon. As a result, the Sullivan show achieved an audience share of 82 percent, a record never equaled until the Beatles appeared years later. It was clear that Elvis was amassing fans; it was clear that people wanted to love him. And that night, Sullivan gave America permission to do so and to invite Elvis into their lives and their culture. Following Elvis's performance, Sullivan walked over to him, put his arm around his shoulder, and told America, with great sincerity, that Elvis was "a fine and decent boy."

From that point on, entertainment was never the same, dividing the history of twentieth-century music into before-Elvis (B.E.) and after-Elvis (A.E.) timeframes. Many would argue that American culture was also forever changed. The young, white, and openly sexual performer created upheaval in many households, causing teens to butt heads with their parents' primarily Victorian values and embrace the statement Elvis made with his risqué on-stage movements. He unlocked the universal trait of teens that has today been accepted as the norm—rebellion. The allegiance fans felt toward Elvis was enhanced by the way they experienced him—through sound, touch, and sight. Teens could hear his music, feel the rhythm and beat, dance the way he did, and watch him on stage (and later in the movies).

Eventually, in an almost "If you can't beat 'em, join 'em" fashion, Elvis appealed to nearly everyone, drawing fans from all walks of life and from generations that initially were threatened by what his music and his style embodied. Why? Because he bonded with people at an extrasensory level through his personality as much as (if not more than) through his songs. His music had cultural relevance in sound and message; his lyrics, style, and delivery reflected his core market at the time; and he influenced how teens danced and dressed. Consequently, he was adopted by the culture, becoming an icon dubbed the King of Rock and Roll, and he ruled the music industry for decades. Today, over 25 years after his death, he is actually more successful than he was in the latter part of his career.

Many rock-and-roll bands followed, striving for the impact and connection Elvis had with his fans. Some were successful; others weren't. But all were aided by the King of Rock and Roll, who paved the way for the mainstream rockers of the 1960s—from Bob Dylan to the Beatles—and opened the door for the next wave—from the Rolling Stones to Led Zeppelin.

Elvis's passion never swayed far from his roots. He loved gospel music; it was his favorite to listen to and to sing. Though he gave a generation of fans a soundtrack of music to live by—"Love Me Tender" for romantic moments, "In the Ghetto" for reflective times, and "Jailhouse Rock," "Blue Suede Shoes," and "Hound Dog" for dancing—he would be most honored and recognized for his gospel works. During the span of his relatively short career, the King of Rock and Roll was nominated for 16 Grammy awards, but ironically never won one for rock and roll. He did, however win three Grammys for his gospel albums. He reminds us that sometimes our greatest successes can be derived from the skills and areas about which we are most passionate, investing in our greatest strengths and evolving without straying too far from our core competencies. Though a Grammy for rock and roll eluded him, he was included in the first group honored by induction to the Rock and Roll Hall of Fame, in 1986.

ACHIEVING CULTURAL ADOPTION

Marketers salivate at the prospect of achieving levels of brand recognition and fan loyalty approaching those achieved by Elvis. He is one of America's most recognizable icons. Even after his death, the loyalty of his fans has been unwavering, with thousands flocking to Graceland each year to pay homage to the King. Though we may laugh at Elvis impersonators and the velvet portraits of Elvis sold at flea markets throughout the country, no one can deny that fans adopted him into their families and lifestyles, and America adopted him as part of its culture. Figure 2.1 diagrams the process Elvis and other legendary rock bands have used to make this type of long-term connection with fans. Studying this process of acceptance by society reveals that a brand's relevance to, representation of, and influence on culture are crucial to creating a long-term relationship and to eventual adoption by society.

Culture refers to the *values, ideas, artifacts,* and *symbols* that help individuals *communicate, interpret,* and *evaluate* as members of society. It is the "blueprint" of human activity, determining the coordinates of social action and productive activity and reflecting influences from factors such as ethnicity, race, religion, and national or regional

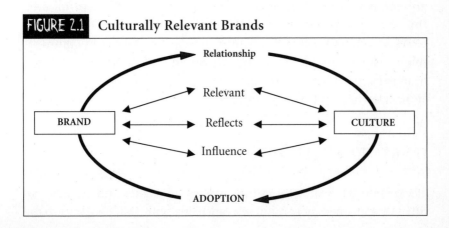

FIGURE 2.1   Culturally Relevant Brands

identity. As these elements change within a society, so too does the culture change. And when changes occur in a culture, branding opportunities emerge—just as the chance emerges for a band to carve out its own space in people's life soundtracks.

Just as the Grateful Dead has done with its legions of Deadheads, successful brands reach beyond the minds of consumers and into their hearts. Building a brand on the key values of its customers causes them to connect with the brand at an emotional level, much more than just a cognitive level, evoking strong responses and connections that differentiate customers from fans. Fans feel, perhaps without knowing why, "This is *my* brand." When this happens on an individual basis, an extrasensory connection is made; and when it happens en masse, cultural adoption occurs.

Attending a rock concert is a valuable way for marketers to experience firsthand the role that emotional connection plays in acceptance of a product—in this case a band or a particular song. Fans like the familiar—if they know a song, they often sing along or at least dance a bit more fervently than they otherwise might. Even during a Paul McCartney concert, fans will sing and dance to the Wings and Beatles songs they know, and head for the restrooms when he announces that the next five songs are from a new CD. Bands know this happens, but they continue to perform the new material for the obvious reason of selling new CDs. But they perform the new material for less obvious reasons as well—to give fans an emotional and memorable experience to connect to the new song, thereby reinforcing relationships with fans, increasing the likelihood of continued cultural adoption, and increasing their longevity in the market. Had Borden followed this strategy in the 1960s or 1970s when the association between Cracker Jack and baseball was ingrained in the American culture, it might have been able to extend the brand and build other Borden brands by piggybacking on the relationship of generations of consumers to the Cracker Jack brand.

IT'S GOT TO BE RELEVANT

The phenomena of long-lasting, successful bands and brands can often be explained by cultural relevance. If a brand isn't relevant to the people who are supposed to buy it, they don't, at least not in the long run. When people say about a brand, "It makes sense; it fits into our lives and our lifestyles," then they are on their way to describing a store or products as "my store" or "my brand," assuming a sense of ownership and pride. A relevant brand name often becomes a descriptive word, such as a "Wal-Mart kind of guy" or a "Tiffany's kind of girl."

The musicians who become rock-and-roll legends are grippingly relevant to the cultural values of a specific group of people—their fans. Similarly, profitable businesses and brands are grippingly relevant to key market segments—those that are currently profitable or possess potential for future growth. The best of the best expand the relationship from one segment to become core, mass-market branding successes. This is more likely to occur when the values and lifestyles linked to a brand are closely aligned with the behavior, whether actual or aspirational, of customers and their culture.

Verizon's recent advertising campaign resonates with American culture today. The slogan "Can you hear me now?" in Verizon's clever television ads reflects the sentiments of people frustrated by poor cellular phone connections. You can hear people waiting in airport concourses or walking down the street uttering the phrase as they try to maintain communication with the person on the phone. It's a slogan adopted by the culture, as much as the phrase "Elvis has left the building."

Achieving cultural relevance is the first phase in marketplace acceptance, but legendary bands will tell you it's also about staying relevant to a culture, using core products to reinforce relationships with existing fans and attract new ones. Hence, the "greatest hits" albums. This is a lesson learned by legendary brands such as food marketer Heinz, which successfully introduced green ketchup, attracting new fans—children who probably enjoy playing with the ketchup as much as eating it. Green ketchup enlisted a new generation in the battle with salsa for market share, but Heinz didn't abandon its classic hit—red ketchup.

During 2002, Aerosmith toured the United States promoting *Oh Yeah!* and the Rolling Stones promoted *Forty Licks,* both "new" albums that featured decades of their greatest hits with a few new songs thrown in to satisfy fans looking for something new. This is beyond repackaging old music and selling it to existing fans; it is really about reestablishing a brand within a culture and creating a transgener-ational fan base. From its latest greatest hits collection, Aerosmith released the "Girls of Summer" single and video, with airplay and cov-erage on MTV and VH1. As new, younger fans became interested in the album for this new track, they were introduced to the band's anthology and music ingrained in the culture for generations.

BRANDS THAT LAST

Some bands remain relevant for decades, releasing albums that com-bine new songs with classic hits and provide a reason for touring—the primary source of income for these artists. Touring also provides the vehicle for classic bands to stay established in the culture, relevant to fans, and on the top of fans' minds. How are classic rock bands doing in this area? Table 2.1 shows the top-10 largest-grossing tours of 2002. Of the top-10 bands, 7 have been around 20 years or more, disclosing the demand for genres of music and artists built to last.

Concerts allow fans to enjoy an experience, but they also establish a connection between performers and fans, spreading a belief among fans that they "know" the individuals in the bands. Corporate brand builders can do the same by participating in special events (such as many do with college students during spring break), distribution of branded products at concerts and festivals, and personal appearances of the CEO and other executives in the media and at public events.

Attitudes toward bands and brands have three primary com-ponents—*affective* (feelings), *cognitive* (knowledge), and *behavioral* (tendency to repeat past behavior). The good feelings (affection) of customers toward brands may be created by creative advertising and favorable word of mouth. These feelings are most resistant to change or competitors' efforts when anchored in the knowledge (cognitive) component of attitude. The more times a consumer buys one brand over others (behavioral component) and is satisfied (rewarded), the greater the probability of buying that brand in the future. For bands, airplay and single sales may create the affective component of favor-able attitude, but it is touring, logo merchandise, publicity, fan clubs, and web sites that build the cognitive component and long-term behavioral loyalty to the classic band winners in Table 2.1.

TABLE 2.1 Concert Gross by Artist

ARTIST	TOTAL GROSS	TOTAL ATTENDANCE	NUMBER OF SHOWS	NUMBER OF SELLOUTS
Paul McCartney	$126,165,542	998,077	58	44
Cher	67,634,323	1,012,037	83	36
Billy Joel and Elton John	66,004,441	613,339	34	24
Dave Matthews Band	52,770,626	1,359,351	67	49
Neil Diamond	52,304,482	911,350	68	50
Britney Spears	43,699,589	779,935	53	36
Aerosmith	38,998,028	779,827	51	10
Creed	37,149,534	889,828	81	23
Crosby, Stills, Nash, & Young	35,018,545	438,022	40	8
Eagles	34,899,563	387,444	31	31

Source: Billboard, December 28, 2002, YE-44.

Technology has enhanced the possibilities for bands and brands to connect with customers both cognitively and affectively. In 1999, VH1 took steps toward upgrading its web site and wound up revamping the old, standby format for expressing fan devotion—the fan club. "Technology brought a new dimension to the fan club," says Darren Layne, interactive television analyst and former director of technology for VH1.com. Light years ahead of the fan club of the 1950s, the online version enabled fans to register on the VH1 site and choose which bands they wanted to follow. They received exclusive access to concert ticket presales and discounts on CDs; they swapped tickets and stories about their favorite bands. "This new-age fan club gave fans the ultimate sense of community—instant, real-time, persistent access to other fans, which allowed the band to become even more ingrained culture and in the lifestyles of the fans."

FIRST MOVER MYTH

Achieving relevance within a culture is also a matter of timing. The *first mover myth,* described in our earlier book, *Customers Rule!* (Crown Business, 2001), shows that innovators are not usually the long-term winners in the market, whether in music or computers. People didn't accept rock and roll from first movers Carl Perkins, Little Richard, and Otis Redding because it was not relevant to their racial and cultural attitudes at the time. Elvis borrowed from first movers, however, and led the rock-and-roll revolution into mass culture. Similarly, Dell dominates the PC market today, even though the first movers in PCs during the 1980s were Commodore, Tandy, and Osborne (not to be confused with the Osbournes!). Word processing and spreadsheets were key applications that caused businesses to put computers on every desktop, but the pioneer brands were VisiWord and VisiCalc, not Windows or Excel. And neither Apple nor Microsoft invented the mouse-driven graphical interfaces that dominate our culture today; the first mover was Xerox. It is similar to the process of emergence and eventual predominance within the world of mass retailing. The Kresge and Woolworth dime stores were first movers, but neither survived to be part of one of today's fastest-growing retail formats, dollar stores.

GAINING CULTURAL ACCEPTANCE FOR INNOVATIVE NEW PRODUCTS

Introducing a new brand or product can be tricky, especially if it is unconventional—different from what has been accepted by the culture to that point. It is difficult to get the attention of would-be buyers anytime, but getting them to try something new usually leaves the best marketers perplexed. The failure to understand the rate of adoption for new technology is one reason many telecom companies are bankrupt, leaving more unused fiber networks than abandoned gold mines. It's the reason people scratch their heads trying to calculate how fast customers will adopt wireless communications, personal video recorders (PVRs, such as TiVo), XML (protocol for exchanging data), Olestra (for reducing fat intake in foods), high definition television, and other innovations. The examples from first mover failures previously described are enough to make anyone pessimistic about how to get a culture to adopt innovative new products.

Now imagine you are a brand-new band, writing and playing a genre of music that is not only obscure but virtually undefined among most audiences. Branding and marketing problems exist not just for the band's brand but for the entire product category. Welcome to the world of new-wave punk music circa 1976.

HOW THE TALKING HEADS GOT FANS TO LISTEN

The Talking Heads not only created a number-one hit with their record "Burnin' Down the House," they ignited the market for a new wave of rock and roll in the 1980s. Their story reveals how to get customers to listen when they don't even know they want the product.

Three young musicians—Chris Frantz, Tina Weymouth, and David Byrne—bound together by the desire to write and play a unique form of music, moved to New York City to follow their dream. Armed with a five-year plan, they spent the first six months watching other bands perform at CBGB (a local, progressive club), writing material, learning how to play together, and developing their talents. Once they developed enough songs for a show, Hilly Kristal, owner of CBGB, put them on stage opposite the Ramones, a band to which they have been linked ever since. "Kristal provided the incubator for bands much like Silicon Valley did for the technology boom a few decades later," says Frantz.

The Talking Heads' music was different—it appealed to a specific type of audience that at the time was at the fringe of society rather than in the middle of it. Seen as smarties who had been to college, they were oddballs in the world of rock and roll, and knew they could attract a niche of cerebral, intellectual fans. Frantz explains, "We were always pretty good about target marketing. We looked for places that attracted people like us and played anyplace we thought would-be fans would be, anyplace we could find a connection with who we thought our audience would be." Their select venues included art galleries and performing arts theaters known for featuring *avant garde* acts.

As each of the bands performing at CBGB got better, the genre of music they were playing became more popular. The bands of the time "schooled" together, deciding that the best way to become noticed, relevant, and accepted in the marketplace would be to band together with others like them and promote their music movement. "We all wanted our form of music to grow, and we were more powerful working toward that goal together than trying to outsell or outdo each other," explains Weymouth. "Together we got more attention from the media and fans and became a part of something bigger than what any of us would have been individually."

When it came time to expand beyond New York City, they united with manager Gary Kurfrist, who understood how to organize, operate, and promote concerts, especially among college markets. He identified college towns in which he thought the Talking Heads, the Ramones, Blondie, and other bands would be accepted, and then found students to act as promoters for campus appearances, often simply finding a place on campus and getting some friends there. The Talking Heads would go in first, and then a few weeks later, another band would come through town. If the audience grew and the music created a buzz among the kids, the promoters would identify it as a hot market and start the next wave. Kurfrist helped them go to the next stage—identifying new acts to book, showing them how to find off-campus venues, and teaching them how to promote the bands and concerts. The process stimulated the entire genre of new wave, punk music.

For no more than $4, college kids could hear a live rock concert of original music—it was a way to encourage trial of a new musical experience and get kids to buy Talking Heads records. Low ticket prices became a motto for the Talking Heads, who even after releasing hit records like "Burnin' Down the House," kept ticket prices low and venues small, opting to play several nights at Radio City Music Hall rather than one night at Madison Square Garden. "It's all about commitment to the type of people that make up our fan base, keeping in closer contact with them, and staying true to what we're all about," says Weymouth.

In typical Talking Heads style, they brought down the house when they played together for the first time in 17 years at the ceremony inducting them to Rock and Roll Hall of Fame in 2002, the year the Ramones were inducted as well. Though the Talking Heads disbanded in the late 1980s, you can still hear their music on radio stations today and buy Frantz and Weymouth's music under the TomTom Club name. The Talking Heads not only participated in a movement, they helped diffuse it from opinion leaders to a wider audience. They also smoothed the way for the success of other intellectual but nerdy superstars such as Elvis Costello, a 2003 inductee to the Rock and Roll Hall of Fame (who even dresses like a nerd). The Talking Heads strategy is a case example of how to move innovative products from obscurity to mass acceptance without mass-marketing resources.

REVENGE OF THE NERDS: GETTING GOOGLED

The Talking Heads' approach to building brands by starting in the intellectual underground is much like the strategy followed by Google, started in 1998 by two doctoral students at Stanford University, Sergey Brin and Larry Page. Although most computer users were content with well-known search engines like Yahoo! and AOL in the late 1990s, a few users, usually quite computer-savvy, learned the quiet secret about Google, a search engine dedicated to the brand promise of *faster and better*. And when these nerds discovered Google's ability to deliver pages more relevant to a query, usually much faster, they told other nerds—much as in the new-wave music network of the 1980s.

Unlike most initial public offering (IPO)–oriented strategies and instant-wealth motivations of Internet companies of that time, Google was dedicated to the customer. Google's Rule 1 is "Put the user in charge." And that's what it does, even to the extent of granting access to its code for other developers to manipulate however they want, limited only by a cap of 1,000 queries a day to prevent server meltdown. With its relentless objective of perfection, Google cuts the time needed for a search by using information from past searches, saving download time on customers' computers, increasing relevance and ease of use. As a result, Google continuously improves on its brand promise of giving users a better experience than its competitors. The open approach to its system and code appeals to nerdy users, who not only develop their own customized approaches, thereby guaranteeing customer loyalty, but also tell others—becoming evangelists for Google.

The strength of the Google brand is not skin-deep; it starts in the heads and hearts of the firm's employees—called "Googlers." The firm attracts the best—it gets 1,500 resumes a day from Googler wannabes—but can hire only a few, spending 87 person-hours per successful candidate to screen down to the 300 or so Googlers it hired in 2002. Google looks for two types of new Googlers. One type is the brilliant, but sometimes a little weird, risk taker. The second type is the certified PhD nerd. When hiring the first category, Google's chief engineer, Wayne Rosing, says, "We look for smart. Smart as in, do they do something weird outside of work, something off the beaten path? That translates into people who have no fear of trying difficult projects and going outside the bounds of what they know." Google also scours the top computer science programs and research labs in the world to hire PhDs who reportedly give the company 90 percent of the best search-engine people in the world. These are the people who can shoot holes in the wild ideas of the weird people. Mix it all up, let people do their own thing in an environment where managers have as many as 160 direct reports, and you get a culture in which people manage themselves. They take lots of risks and create plenty of failures along the way, but all in a culture dedicated to the relentless drive to deliver on the brand promise of faster and better. Google does it better than perhaps any other computer firm in the world, something nerds understood about the brand from the beginning.

Its systems may be open, but its financial books are not. Private, secretive, but apparently highly profitable, the company is estimated by some analysts to be reaping several hundred million dollars a year, accounting for three-quarters of all web searches. When *Fast Company* featured Google in its April 2003 issue, it concluded, "The cardinal rule at Google is, if you can do something that will improve the user's experience, do it. Because it's not perfect, being dominant isn't good enough. And the maniacal attack on imperfection reflects a genuine belief in the primacy of the customer."

Similar to the sense you get in talking to Weymooth and Frantz about the Talking Heads, there's something about the Google brand that makes it feel pure—less of a commercial sellout than many Internet inhabitants, even though it now partners with Internet giants such as AOL. Without the ballyhoo of an IPO or expensive advertising, Google lets its customers do the evangelizing for it. First, win the nerds; then let them win the rest of the world. It worked for the Talking Heads, and it's working for Google.

REFLECTING SOCIETY TO MAKE AN EMOTIONAL CONNECTION

Businesses, not-for-profit organizations, and government leaders, to name just a few types of marketers, are wise to study popular music for a very important reason. Popular music often predicts changes in mainstream culture well before mainstream culture recognizes the change. In the 1960s, when mainstream America and the political leadership were still supportive of the Vietnam War, they could have detected the winds of change by paying attention to the music of Peter, Paul, and Mary; the Kingston Trio; Bob Dylan; and others. Madonna was a leading indicator and reflector of changing sexual mores in the 1980s and continues to be on the cutting edge today (see Chapter 7). From Cat Stevens to rapper Jay Z, music changes as society changes—reflecting changes in people's lifestyles and moods.

Winning marketers monitor changes in the culture and its music and reflect them in their brands. Why? Because problems arise from life, and firms that address top-of-the mind issues by developing solutions to perceived problems—and do it well—are rewarded with robust sales, brand loyalty, and willingness to pay premium prices even in difficult markets.

Lifestyle trends affect a myriad of marketing strategies and tactics, including product design, positioning, packaging, advertising, and distribution. Witness Campbell's recent introduction of soups that come in heat-and-drink cups, designed specifically for people who don't have time to eat anything requiring a table or utensils. Similarly, a recent ad for Tide laundry detergent focuses on a single mother getting ready for a date, dressed in a freshly washed sweater and armed with dating advice from her teenage daughter—a far cry from June Cleaver themes of the past. Typically, brands are analyzed from the perspective of products—either consumer or industrial—and services ranging from financial institutions to health care systems. Most books on branding, including this one, reflect this emphasis. The nature of brands and winning strategies that make them culturally relevant is more comprehensive, however, recognizing an increasing importance to develop culturally relevant brands for retail organizations, for professional persons, and ultimately, for the most important brand of all—the brand called *You*.

RETAILERS AS BRANDS

Major retailers of the past were usually sellers of other firm's brands. Grocery chains sold brands of products from Procter & Gamble and Kraft. Department stores sold fashion brands ranging from Levi's to Tommy Hilfiger. Hardware stores sold Stanley tools and Kohler plumbing fixtures. That's changing. To be culturally relevant today, the goal for retailers is to be not just a seller of branded products, but *to be the brand* in the minds of consumers. This is fueled partly by the fact that an increasing proportion of sales and margins is derived from store brands ("private brands") at most retail chains. More important, in an era of too many retailers chasing too few consumers, it's fueled by the need to be positioned in consumers' minds as the place that delivers the satisfaction of a Stones or KISS concert. It may not matter to consumers whether that satisfaction is derived from manufacturers' brands, the store's brands, or the right combination of both. In consumers' minds, it's the total experience that creates a retailer's brand. Are the right products in stock? Are prices in the expected range? Are personnel knowledgeable and friendly? Do the location, atmospherics, and in-store logistics invite consumers to the store, delighting them so well that they return and tell their friends?

Some retail brands are succeeding, none so well as Wal-Mart, as you'll see in Chapter 4. No retailer has had faster growth in sales recently than Florida-based Chico's, the boomer-oriented retailing champion in ability to relate to consumer lifestyles. Kohl's, Container Store, and 99 cent stores are other big winners in understanding changing lifestyles and relating to them.

Probably no type of retailer is more challenged in adapting to changing lifestyles than department stores such as Dillard's, May, and Federated. Caught in the vise of price competition from mass merchants and the segmented appeal of specialty stores, some retail analysts see the future for department stores about as bright as that of prehistoric dinosaurs.

Federated Department Stores is attempting to reinvent its future, however, by becoming a lifestyle brand. Its Lazarus store in Easton Town Center in Columbus, Ohio, captured the National Retail Federation's 2000 Store of the Year award for implementing a host of "Reinvent Strategies" based on its customers' changing shopping preferences. With Federated's global sourcing capability, the store's brand represents not so much a place to buy products as a purchasing agent for the customer—finding the best mix of brands, products, and styles that the customer wants to buy. Included in the brand is the ability to stretch beyond what customers say they want now to something they might not know is available or possible. That's where the surprise element, the unexpected, comes into play, leading to a moment when the customer may say, "I didn't know about that style or that look, but I like it."

Federated's energetic CEO Terry Lundgren explains, "Our 'Reinvent Strategies' focus on how to make both the *buying* and *shopping* experiences better for our customers. There are times that our customer is going to enter the store, know what she's looking for, and want to get in and out as quickly and efficiently as possible. For those times we simplify her shopping experience, easing her movement through the store with shopping carts, clear signage that looks somewhat like street signs, and scanners that show her exactly what the price and savings are on the product she wants buy. But we also want to improve on the social and emotional aspect of shopping that we believe our customers still want to experience. When she wants to spend more time in our stores, we've added things like cafes that serve Starbucks coffee, soothing lighting, different types of music in different departments, flat-screen TVs, and nuances to put some wow back into the shopping experience."

The most successful retailers and brands, like legendary rock bands, reflect changes in consumer mood, affecting not only what people relate to and connect with, but also what they buy and consume. During times of war, the lyrics and mood of popular songs reflect sentiments different from those during high-flying times of economic booms. Songs by Peter, Paul, and Mary and Bob Dylan provided unofficial anthems during the 1960s, while Cyndi Lauper's "Girls Just Wanna Have Fun" reflected the sentiment of society in the carefree 1980s.

Few things affect mood more than music. Just as some bands strike a chord with fans when they reflect the societal mood, some find success by creating music to change the mood, providing an escape from the pressures of the real world. Retailers may be victims of consumer mood during times of global conflict and stock meltdown, but they can also be change agents of consumer mood, creating havens to which consumers want to flock. Engaging consumers through all of their senses—from colors that convey happiness and security and scents that are inviting—makes them want to spend more time in the store. Certainly price counts, but so do friendly faces, helpful associates, and security measures, inviting consumers to turn off the depressing news on the television and spend time in retailers' stores.

Retailers might not be able to change dramatically the number of shopping bags leaving the store during periods of depressed consumer mood, but they can create places people want to *be*. Ultimately, consumer mood changes, and the stores that invest in an emotional relationship with their customers, even when customers aren't buying, are poised to reap the rewards when mood and financial circumstances turn upward. Like the success of the tours of legendary bands, today's emotional connection often turns into tomorrow's financial transaction. Look at the popularity and success of Paul McCartney's 2002 tour in Table 2.1, built primarily on the emotional connection he has with fans from his time with the Beatles and Wings. Just because his fans may not continuously buy all his music, they are willing to invest time with him when he tours.

PEOPLE AS BRANDS

In addition to retailers being brands, so too are people. In fact, one type of brand that is extremely relevant and just as connected to customers as the traditional kinds of brands (products, retailers, and organizations) is the brand of professionals—physicians, attorneys, insurance agents, architects, or even funeral directors. These brands are as important to consumers at critical moments of their lives as many of their personal relationships, yet few professionals receive training during their academic studies or from their professional societies on how to build a brand that delights their clients. And most professionals appear to give little thought to how to create a brand that turns clients into fans who refer friends to their favorite doctors or professional practices.

One professional person who works hard at correcting this omission is Gary Kinman, an award-winning landscape architect and founder of Kinman & Associates. Kinman's client approach is marketing-driven, which makes him a unique brand among the others in his field, most of whom see themselves as sellers and installers of horticultural products. Rather, Kinman defines his brand promise as shaping the earth to enhance the life of his clients. "The first thing I do is understand the psychology of the customer," he says. "How do I connect with my customers and what is relevant to their lifestyles? People buy because of emotion. If I can find the motive or emotion they connect to, I can create a product that will create value way beyond the cost of physical materials."

Another dimension of Kinman's brand is his commitment to teaching others and elevating the entire industry. He founded the

Kinman Institute, where he trains other architects and professionals on everything from business operations to branding. He teaches attendees, who already know most of the functional basics of balance, scale, proportion, materials, and so forth, a great truth of branding: "You can't understand how to do what your clients want you to do unless you understand them and what constitutes value for them." Whether it is a minor change in a modest home or a million-dollar landscape project for a suburban estate, Kinman shows his students how to create value by connecting with customers and how they have to take on marketing roles themselves.

As professionals such as Kinman demonstrate, the term *marketing* should no longer be considered taboo, regardless of your industry, even in the world of medicine. Physicians who take time to help their patients, show them care and concern, and connect with them are the ones people want to visit—they are the ones with thriving practices and the ones that receive the most referrals. And while taking a lot of time with patients isn't always feasible, it speaks volumes about the brand of the person and the healthcare organization.

Ultimately, the most important brand developed by any person is the brand called *You*. Whether you have to promote yourself to win clients or get a job, customers will make choices about you based on your personal brand. What makes some rock-and-roll stars more successful than others often stems from what they are like as people and how that translates into their brands. The musicians featured in this book offer lessons on how to handle controversy, how your personal brand connects to the brand of your professional practice, how personal values can affect people's perceptions of your brand, and how you will most likely be your own best marketer. In addition, the CEOs described in this book such as David Neeleman (JetBlue), Leslie Wexner (Limited Brands), and Betsy Holden (Kraft) provide lessons on how personal brands intertwine with their professional or corporate brands.

THE INFLUENCE OF BRANDS ON SOCIETY

Music not only *reflects* societal values; it can significantly *influence* the values of individuals. Unlike animals, whose behavior is more instinctive, humans are not born with norms of behavior. Instead, they learn through imitation or by observing the process of reward and punishment in a society whose members adhere to or deviate from the group's norms. When highly rewarded rock stars—or sports heroes and politicians, for that matter—adhere to or deviate from social norms in dress, food and beverage preferences, and social behavior, millions of fans learn what is rewarded and follow suit. The key to creating a cool brand is often to associate it with the people and behavior admired by the market segment to which the brand is targeted.

A majority of the rock stars discussed in *Brands That Rock* have one thing in common—they didn't fit in with the other kids in school. They were different, delightfully odd in their own sense of the word. "They all came from outside of society and became the inside," says Bruce Springsteen in a film featured at the Rock and Roll Hall of Fame.

Although they did not fit in the mainstream, they were able to channel their creativity, energies, talents, and idiosyncrasies into the world of music, which is still known for accepting individuals who are misunderstood by society. The irony is that their talents and creativity were most likely ignored by traditionalists—retailers, manufacturers, and the like—who probably thought they had nothing to offer to the world of commerce. But these people were able to catapult their status from outcast to megastar, from those who were *outside* the culture to those who help *define* it.

Legendary bands influence the culture, and the best allow the culture to influence them as well. Just as Madonna influences fashion and even exercise trends, Gene Simmons and KISS listened to their fans and figured out how to sell more records by packaging the KISS experience (a key lesson examined in detail in Chapter 6). Bands have even influenced people's definition of good music, creating acceptance of a style or quality level that might have been unacceptable previously.

"It's not always about how well you sing, especially in the traditional sense of the word, because standards of what is good or bad change," says Chris Frantz. "Bob Dylan, for example, proves that the message can overcome a lot of other things that we think are important in being accepted. There are a lot of breakthroughs that occur because of things beyond traditional product quality that center more on message and [emotional] connection that eventually change the standard."

Though its hamburgers may not win as many taste tests as gourmet burgers, McDonald's created a new standard in food retailing based on convenience, speed, consistency, and emotions that influenced what was acceptable and even desired by many Americans in terms of their food choices. Similarly, Starbucks has set a new standard for good coffee, and Wal-Mart has set a new standard of what people expect to pay for products.

Elvis brought ethnic music to the mainstream, helping part of a minority culture become part of the majority culture, a lesson of massive importance for brand managers and marketers. Until then, fashion, product, and consumer trends were assumed to trickle down from the upper classes to the lower classes. Rock and roll changed the sociology of marketing to a new model of product innovation and brand acceptance—the *trickle-up* process of brand development. In today's world of branding, everything from urban styles to slang words are trickling up to mainstream culture, following in the footsteps of their musical predecessor—rhythm and blues.

Today's most relevant example is Eminem, the foul-mouthed, white rapper who says things in his songs that most of us would never admit to thinking. The 30-year-old prodigal son of Dr. Dre (one of the founding fathers of rap music) spews out sentiments of hate, homophobia, murder, gay sex, rape, and hating his mother. (If there are any additional disparaging topics you can name, he's probably sung about them.) But ask critics and fans alike, and they'll tell you his lyrics are a bit tongue-in-cheek, and if you really look behind the façade of hate, you'll see the humor in his words. Okay. The only person he seems to care for is his daughter, to whom he declares his devotion and love. These sentiments touch a nerve with many of the kids who make up his fan base—kids who don't have fathers and wish someone would love them as much as Eminem professes to love his daughter. His association with Dr. Dre has given him credibility in the hip-hop community and has helped him craft a strong beat and musical sound, and his whiteness has let him connect with suburban kids—and, believe it or not, some of their parents.

Eminem's major debut album in 1999, *The Slim Shady LP,* hit an emotional chord with a variety of fans—some loved it and some hated it. Its popularity fueled the 2000 release of *The Marshall Mathers LP*, which poked fun at celebrity and controversy in Eminem's typical hip-hop mockery fashion. His most recent album, *The Eminem Show*, is a tamer, simpler version of his first releases, which built his rebel image and brand among urbanites and suburbanites alike. By the summer of 2002, you could find urban kids, mostly white suburban kids, and soccer moms rapping and bopping to "Without Me," a hit single. Critics, who prefer the harsher, "more pure" version of Eminem, cite his new, tamer music as a way to grow his brand based on the formula that has worked for him in the past. Jon Pareles, of the *New York Times,* writes, "Eminem has now decided what his brand image is; he's the spokesman for suburban adolescent rebellion coupled with self-pity, for 'so much anger aimed in no particular direction.' "[1]

USING MUSIC TO CREATE A RELATIONSHIP WITH CULTURE

The common characteristic tying iconic brands together is the relationship to fans. Elvis definitely has that deep emotional connection with his fans, as do other bands described in this book. Retailers and product marketers continue to search for new ways to break the ice with customers and reward their loyalty, whether by frequent shopper discounts and loyalty cards or special sales and events held only for top customers, all designs to create connections with customers, capturing their loyalty and dollars. Customer relationship management (CRM) software, all the rage among marketers, helps identify behaviors of the most profitable customers and encourage those behaviors among other segments of the customer base. It helps marketers cross-sell other products to loyal customers and increase the productivity of marketing resources. However, CRM can only guide strategies and tactics to develop profitable customer relationships. The human, emotional side of relationship building and connection goes beyond even the best computer software.

Scott Elias, founder of New York's Elias Associates, a firm heavily involved in music-partnered commercials, explains, "Classic rock has been effective because it's nostalgia, something people know and love."[2] His analysis indicates that about 75 to 80 percent of national television ads now add music to the ads, compared to only 25 percent just a few years ago. Compared to words in the content of an ad, Elias states, "Music is more primal, and is the most effective emotional communicator. You can communicate with smells, words, and pictures, but the most direct and powerful is music and that's why it's the universal language."

MAKING CONNECTIONS WITH MUSIC

Central and peripheral processing of messages, the focus of much research in consumer behavior, explain how music affects the personality of a brand. When direct claims are made about a product and its attributes—the brand promise—they are processed cognitively by the consumer. Consumers understand what the brand claims to be and evaluate it using their reasoning abilities. Peripheral processing involves cues that the consumer doesn't usually think about—things such as background music, the color of the ad, feelings toward the actors, and other elements that pass into the brain without thinking about them, passing into the consumer's memory without the filter of conscious thought. Music is one of the most powerful of the peripheral cues, going directly into the brain, and hopefully resonating in the mind at the time the consumer drives by a store or searches among brands on a shelf. It doesn't pass through the cognitive filter that evaluates the more direct, or central, messages contained in the ad claims and copy.

When consumers carefully consider the message's content, then the presence of compelling claims about the advertised brand is essential to develop favorable attitudes toward the brand. However, when consumers do not think carefully about the message claims—probably the reality with many products ranging from colas and beers to personal care and household items—the strength of the ad claims becomes less important. Instead, the ad's persuasive impact depends on whether it contains positive peripheral cues. This is why background music by the Rolling Stones or Elton John may affect attitudes toward the brand even without much conscious awareness of the music. Ad practitioner Elias explains, "I'm not sure that the consumer listens as much to the copy as the advertiser might think. I think the personality of the product is shaped by the type of music chosen."

Music and promotional tie-ins to music help marketers position a brand as up-to-date and reflective of current culture, as well as develop stronger relationships. Macy's teamed up with *GQ magazine* and designers ranging from Kenneth Cole and Geoffrey Beene to Perry Ellis and Tommy Hilfiger to create a promotional campaign blending retailing, fashion, and music. In an eight-page 2002 holiday ad, Macy's created an up-to-date men's collection featuring musical artists clad in designer duds, with a description of the apparel, the artists, and their upcoming releases. Each designer brand was connected with a music brand, connecting to an established fan base and reflecting a lifestyle segment. Macy's customers who spent $75 or more on any of the fashions featured in the ad could send in a copy of the receipt to GQ Promotions and receive a free CD by the featured artists. Macy's rewards its customers with free music (and shopping suggestions), promotes its vendors' labels, creates awareness for the bands' upcoming releases, and connects its own brand as well as those of the designers and artists with customers. It's a quad-win proposition for building relationships at multiple levels.

Consumer research indicates that credible sources usually enhance persuasion. Physically attractive sources are more persuasive, especially for sources that are likeable, hold celebrity status, or are similar to the target audience. The surrounding content of television programs, radio music, or magazine content also may enhance an ad's credibility.

Celebrity endorsers, whether rock musicians or Michael Jordan, shape consumers' interpretation of the ad and the product through *meaning transfer*—the process by which the meaning of one object (a rock song, for example) is transferred to another object, the product being advertised. Products take on some of the characteristics consumers associate with the endorsers or the music they hear in the ads. When the endorser is trusted by consumers, they are more accepting of the ad claims, depending on how well the product and the endorser fit together. That's one reason the Elton John ads endorsing Diet Coke work so well—he obviously needs the product and appears to really like it.

EVERYTHING GOES BETTER WITH COKE

One of the most memorable television commercials of all time featured Elton John promoting Diet Coke. In the ad, Elton John plays a piano in a nightclub, joined by famous celebrities from the past. Using high-tech recreation, Louis Armstrong blows a trumpet riff from a Diet Coke jingle as he stands next to John's piano. Humphrey Bogart walks into the nightclub as though he is Rick Blaine, walking into his own club in Casablanca. James Cagney orders drinks and appears to smile at his modern lady companion as she rests her elbow on his shoulder. The shots of Bogart came from *All Through the Night* (1942), Armstrong was lifted from *High Society* (1956), and Cagney was heisted from *The Roaring Twenties* (1939) and *Public Enemy* (1931). Computers black out the background of the old movies frame by frame, keeping only the images of the stars, all now appearing to be in a contemporary setting.

This transgenerational ad not only spans the ages of film, it spans the ages of cola markets, and John delivers the punch line with a truly inspired slogan—"Drink Diet Coke—Just for the Taste of It."

Advertising experts for many years have understood the power of a USP—a *unique selling proposition*. "Just for the Taste of It" is a short, memorable statement of the principal benefit desired by customers. Elton John and his famous pals from the past deliver it in a manner guaranteed to attract the attention of television audiences and download the message into their long-term memories. That's what a great commercial should do, allowing consumers to retrieve the USP when they're ready to purchase.

Elton John also relates to his fans beyond the television commercial. At his concerts, an ice bucket is always nearby, and the seemingly bottomless Diet Coke can is in his hand between songs and by the piano during the performance. But it doesn't stop there. We've watched his performance, admiring his marketing flair as he makes sure the Diet Coke logo is displayed to the audience, usually in a position that the I-Mag projection cameras can't miss. Add to the campaign his credibility as an endorser because of his lifelong struggle with weight, and it's easy to understand why the relationship between Diet Coke and Elton John is one of the classic success stories in the role of sponsorship in brand building.

UNDERSTAND, EMULATE, INFILTRATE

Unless management acts, the more successful a firm has been in the past, the more likely it is to fall in the future. Sound counterintuitive? Actually, this statement is dead on, because many strategies that are successful in the marketplace are effective only so long as the environment is held constant. And especially in today's rapidly evolving consumer environment, that isn't very long.

Legendary rock-and-roll bands achieve their status because they stay connected with fans and remain relevant to the culture. For many, this includes evolving the total band experience over time, from how, where, and when fans hear and experience the band to the look, sound, and overall image of the artists and their music. In addition to creating new music, legendary bands reinvent themselves and avoid becoming outdated and irrelevant by:

♪ Touring—to spark renewed interest in the band and bring it into a new point in time for fans

♪ Collaborating with new artists—to associate themselves with new and contemporary sounds, introduce them to new fans, and accompany new memories

♪ Promoting and aligning with products and brands that are relevant to fans

♪ Releasing greatest hits albums—to rekindle loyalty, stir memories and emotions, and introduce new fans to already adopted music

♪ Embracing new media outlets—to reach audiences through new but accepted technology, from videos and DVDs to the Internet

♪ Repackaging (of music and personalities)—to reflect changes in accepted visual imagery, language, and topics and desired physical appearance

Although these strategies focus on change, they demonstrate that an important key is to evolve without abandoning what has made the bands successful in the past. As long as people listen to the music of Bob Seger, the Rolling Stones, and Elton John, these performers will remain an active part of their fans' lives and part of our culture. If they continue to relate to their fans and stay in tune with their fans' lifestyles, these legendary bands will continue to build long-term loyalty. As a result, they command a major share of fans' entertainment dollars and increase their value to the marketers of consumer products looking for ways to connect with certain segments of the culture. And, perhaps more important to the artists themselves, they will capture a position in music history.

Anyone with the responsibility for managing an organization's brand needs to start by understanding the culture of its core customers. Brand management should always be focused on evaluating, emulating, and, if the market segment is sufficiently attractive, infiltrating the culture of the largest and fastest-growing groups of its market.

Brand evolution is not reserved for just legendary rock bands or consumer products companies. The National Football League has undergone a significant transformation over the past several years to gain a strong foothold in American culture.

"The NFL is an established brand, with 80 years of equity, but a few years ago there was a sense among ownership and senior management that it had become more of a licensing company," explains John Collins, NFL's senior vice president of marketing and entertainment. "In order to redefine the NFL, we stepped back and thought about our place in the world of brands—what we stood for and how we could evolve. When we talk about ourselves today, we talk about being premier entertainment."

Rock and roll has played a key role in the NFL's brand transformation. Fans who religiously fill stadiums on Sunday afternoons and Monday nights are treated to mini–music fests, as music blares between plays and quarters. And then there are the much-awaited Super Bowl halftime shows, which have featured superstars from Michael Jackson to Aerosmith (with Britney Spears and 'N Sync) to U2.

To celebrate its first-ever season kickoff in 2002, the NFL turned to Bon Jovi to headline what was being billed as the world's largest tailgate party. Known for its classic rock sound and the movie-star good looks of its lead singer Jon Bon Jovi and lead guitarist Richie Sambora, the band connected with fans as it played a string of hits and an emotional rendition of "America the Beautiful." Bon Jovi's popularity among guys who like good old rock and roll and women who like great-looking sexy guys appeal to NFL fans of either gender. The ultimate tailgate party attracted over 500,000 fans to Times Square and millions more in 226 countries with 13 live broadcasts of the event. In fact, more people watched the kickoff than voted in the prior presidential election.

Although music has become an important dimension of the NFL brand, Collins points out, "We're not trying to be in the music business, but we are trying to be in the fabric of the American culture and be ubiquitous in terms of where that shows up. It's all part of trying to be where people are and becoming part of their culture."

The tricky part is that culture changes. If it didn't, we'd all still be swinging to Glenn Miller or waltzing to Mozart. Instead, legions of fans rock to the Rolling Stones, Aerosmith, and KISS, sing along with Elton John and Neil Diamond, and dance to Madonna. They have been adopted by the culture as fervently as Coca-Cola, Starbucks, and Wal-Mart have, with even more emotion and devotion from their fans. The remaining chapters reveal the strategies that these artists have used to win fans and create profits.

3

ELTON JOHN:
MUSIC MAN, MARKETING MAN, ARCHITECT OF A BRAND

Rock and roll, man, it changed my life. It was like the Voice of America, the real America, coming to your home.

—BRUCE SPRINGSTEEN

Elton John has had at least one top-40 hit every year for 30 straight years; not even Elvis, with 23 years, matched John's record! From behind his piano, John has reached the hearts and souls of millions of people with a music montage ranging from romantic ballads to toe-tapping rock and roll. "Your Song." "Rocket Man." "The One." Chances are you and your teenage kids can name at least three Elton John songs without too much effort. While you may remember his hits from the 1970s, the names of songs from Disney's films *The Lion King* or *The Road to El Dorado* may roll more readily from your children's tongues.

Elton John's appeal has spanned generations as few entertainers' have; studying his career quickly reveals that there is more to creating hits than just making good music. Fans have watched him transform from what might be described as the Liberace of rock and roll—clad in wild sunglasses, outrageously sequined outfits, and flamboyant hats—to respected artist, statesman, and AIDS activist. They've seen him appear on magazine covers, television shows, television advertisements, and alongside some of the hottest entertainers of the moment. They've followed his personal life in the media, including his struggles with substance abuse, weight gain, sexual preference, and personal finances. They've also watched him push the envelope of artistry with his Disney movie soundtracks and his Broadway triumphs with *The Lion King* and *Aida.*

As a result, John achieved unprecedented success with his tribute to Princess Diana set to "Candle In The Wind," which he performed only at her funeral. "I was singing on behalf of all those people who had stood for 13, 14 hours to pay tribute to someone they obviously thought a lot of," he says. He donated the proceeds of the record sales—$32 million—to Princess Diana's favorite charities. This song became the number-one-selling song of all time, eclipsing sales of the previous record holder, "White Christmas" by Bing Crosby. John's fans have propelled him to sales of over 200 million albums worldwide, with 10 multiplatinum, 24 platinum, and 33 gold records in the United States alone. Along the way he accumulated an Academy Award for *Can You Feel the Love Tonight* in 1995, five Grammys, a People's Choice Award in 1999, and a Tony Award for his musical *Aida* in 2000. He's been honored with fashion, music video, and social responsibility awards as well.

Elton John's ability to amass critical acclaim, fans, and profits stems from his two primary strengths—his artistic talent and his marketing prowess. He recognized early that one without the other usually leads to moderate success at best, and the brand that is Elton John certainly doesn't stand for moderation.

MUSIC MAN

Reginald Kenneth Dwight was born in 1947 to a musical family in Pinner, a London suburb, where his father played trumpet in both the Royal Air Force and in an American-style big band. Young Reggie grew up with records by singers like Rosemary Clooney, Frank Sinatra, and Frankie Laine and pianists such as Nat "King" Cole, George

Shearing, and Winifred Atwell, who played both popular and classical music and quickly became one of his favorites. After listening to her classic recording of "The Skater's Waltz," he sat down at the family piano and played it perfectly by ear. He was three years old. By the age of four, Reggie was "on stage" for family gatherings, and he performed at his cousin's wedding at age seven, when the band was late.

Piano lessons and an ability to listen to and then play classical recordings to near perfection won him a scholarship at the Royal Academy of Music in London at the age of 11. At the academy, he excelled in mastering the music of Handel, Chopin, and Bach and sang in the school's choir. As busy as he was with his studies, he found time for a part-time job as a newspaper carrier.

Although a model student in many ways—polite and highly capable—he was less than diligent in his studies, perhaps because he didn't find them challenging. He could mimic the classical masters without much effort, and after five years, he left the venerable Royal Academy. He did return, however, in July 2002, when he became the second person in the school's 180-year history to receive an honorary doctorate degree. What happened between his departure from the academy and his return would make music history, deserving of an honorary degree in marketing as well.

MARKETING MAN

As a young boy, Elton John's mastery of the classics gave way to his love for rock and roll, fueled by the likes of Elvis Presley, Bill Haley, Little Richard, and Jerry Lee Lewis. He worked hard to go from standing in front of a mirror, pounding out songs on the piano and pretending to be Lewis, to performing live at Dodger stadium in 1975 to a sellout crowd of 55,000.

John isn't just a music man; he is a marketing man—that's what has propelled him to phenomenal heights of success and made him a household name. When we study John's career, we begin to realize that *marketing* may be one of the most misunderstood words in the common business vernacular. It's often equated with *selling* or *advertising* when actually it's about *creating, changing,* or *evolving* a product into something that people will buy. Simply put—*selling* is getting people to buy what you produce, but *marketing* is about producing what people will want to buy. Sometimes marketers are accused of manipulating people by trying to persuade them in some way. John would probably agree, but with one caveat—recognition of precisely who is being manipulated in the marketing process. Marketing is not about a marketer manipulating consumers; it's about understanding consumers well enough to let them manipulate the marketer to produce what will sell more easily.

Walking the fine line of what "more pure" artists would consider selling out, Elton John is a great example of what it takes to create a complete brand, as you'll see in this chapter. His career has flourished because of his understanding of what consumers want, his ability to create what his fans will buy, and his willingness to compromise between artistic purity and commercial appeal. As you see John's branding story unfold, you'll see how his success provides lessons on:

♪ Adopting a marketing rather than a sales orientation

♪ Developing transgenerational brand appeal

♪ Developing both the functional and emotional elements of the brand to create a unified message and image in the market

♪ Understanding how brand attributes work together to drive positioning and "heart share"

♪ Creating brand personality and promise that connect with fans

♪ Changing a brand image when it becomes irrelevant to fans or no longer represents the promise

♪ Understanding how the image of the CEO or spokesperson affects the image of the brand of the product and the company.

John probably could have been very successful as a classical pianist. He had the natural talent and the training for it, but he chose a career in rock and roll, which is perhaps one of his most revealing marketing lessons. He understood that being successful in the classical recordings arena probably meant sales of a few hundred thousand records, while success in the pop music market meant larger, mass audiences, more market impact, and bigger bucks—over $200 million and rising for his recordings alone. It was also where his passion resided, certainly not an insignificant factor in his success, and a key lesson for marketers of any service, product, or brand.

MUSIC MEETS MARKETING

In order to appreciate fully the name Elton John made for himself, it is helpful to understand the foundation of the brand he created. Reggie Dwight, as he was still known in the early 1960s, banded with a local group of boys to form Bluesology, in which he played the organ (primarily because of its aggressive, intimidating qualities). The group added a trumpet player and a saxophone player who were older, experienced jazz musicians with contacts in the industry. Not only did they help get bookings in better venues, they helped put together a demo tape in 1965 of a song Dwight had written, called "Come Back Baby." The key was too high for the band's lead singer, so Dwight stepped in, and because it was a ballad, he swapped his organ for the piano. In a sweet, clear voice he sang the song that beckoned his love to come back to him, as his fingers danced along the ivories—a combination that would separate him from many other rockers and eventually lead him to superstardom. Few people, however, would hear his breakthrough piece.

Success was far from instant, as Bluesology worked for several years as a backup band for touring soul groups such as Patti LaBelle and the Blue Bells, the Ink Spots, and as an opening act for his boyhood hero, Little Richard. Years later, John recalled, "When I saw Little Richard standing on top of the piano, all lights, sequins, and energy, I decided there and then that I was going to be a rock-and-roll piano player!"[1]

Bluesology also backed up a blues singer named Long John Baldry, who had a number-one hit in England, "Let the Heartaches Begin." Not only did Baldry stand nearly a foot taller than the short and generally overweight Dwight, he became Dwight's hero musically and in other ways. Soon thereafter, in 1967, Reggie Dwight made some changes. "Being called Reggie was kind of like a nightmare when I was young. I couldn't wait to be somebody else," he stated in a 1988 radio interview.[2] He took the name "Elton" from Bluesology's sax player, Elton Dean, and "John" from Baldry. Armed with solid experience ranging from the classics to the blues, plenty of ambition, and a new name, the stage was set for him to move from backup to big time. All he needed was a special spark to light the fire within him. That spark was Bernie Taupin.

UPSIDE-DOWN CREATIVE PROCESS

Elton John's career as a pianist and as a singer was stalled; he even flunked a voice audition in 1967 at Liberty Records. He did, however, get work as a studio musician at Liberty, where Ray Williams, the head of A&R, handed him a bunch of lyrics written by a "fellow from Lincolnshire" who couldn't compose music, named Bernie Taupin. By the autumn of 1967, John (although he was still called Reggie Dwight then) had put music to several of Taupin's lyrics including "Scarecrow" and "A Dandelion Dies in the Wind" and mailed them to him. Both were folk songs reflecting Taupin's life growing up on a farm. Eventually Williams brought Taupin to the recording studio where John was doing session work and with the simple words "meet Bernie" ignited one of the longest-lasting and most commercially successful partnerships in the music industry.

Perhaps an unconventional pairing, the synergy between John, trained in classical music, and Taupin, a farm boy who nevertheless loved classical poetry by Coleridge and Tennyson, birthed some of the most emotion-evoking songs in music history. Taupin was impressed with how much John knew about music; John recognized that Taupin's lyrics, though sometimes cryptic, had an intriguing, mystical, earthy quality that connected at a deeper emotional level than anything he had written himself. It wasn't long before Taupin (who soon became the brother John never had) moved into the home where John and his mother still lived. Their brotherhood would provide the foundation for a lifelong collaboration and help them survive strains that might sever other, less personal partnerships.

The team tackled the creative process just as they had on their first collaboration, which would become a hallmark difference between their collaborative team and others in the business. Taupin wrote the lyrics first, then handed them off to John, who wrote the music around them, abandoning the traditional process in which lyrics are written after the music. As a result, the music is lyric-driven rather than music-driven, and to this day, that is how the team works. "I'm a musical mouthpiece for his lyrics, which I love," John explained on VH1's *Behind the Music*.

Although confetti didn't fly with the release of the team's initial recordings, some songs did catch the attention of other artists. For example, Three Dog Night included "Lady Samantha," written and composed by the duo, on its *Suitable for Framing* album in 1969—a form of flattery if not success for John and Taupin at that point in their careers. *Empty Sky*, released in 1969, was the team's first album featuring Elton John. Overall, it was far from a perfect product, selling only 4,000 copies, but it demonstrates that everyone—whether entrepreneur or musical group—has to start somewhere, even with little initial success.

YOUR SONG—GIVING FANS WHAT THEY WANT

Up to that point, John and Taupin had been trying to sell—generally unsuccessfully—what they had created, relying only on their own ideas and creative talents. But sometimes those most involved in the creative side of business are those least likely to have a connection to what customers really want to buy because of an all-too-common disconnection from mass-market audiences.

The shift to a marketing orientation started with changing their product. Taupin and John continued to do what each did best, but they added producer Gus Dudgeon, an industry veteran with the experience needed to elevate the music quality, and an arranger, Paul Buckmaster, who offered up elegant string arrangements, complete with a studio orchestra. The result was a product with substantially more depth than the compositions and performances they had tried to sell by themselves.

The result was *Elton John,* their second album, released in the summer of 1970. It could serve as a textbook on consumer behavior, demonstrating how to reach consumers by appealing to basic human emotions. Just as companies with high sales and brand loyalty often design products that appeal to the needs, drives, problems and feelings of consumers,[3] so too did the album *Elton John* appeal to basic human needs and motivations. It encompassed a wide range of demographic and cultural segments, and served as a blueprint for the brand that John would build over the next three decades.

The featured track, "Your Song," which became his first number one hit, spoke about giving the beautiful gift of a song to a lover—a simple sentiment but one that connects with anyone who is in love or wants to be, which is just about everyone. This song's significance would only increase throughout John's career, becoming one of the most requested by fans among the string of hits that would span the next 35 years. And while it is about a lover's gift, it symbolizes the gift of song from John to his fans—the ultimate marketing gesture. Giving back to fans—rewarding them with something they feel has been created for them—helps move the relationship to a more intimate level.

The album also contained other culturally relevant songs, connecting with people of all ages. "Sixty Years On" related to the loneliness of old age, telling with words, harpsichord, and broken piano chords the poignant story of a veteran returning after the war to the isolation of old age. "First Episode at Hienton" spoke directly to the feelings of every teenager, telling the story of a young man's first sexual experience with a girl named Valerie. On "Take Me to the Pilot," the meaning of the words was more cryptic ("I haven't a clue", says Taupin) apparently explained only by Taupin's interest in science fiction at the time. And while the meaning might have been foggy, the emotional charge of the music was clear, grabbing the psyche of listeners, taking them to a crescendo of synthesizer-enhanced, full-orchestral climax. "The Greatest Discovery," in contrast, was a piano lullaby describing one of life's most emotional experiences, the birth of a baby.

Other songs spoke of the cultural gaps associated with poverty ("No Shoestrings on Louise") in a country melody, similar to what the Rolling Stones were recording at the time. Race relations and the consequences of bigotry were encompassed in "Border Song," with soul themes so profound that Aretha Franklin recorded a cover of the song the next year—the first major star to do so. The final song, "The

King Must Die," was interpreted in the culture of the time to be about the death of Martin Luther King, although Taupin actually wrote it about assassination plots through the ages.

A TRANSGENERATIONAL APPEAL

This album, and subsequent others, connected at the deepest level with people of all ages, genders, and cultural groups. It laid the foundation for Elton John's transgenerational marketing strategy—creating a product that may be designed for a specific segment but whose appeal transcends a variety of age groups rather than just teens or just boomers. Other artists have had success with a similar approach, although few are really able to create a music product that appeals to multigenerational audiences. The fact that the classic rock bands highlighted in this book have been around for so long helps to explain why they are more likely to attract varied audiences today, but it isn't often that new artists can attract the same mix.

One breakout example of late is Norah Jones, whose fairytale success story began with the release of her album *Come Away With Me* in February 2002, culminating in eight Grammy awards, ranging from Best New Artist to Album of the Year. But this Cinderella's night at the ball was not the result of an invitation by the prince, rather because the townspeople drove her to the palace and pushed her inside. Her voice is sultry, her look exotic, her sound lush, her talent enormous and genuine. With low expectations for the commercial success of the album, critics and fans alike were surprised by the runaway acceptance of her style of music, and no one was more stunned than Jones herself.

"If anyone says there was a formula for predicting the success of this album, they're lying," says Ray Gmeiner, vice president of promotions for Virgin Records. "She's sold 6 million records so far simply because her sound hits a chord with people." The key is that the chord belongs to people from 16 to 66, who enjoy her voice, the mood she creates, and the emotions she stirs. Younger fans are in fact a little surprised that they like the album as much as they do, because it's a collection of songs closer to what their grandparents might have lying around than to what they've listened to in the past.

Jones's rise to stardom may have been unexpected by most, but what isn't surprising is that her approach works, similar to the way Elton John's has. At a time in our culture when unity and family are top-of-mind concerns to people of all ages, Jones's music, like John's, is something that children, parents, and grandparents can enjoy together. And because her album features more than just one hit, it has overcome the download mentality rampant among young consumers who don't perceive enough value in an album to part with $15.

Her hit album is reminiscent of the sentiment and appeal of Elton John's works. *Elton John,* in a sense, was a prototypical product with lyrical and melodic themes connecting at the deepest emotional levels to multiple market segments—a prototype that helps explain the appeal of Harry Potter books.

CREATING BRAND ELTON

The album *Elton John,* if not perfect, was excellent. It delivered both lyrics and musical qualities a cut above everything else on the market, displaying John's foundation in classical music and Taupin's classic poetic content layered onto his country roots. However, a great product is not enough to attain a legendary position in the industry; it takes a great brand to create star qualities and legions of loyal fans.

A brand, whether it is Elton John, Krispy Kreme, or JetBlue, is a product or a service with an identifiable set of benefits wrapped in a recognizable personality. It creates an image and an identity for a product, line of products, or a company, and makes a promise to others (customers, vendors, regulators, shareholders, and everyone else), telling them what they can expect and whether they can trust the product to fulfill those expectations. Successful brands start with a blueprint that describes the needed building blocks, where they are to be placed, and how they should fit together to create a profitable venture.

A brand strategy needs to consider both the functional and emotional elements of a brand, as seen in Figure 3.1. Functional elements may include the quality of the product or the service experience, for example. In the case of JetBlue, described later in this chapter, the

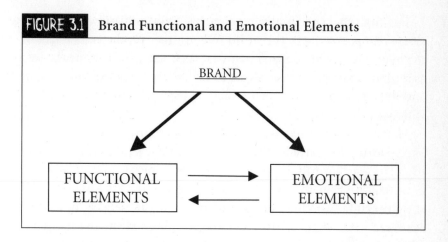

FIGURE 3.1 Brand Functional and Emotional Elements

functional attributes of the brand include all of the interactions customers have with the JetBlue experience, from ease of check-in and comfort of the seats to price and safety. The emotional attributes, on the other hand, include the brand image, personality, and promise that help create a connection with customers. Some functional elements, such as the design of the Volkswagen Beetle, create emotional connections with consumers, while some emotional elements, such as the Pez candy dispenser, have functional qualities that attract customers.

The process of creating one unified identity that encompasses attributes in both of the categories comprises the architecture of a brand, and Elton John provides an amazing case study in this area. John demonstrates how the functional and emotional elements relate to create an overriding brand image and position. It is clear how he has worked over the years to develop his musical talents and performance skills to perfect the functional attributes of the Elton John brand. While those attributes seem difficult to master, honing the emotional elements of his brand proved to be challenging as well.

DEVELOPING ELTON'S EMOTIONAL SIDE

Before the success of *Elton John,* John's career was progressing modestly. But to become a star, a master of music marketing, he needed to continue the transformation of his brand personality. John needed to look and act more like what he aspired to be—a rock star.

His first challenge was changing his look, otherwise known as *design and packaging* in the world of consumer products. The fact of the matter is that there aren't many fat rock stars, and at times he was as rotund as the spectacles he wore as a child. He needed to lose weight, and did, although it has been a lifelong battle that has haunted him with bouts of bulimia.

His second challenge was developing a commanding stage presence. During his early live performances, John stood on stage or at the piano, awkwardly holding the microphone, devoid of any real personality. Clean-shaven with short bangs across his forehead, this shy guy exuded anything but confidence to his audience—in fact, he appeared somewhat embarrassed to be on stage. He hadn't mastered what superstars know—winning over audiences is easier when entertainers project self-confidence. Addressing the limitations of his shy nature, John changed his appearance and his personality, with a vengeance, to become one of the best rock-and-roll entertainers of our time.

The turning point for John's career came on August 25, 1970, when he appeared at the Troubadour Club in Los Angeles amid much anticipation and hype. Promoters put up billboards and posters, bought radio time, and arranged for John to arrive in a British-style double-decker bus. The attention and fanfare made him a little uncomfortable, especially when he found out that people like Gordon Lightfoot and Henry Mancini would be in the audience and that Neil Diamond was going to introduce him. These were his heroes, not his audience. He was nervous.

Instead of conservative dress, which would have matched the dark, staid cover of the *Elton John* album, the promoters talked him into wearing light-colored bell-bottoms with a huge belt of stars and moons, and a long-sleeved shirt with large letters spelling out "Rock 'n' Roll." Elton's transformation occurred on stage that night when he grabbed a tambourine, involved the audience in a sing-along, and brought down the house with a rousing rendition of "Burn Down the Mission." His new persona connected with the audience in a way he had never experienced before. The experience fueled a further transformation that would later include a wide array of costumes, from jumpsuits and bib overalls to white boots and star-spangled T-shirts.

And then there were the sunglasses—hundreds of pairs, for which he is now legendary. These were no ordinary sunglasses. Oversized, covered in stars and sequins—to this day fans still comment on the wild sunglass designs, referring to them as "Elton John glasses." Beyond their flash, they symbolized something very revealing about his real personality. "I'd always been very shy and the dark glasses were really a shield," John says. "I could hide behind them."

Elton John's brand personality evolved as his music and his career escalated to new levels. It wasn't long before songs such as "Take Me to the Pilot," "Your Song," and "Border Song" were all over the radio dial, making the once-awkward British teen the darling of the American media; Reggie Dwight, geeky teenager, had transformed into Elton John, rock star. The press and the critics alike were unusually kind to John—unlike the reception his rock-and-roll contemporaries received—with magazines such as *Time* and *Life* describing him as an "emerging superman." Critics focused on his underlying musical talent, rather than extracurricular antics as with other rockers.

What once was a weakness for John would become one of his strengths. He recognized early on that gigs on the road were more important than being at the top of the pops, because concerts were where people would find out what he could really do and what he was all about. On the road, he could meld the functional and emotional elements of his brand to turn customers into fans.

John was at a disadvantage compared to guitar players and other front people, however. They could jump up and down and dance around the stage and even more into the audience. It's a little difficult to carry a piano around the stage, so instead, he jumped up and down and around the piano. Today, he still plays some songs from underneath his bench, bringing fans to their feet. It's a great example of transforming a plain functional element into an emotional connection with fans. He didn't have a guitar's natural advantage of high-voltage amplification either, so he made up for that with sheer, unrestrained energy—pounding the keys so hard that his fingers sometimes bled by the end of a concert. With his piano, he capitalized on what others might have considered a restraint and created a differential advantage, introducing a sound different from that of other rock-and-roll musicians of this era.

THE PROMISE OF THE ELTON JOHN BRAND

Brands are shorthand for the promises a company makes to consumers and supply-chain members about the products it is selling. If there were a pledge companies made to consumers through their brands it would contain commitments about product and service quality, satisfaction with the product experience, fixing problems if they occur, trying to meet customer expectations, and living up to the hype created by advertising. This pledge conveys a brand's superiority over and differentiation from competitive offerings.

Brand promise is a principle that works for people as well as for products. How individuals behave, speak, dress, and make others feel determines how people perceive them, which can affect anything from attracting new clients, in the case of an attorney, or landing a new job, in the case of a student. Just as in the case of any other well-developed brand, the Elton John brand came to symbolize a promise to its fans of quality music, evocative lyrics, and variety of sound— from orchestral ballads to heavy-beat rock songs. John's brand promise also became focused on the concert experience, which included great music, performed with high energy and accuracy, and an array of flamboyant costumes and accessories.

Fans came to expect glitz, glamour, and flash when they saw Elton John perform, and their expectations escalated from one performance to the next. He seemed to operate under the philosophy that consumer *satisfaction* is not enough to build brand loyalty; rather, it is exceeding *expectations* that creates delighted customers and fans. Sometimes, as in the case of John, trying to exceed expectations begins a vicious cycle that can frustrate marketers as companies search for ways to one-up themselves.

For marketers, increasing expectations in an economy of hyper-competition creates constant pressure to evolve the brand. Retailers, for example, face the pressure of *positive comps* (increased sales at the same stores compared to the previous year), constantly refreshed product offerings, and ultimately expectations to make better earnings every year than the year before. Rock stars deal with a lot of the same pressures, heaped on them by their fans, their managers, and themselves. As John's personal life embraced excess—in terms of food, alcohol, drugs, and fame—so too did his on-stage persona. Nonetheless, concerts remained the primary way for John to showcase his musical talents, project his personality, and connect with his fans.

Elton John, the personality, became the center of the Elton John concert experience to the point that it overshadowed the music. "In the end," admits John, "it (the costumes) got too much." Many critics would agree that the feathers and sequins ultimately became more of a distraction than an enhancer to the core of the Elton John brand. It would be something that he would adjust in the latter part of his career.

ROCKET MAN

Following the release of *Elton John,* John and his band embarked on their first world tour in the spring of 1971. This would mark the beginning of a five-year period, which John today refers to as the years in which he could do no wrong. By the end of the tour, the band would have four albums in the top 40. The 1972 album *Honky Chateau* was a sales breakthrough, with hits such as "Honky Cat" and "Rocket Man." It was followed with more chart toppers including "Crocodile Rock," "Daniel," "Bennie and the Jets," "The Bitch Is Back," and "Yellow Brick Road." *Tumbleweed Connection* contained rich acoustic sound on tracks such as "Love Song" (a duet with its writer, Leslie Duncan) along with some of John's most expressive songs. He enjoyed the high of having a string of seven number-one hits.

There seemed to be no stopping Elton John's success in the 1970s. In 1975, *Captain Fantastic & the Brown Dirt Cowboy,* his twelfth album in five years, became the first album ever to enter the *Billboard* charts at number one. It included the smash hit "Philadelphia Freedom." Bernie Taupin recalls, "As soon as that happened we went, oh we're in trouble now because where do you go from number one? Then the next album we had out was *Rock of the Westies,* and that went in at number one too, and we thought now we're *really* in trouble."

As the hits kept coming, John's confidence skyrocketed and his public persona became more outrageous. "It got to the point where everything was coming in at number one, and the only dangerous thing about that is that you assume that everything else should come in at number one," he recalls. But what was happening to him professionally, for all the world to see, was worlds apart from what was happening to him personally. He had been in a solid, romantic relationship with his manager, John Reed, for several years, which brought him great comfort. But hiding it from the world became more difficult, as his life mirrored the words in "Rocket Man"—"I'm not the man you think I am at home." As with many relationships, this one ended, which was difficult for John, but he tried to mask his grief and maintain his wild persona in public.

The next stage in his brand evolution would focus on the effect his personal life had on the image of his brand among his fans. It was similar to the impact that changes in the personal lives of company owners, CEOs, and spokespersons have on the image and public perception of the companies and brands they represent.

INTERTWINING THE PERSONAL MAN AND THE PROFESSIONAL BRAND

In an all-too-common story in the music industry, money, fame, and power made indulging in alcohol and drugs easy. A self-proclaimed "goody two-shoes," it wasn't until a few years into his career that Elton John tried drugs, although he knew that his band members had been using for a while. As he says, the blow made it easier for him to overcome his shyness, talk to people, and break out of his shell. Drugs and alcohol also allowed him a temporary escape from other issues in his personal life.

Rumors about his sexuality hovered, but it wasn't until Cliff Jar of *Rolling Stone* magazine asked the bisexuality question during an interview that it became public. John explains, "I thought it was okay to say yeah." He just didn't care anymore who knew; it was the beginning of the process of recapturing himself. But it was the 1970s, and many of his fans were shocked by the headlines that screamed of his proclaimed bisexuality. It hurt his brand because mainstream culture wasn't ready to deal with sexual preference publicly. *Blue Moves,* the album following his announcement, didn't come in at number one. In fact, it peaked at only number three—which although disappointing after a string of chart-topping albums, proved that the news had damaged his career but hadn't killed it.

His personal highs and lows affected his career to a certain degree, but even in the early 1980s he was able to release a whole new string of hits despite the minor differences he had had with Taupin along the way. This period brought hits such as "I'm Still Standing," "I Guess That's Why They Call It the Blues," "Sad Songs," and "Nikita." But his surprise marriage to sound engineer Renate Blauel in 1984 and full-blown drug addiction distracted from the professional success he still managed to create.

The straw that almost broke the proverbial camel's back was a series of articles printed in a British tabloid, the *Sun,* accusing the superstar of participating in wild sex orgies with young male prostitutes. To that point, he had faced adversity, but never an all-out assault on his character. The Elton John brand, what it and he stood for among fans, was under attack. The performer was devastated. He recalls, "For a time I wouldn't go out of the house."

In October 1988, the *Sun* settled out of court for £1 million and a front-page apology. Despite those difficult times, he turned to work as his salvation and released *Reg Strikes Back* in 1988; the album spent five months on the charts. "It wasn't one of my best albums," he admits. "But it got me doing something." After its release, he auctioned off his glitter-rock costumes and returned to the core of the Elton John brand.

This chapter in John's life provides a valuable lesson in personal branding. When controversy rears its ugly head in the form of scandal or bad press, you have to remain active, try to function in a business-as-usual mode, and fix whatever is broken. This difficult time in John's life shows that negative publicity can damage careers and lives but won't kill you; in fact, it can change lives for the better.

Elton John's image rebirth was in its embryonic stage, sparked by his connection to a young boy, Ryan White, who had been a loyal fan, and the friendship he formed with Ryan's mother after the boy's tragic AIDS-related death. The emotional experience he went through over the child's death gave him new perspectives and led to a lasting bond between John and AIDS activism. The experience forced him to take a long look at his life. By the age of 43, he'd become a white-haired, overweight addict hiding behind a Steinway. "I looked like a 70-year-old man playing the piano." The time had come to save himself from bulimia, alcohol, and drugs.

He spent most of 1991 out of the public eye, then reemerged sober, fit, and filled with a new lust for life, on George Michael's remake of "Don't Let the Sun Go Down on Me." Taupin summed it up best in a VH1 *Behind the Music* interview: "He made mistakes, he got into a rut, he got himself out, case closed."

The 1990s brought another string of hits, among them "The One," which became his first number-one hit in 16 years. It struck an emotional chord with old fans from the 1970s and 1980s and new ones from the 1990s. Perhaps the greatest impact on what the Elton John brand stands for today began with an announcement he made during a press conference in 1992. John told the media, "Every single I release in America from this point . . . all my proceeds will go to AIDS research and AIDS charities." To date, John has raised well over $20 million for the cause, making him a hero in the eyes of fans and critics alike and giving fans another reason to remain devoted to him.

During this brand reformulation, John traded in his feathers for designer Versace duds (although sequins still appear from time to time as part of the image). But he got back to the core of his brand— great piano-based rock and roll, entrenched in his understanding of the musical masters. "I stress (to young musicians) to listen to the great masters who came before us," he said at the 2003 Rock and Roll Hall of Fame induction ceremonies. He did just that, and in the process figured out how to manipulate the peripheral cues (from personality to staging and dress) to present his core strengths best, rather than use them to cover up and distract from what really makes him great—his music.

REACHING MULTIPLE SEGMENTS WITH ONE UNDERLYING THEME

One secret behind Elton John's abundant success and mass appeal is good old market segmentation strategy. Over the years, he has reached a number of audience types, spanning beyond traditional age, income, and gender boundaries. In the past decade, he has attracted kindergarten-age fans and their grandparents with "Can You Feel the Love Tonight" and "Circle of Life" from Disney's megahit, *The Lion King.* After conquering Hollywood by winning an Academy Award for his work on *The Lion King,* he took on Broadway, collaborating with

Tim Rice on *Aida*. "I was scared to do *Aida* because I hadn't done anything like that before," recalls John, "but the scary things are the most enjoyable, and you need the scary; you can't be complacent."

He has been anything but complacent over the years. He has stayed fresh and relevant to numerous market segments with intense cobranding efforts. Not only did he tour with Billy Joel to offer audiences around the globe a piano recital like none had ever seen; he released duets with LeAnn Rimes (hitting country audiences), Moby (reaching dance-music audiences), Miss Piggy (connecting with the kid in all of us), Janet Jackson (hitting R&B audiences), and Luciano Pavarotti (finding classical music lovers), to name a few. His *Duets* album teamed him up with everyone from k.d. lang and Little Richard to Bonnie Raitt and Don Henley.

Perhaps the most controversial pairing occurred at the 2001 Grammy Awards, when John performed live with Eminem, the white rap superstar, known for songs that outrage a majority of people at any given time. The announced duet shocked fans and outraged several of the gay-rights groups that had heralded John as one of their celebrity supporters. In a press release, John said, "I'm a big fan of his music, and I said I would be delighted to [sing with him]." John, who dismisses some of the seriousness of the lyrics and chooses to see the humor that Eminem says is the core of his music, adds, "If I thought for one minute that he was [hateful], I wouldn't do it."

So why would he perform with Eminem, knowing that many fans would protest? Perhaps it was his admiration for a young artist willing to go against the grain of acceptability to impact the culture. Perhaps it was to help create dialog about topics that still divide society. Perhaps it was showing tolerance for differing opinions. Or perhaps it was a little bit of all of these plus the enormous publicity value from everything that goes along with a professional alliance with the hottest music act to hit young audiences in the past decade. This type of cobranding strategy has also worked well for Carlos Santana; he has teamed up with Rob Thomas, lead singer of Matchbox Twenty, and most recently with Vanessa Carlton, the 2002 newcomer who was up for her first Grammy in 2003.

Another motivator for John may be the positioning that goes along with recognizing new talent and appreciating where a new artist is destined to go in the next few years. If fans see Elton John as a visionary in discovering and performing with groundbreaking talent, doesn't that position his brand as cool, relevant, and groundbreaking as well—an approach that has worked well for Quincy Jones and Prince. Regardless of why he performed with Eminem, rest assured that the effect on the Elton John brand was considered before he agreed to do it.

Elton John's brand architecture stands as a grand example for how to establish a brand in the marketplace. Developing both the functional and emotional elements of the brand, creating a distinct personality to which customers can relate, formulating a brand promise, and promoting a unique brand position and message to customers are all part of establishing a powerful brand among a host of also-rans.

NEELEMAN IN THE SKY WITH DIAMONDS

The Elton John brand is different from many others in that Elton, the man, is Elton, the brand. But entertainers aren't alone in this arena. Companies that hire spokespeople—or, even more important, use their CEOs as front people—also have to figure out how to handle this intricate intertwining of personalities. Enter David Neeleman, CEO of JetBlue, who plays a vital role in the growth, popularity, and profitability of his unconventional airline.

TAKE ME TO THE PILOT

Amid headlines proclaiming financial woes among almost all major airlines, JetBlue Airways has emerged as a darling of the air-travel industry. Armed with a fleet of new planes (equipped with leather seats and DirecTV programming), low fares, friendly service, state-of-the-art check-in technology, and a healthy dose of entrepreneurial spirit, JetBlue is connecting at the deepest level with travelers who are fed up with the business-as-usual service of the major airlines. JetBlue's brand encompasses a unique combination of product, personality, and promise that is changing customer expectations about travel.

In the company's pilot seat is David Neeleman, who set out to create a successful low-fare airline based in New York City. His goal was to "bring humanity back to travel and to make flying more enjoyable." Sound challenging? Critics thought so. They scoffed at the notion of developing a unique product in the less-than-creative airline industry, not to mention finding quality employees able to carryout the rigorous standards that the JetBlue team envisioned.

Neeleman began developing the functional attributes of the Jet-Blue brand years prior to the official birthdate of the business. As president of Salt Lake City–based Morris Air, the first airline Neeleman founded, he began creating a formula of innovative, high-quality airline service coupled with low fares to attract a strong and loyal market. After selling Morris Air in 1993 to Southwest Airlines, he helped launch WestJet, a successful Canadian low-fare carrier, and further developed the e-ticketing system he first instituted at Morris Air. Called Open Skies, it was positioned as the world's simplest airline reservation system and was sold to Hewlett-Packard in 1999.

With three successful aviation businesses under his belt, Neeleman decided the time was right to bring his airline formula to the world's largest aviation market, New York City. In July 1999 he gathered a hand-picked management team and $130 million in capital funding, and on February 11, 2000, JetBlue Airways took to the sky. It hasn't looked back, expanding from its inaugural service between New York City's John F. Kennedy International Airport and Fort Lauderdale, Florida, to over 20 cities around the country.

CREATING THE JETBLUE BRAND

With the operating strategies and corporate structure in place, it came time to develop and maintain the JetBlue brand, supported in part by Magnet ID. Though JetBlue is not Magnet's largest client, the account is a huge source of pride for the agency. Except for advertising, it has been involved in every part of the branding process, focusing on every visual component and every instance in which a customer encounters the brand.

"Magnet often acts as JetBlue's identity conscience; we have worked with them from the eary days before my firm Christopher Johnson &

Associates was acquired by Havas and transformed into Magnet," says Christopher Johnson, head of Magnet's brand identity group. "Collectively, we helped to build a brand that is visually interesting but far from over the top. It's not trying to be hip or trying to be edgy. It's clean; it's current. The other airlines are constantly rebranding, and they look and feel like big corporations. JetBlue doesn't; instead, you feel like you're flying with your family when you fly JetBlue."

Johnson recalls having some of his first meetings with the JetBlue team on its planes, which at times had just finished flying a leg and hadn't been cleaned yet. "When we got on the planes, you can imagine what everyone in the meeting did, including the president—they cleaned the plane, and we helped do it too because we were a team. From the beginning it's been this 'roll up your sleeves, we're gonna build this thing together' type attitude," he explains.

Neeleman and his team designed JetBlue's brand promise and have stayed true to that through its growth. "The brand is all about having fun when you fly, which from a product standpoint includes new planes, low fares, and television at every seat," says Neeleman. "From a company standpoint, it means that employees are nice to customers, being both lighthearted and friendly but also responsible and professional." The functional attributes are carried out so efficiently that they become emotional brand elements as well. DirectTV at every seat is like Elton John pounding the keys from below his piano.

"The JetBlue brand promise dictates how employees execute at the various stages of the customer experience, from the time customers checkin at the gate to the time they land and claim their luggage. And consistency in the experience is key, or else the brand suffers," explains Neeleman. "The brand is so much deeper than any ad could convey; it's about how to treat customers and how to treat employees, understanding that how you treat one affects the other."

If JetBlue employees are the purveyors of the brand, then Neeleman is the steward of it. "We believe that the brand's personality and promise has to come from the top for it to become ingrained throughout the rest of the organization," says Johnson, "and at JetBlue, the CEO believes it; he walks the walk and talks the talk, and his commitment to the brand filters down to all 4,000 employees and millions of customers."

FLY WITH PERSONALITY

The human characteristics of the JetBlue brand come from David Neeleman and his personality; he's likeable and charismatic, both of which are traits of the JetBlue brand. Although he didn't start that way, today he is the leader of the brand—JetBlue's front man—which comes naturally to the customer-oriented CEO. He likes to engage the public and gather information that he can use to improve his company. He rides the planes once a week, talks to customers, and asks them questions. Approachable, friendly, concerned, and interested in what people have to say—that's part of the personality he brings to the brand.

JetBlue's personality can also be described as cool, a travel alternative for people looking for a different experience. "In building the JetBlue brand and personality, we realized that there really wasn't anyone in the airline industry that was cool," says Johnson. "Being different, being cool became important to the universal message of the brand."

One challenge is that *cool* means different things at different times to different people. Some JetBlue fans like the humor; some like the efficiency; some like the value. It is the combination that gives the brand its unique position in the minds of customers. For example, in the tough economic climate of 2003, frugality was in; rather than being embarrassed about looking for deals, people saw it as a way to show their shopping savvy and prowess. And companies that can appeal to that need and attitude in such times without making consumers feel like they are buying something cheap may capture their loyalty. JetBlue does this with leather seats, DirecTV, and top-notch service for low prices, showing customers that they don't have to sacrifice quality when they fly with JetBlue.

Just as Elton John has chosen to cobrand with other performers to remain relevant but also cool in the marketplace, JetBlue has chosen to partner with Crunch gym to develop a series of yoga exercises designed to help passengers relax, loosen up, and feel invigorated. The significance of partnering with Crunch may escape some customers, but those with an affinity for coolness know that though Crunch doesn't necessarily try to be cool, it is. The two brands have very similar messages and core values, which focus on fun and not taking things too seriously.

But ask any rock star and he or she will tell you that being cool is tough to attain and even tougher to maintain, because the minute someone claims to be cool, they begin that slide toward uncoolness. "Being cool stems from that lack of self-consciousness and a trueness to the brand promise," explains Johnson. "JetBlue simply followed the notion of making an airline that people would want to fly. And they instituted an attitude that flew in the face of traditional airlines, and inherently that honesty of the brand came forward, and it remains there. It is not a contrived coolness; it is one that stems from the honest intent of the company to be different and appeal to people's emotions."

Like Elton John's music, the JetBlue brand appeals to a transgenerational group of customers. Its universal brand message and product appeal to people who are hip and style-conscious and who think of JetBlue along those lines. Yet 65-year-olds like the company and appreciate the friendly service. A common thread among a majority of JetBlue fans is that they write and call the company with ideas for how to paint the jets and improve the product. They also send fan mail to Neeleman and his company. And most important, they love to spread the word about the airline. A high proportion of JetBlue customers become avid fans because of the strong emotional content of the brand. They appreciate the humor that JetBlue tries to interject into the increasingly stressful activity of travel. They relate well to Neeleman, who has given the brand a very human touch. Ultimately, they end up smiling when they think of the brand—it creates an emotional response before many of them formulate the words to express their feelings.

So, is JetBlue catching on? You bet. As Neeleman explains, "You can begin to hear people say, 'I took JetBlue to Florida' instead of 'I flew to Florida,' which indicates to us that they have a sense of ownership and affinity for the brand." And that is one of the ultimate indicators of when a brand has become a part of culture, when its name enters the everyday vernacular—such as Kleenex, Vaseline, or Elton John sunglasses.

Success attracts competitors, however, making it more important than ever that JetBlue hone both the functional and emotional elements of its brand. And as Delta and United eye the low-fare market, one thing they can't duplicate is the DirecTV offering. In 2002, Jet-Blue bought the technology that enables satellite transmission to aircraft, because it saw that as a key advantage of its product and wanted to protect the brand.

Critics wonder if large corporate structures such as United and Delta will be able to replicate the JetBlue formula of expense control and customer orientation. Just as there existed many pianists with as much talent as Elton John, not many were able to make it big in the market. Elton John and JetBlue demonstrate that success in the market requires both mastering the functional attributes of a product and conveying the emotional elements.

Recognizing that the JetBlue brand is one of its greatest assets, Jet-Blue and Magnet continue to work together on a process they define as *brand collaboration,* in which they share ideas and creative thoughts on furthering the emotional attributes of the brand. The team refuses to adopt the philosophy of continually throwing money at problems; rather, they try to do the opposite and figure out ways to address issues without investing much, if any, new money. One of these ideas, designed to connect with frustrated travelers, was to install punching bags with humorous thoughts about travel written on them. With phrases like "I left the coffee maker on at home," passengers can read them or hit them—either way releasing a little tension and often ending up laughing.

The beauty of something so simple is that in the case of JetBlue, it doesn't seem contrived, because of the history of the brand personality. The company's strong financial performance causes its name to be trumpeted in the first paragraphs of many business articles written about the airline industry—and now the world of branding. But all of the attention does bring the danger of overexposure. "JetBlue continuously walks the fine line of how much exposure it wants for the JetBlue story because they don't want it to become a trite brand image," explains Johnson.

A real challenge for brand managers is to understand how to keep telling a story to get into new markets, without becoming so ubiquitous that people tune out a brand's nuances. This is one reason that most bands don't tour every year—they wouldn't be new or novel enough and often are too expensive to attract fans that often. The challenge also becomes how to replicate both the functional and emotional aspects of the brand in new and different markets. Spreading corporate culture, which is an important part of the most successful company brands—especially Wal-Mart—is a task that can trip up even stellar firms. Sam Walton was the most important ingredient in spreading the Wal-Mart culture within his company because he lived, breathed, and embodied the brand. After his death, the company focused on ways to keep his vision and passion throughout the organization and instill it in new hires who had never met him. Videos of him and old-fashioned traditions became paramount in keeping as much of the original Wal-Mart culture alive as possible.

Neeleman finds himself in a similar position as he becomes the evangelist of the JetBlue brand within the organization, to the financial community, and to its fans. By the end of 2002, JetBlue found itself 4,000 employees strong. JetBlue has stayed true to its core strengths, not allowing image to detract from its real value in the market. As with Elton John, the total customer experience will keep JetBlue focused on delivering the right combination of functional and emotional brand attributes to see the organization through expansion with its reputation intact.

STILL STANDING

Learning from the case of Elton John, in which he eventually became more about personality (costumes, wigs, and stage antics) than just about music, JetBlue's commitment lies in a healthy combination of improving the functional aspects of its brands as well as its emotional components.

At a time when branding seems to be all the rage, there are those who caution against becoming too branding oriented just for the sake of creating a name in the marketplace. Ron Frasch, CEO of Bergdorf Goodman, explains that in the world of retailing, branding will get you only so far, for so long. "For us, it still comes down to the quality of product and service that we provide to our customers, whether we use the term *branding* or not. The danger for some of our vendors is that if they see their brand as 'designer jeans' and have built their primary message to consumers on that limited platform, they often don't change when the market doesn't want jeans."

He hits on a problem that has permeated the marketing world in the past few years. *Brand* has become the go-to buzzword among marketers, advertisers, publicists, and executives to describe everything from advertising to the product itself. A multitude of meanings of the world float on the surface of the vast sea of marketing. In cases like the one Frasch describes, a principle rule of branding has been broken—great brands evolve both to reflect changes among people and to influence them just enough so as not to be rejected by their current fans. It is an overall marketing philosophy that has to drive the branding process; otherwise, a brand becomes nothing more than a picture of an aluminum can or a photograph of a beautiful model wearing a pair of jeans. And in an age when technology allows a lot of competitors to flood the market with similar-quality products, everyone is looking to capture that special something that will make a connection with customers.

Frasch adds, "With everyone talking about creating better brands, I've seen a lot of sameness out there, perhaps because the messages or images seem to be more contrived rather than naturally emanating from the real creative core of the product." The evolution of Elton John's personality did cross that line of manufactured versus natural that Frasch points out, and it demonstrates the disconnection that can occur because of overexposure, going over the top, and being too concerned with image and not enough with substance and product. The success that followed John's return to his core strengths and the way JetBlue is changing air travel prove that great brands must master both the functional and emotional elements in order to develop and grow a fan base.

To paraphrase his hit song of the early 1980s, Elton John is still standing. In fact, he continues to stand tall among a host of newer and younger musicians and entertainers for several reasons. Paramount to his continued success is his musical talent, but also important is the person he has become in the past decade. The Elton John brand has evolved to stand for much more than loud costumes and excess; it stands for human rights, AIDS activism, charity, and good music. Some critics might say it also stands for commerciality, which he joked about while inducting Elvis Costello to the Rock and Roll Hall of Fame in 2003, cracking, "I've gone the commercial route, but hey, someone's gotta pay for this hair." We prefer to think of Elton John as simply a savvy marketer.

4

KISS:
KEEP IT SIMPLE, STUPID

We would be KISS, or we would be nothing. —GENE SIMMONS

It's hard to believe that four guys who look like they just ascended from hell—clad in outrageous makeup, black spandex costumes, and platform shoes—could become an endearing thread in the fabric of American music. KISS invaded the music scene in the 1970s with hard-hitting rock-and-roll tunes and shows that broke the rules of the concert experience of that day. It wasn't long before legions of kids sang the band's songs and sported its makeup, much to the dismay of parents who wished they would behave more like those nice Brady kids on television.

But following KISS became a lifestyle for a lot of fans. Much like the Grateful Dead's Deadheads, the KISS Army, as its most dedicated fans were known, followed the band from city to city in full makeup and dress and communed with other zealots.

Unlike the other bands featured in this book, however, KISS's rise to stardom didn't bring with it a number-one record or great critical acclaim. Nor did the band go on to win a coveted Grammy award, or many other major awards, for that matter. KISS did, however, win over fans and score big at the cash register, generating hefty profits for the band.

Fast-forward 30 years and picture yourself in a meeting with a group of millionaires, and you probably wouldn't envision yourself walking away thinking, "All I ever really needed to know about how to build a brand, I learned from KISS." But underneath all of the makeup, spandex, and hair is a group of intelligent people who carefully crafted the evolution of the KISS brand. At the helm of the organization are Gene Simmons—the long-tongued, fire-breathing, marketer extraordinaire—and Paul Stanley—cofounder, visionary, and philosopher. Perhaps the greatest business lessons they offer lie beyond the marketing and branding tactics the band employed; rather, they lie in the area of strategy. KISS is living proof that you have to get the strategy right before you can get the brand right.

Sound complex? *Au contraire.* The beauty of the KISS equation for mass acceptance and financial success is in its foundation of simplicity. Have vision; define an image; talk to people; give them what they want; package it with a dose of fantasy; and make them a part of something bigger and more exotic than they could be on their own. But simplicity doesn't mean absence of strategy, nor does it mean anything less than precise execution.

"We always envisioned ourselves playing to huge audiences," explains Simmons in an interview on VH1's *KISS: Beyond the Makeup.* Stanley adds, "We wanted to look like the band we never saw, sound like the band we never heard. We wanted to be the ultimate combination of all the things we loved." KISS's simple strategy was executed with such distinction that since 1972 it has sold more than 80 million records and is the music industry's all-time merchandising and licensing leader with over a billion dollars in revenue—half of that generated in the past five years. Its merchandise portfolio includes 2,500 licensed products sold around the world.

Never conclude that the strategy you are about to see unfold is just about the brand power of a winning rock band. KISS made the transition from fledgling to icon with the aid of a host of strategies from which entrepreneurs, marketing managers, and retailers looking to enhance the shopping experience in their stores can learn. The KISS saga focuses on:

♪ Building a fan base by capturing markets competitors deem secondary

♫ Capturing a unique position in the market by developing the entertainment value of your product experience

♫ Developing a two-way relationship with customers that not only lets you connect to fans but lets fans connect to you

♫ Creating a vehicle for your customers to participate in and live your brand

♫ Creating and licensing a brand to expand global reach and adoption.

In fact, KISS flourished with strategies similar to those employed by many great organizations, including the largest corporation in the world. Both KISS and Wal-Mart demonstrate that sound marketing, product, and customer satisfaction strategies build market share and that brilliant execution of those strategies throughout the channel maintains it. While the execution—and perhaps the values of the organization—may be different from those of other businesses, the strategic nature of KISS branding remains the same for dominant firms of any kind.

IT STARTS WITH A KISS

For most of us, the thought of a kiss conjures up a refrain of pleasant emotions. Perhaps it's a quick kiss on the cheek by a beautiful young woman that captures a man's heart, or a passionate exchange on a starry night in a horse-drawn carriage that marks the beginning of a life together. A kiss symbolizes emotion, electricity, excitement, and anticipation for something more in a way that the anatomical description (the tightening of lip muscles held against each other) fails to capture.

For the KISS Army, the word conjures the same emotions, but a very different visual. The sometimes raucous and always passionate entertainers stirred emotions, generated energy, and sparked enthusiasm with their unorthodox concerts, which they held in small towns and cities that had never been exposed to such an out-of-mind emotional experience. Not only did KISS elevate the concert standard in venues where other larger acts didn't bother to play, it affected the standard throughout the rock-and-roll industry.

Today, KISS is credited with leading the way for performers like Britney Spears and 'N Sync, and those who take animals on stage (as Britney did in her 2002 tour) or use pyrotechnics (as Kid Rock does) to create multisensory experiences. But it is safe to say that the impact of KISS on fans and the industry would not have happened were it not for Gene Simmons. His is a story of ambition, vision, ego, and business savvy, and just like those of other great entrepreneurs studied in MBA programs, it deserves close examination to uncover the influences that shaped his career and success.

IMMIGRATION, FASCINATION, AND INFATUATION

Chaim Witz was born in 1949 in Israel and came to America with his mother at age eight. Changing his name to Gene (it was more American than Chaim) Klein (his mother's maiden name), he assimilated into his new neighborhood—the Williamsburg area of Brooklyn—and overcame the challenges of living in a single-parent household and having only limited English skills. Gene attended yeshiva, where the first half of the day was devoted to the Old Testament, Torah studies, and Bible stories, followed by an afternoon of traditional academics, then Bible study until 9:30 P.M., and plenty of homework after that. This was young Gene's routine, six days a week, and it fostered a disciplined lifestyle of hard work that was to characterize much of his later success.

America represented many things to Gene, especially vast economic opportunity, but above all it meant entertainment. In his autobiography, *KISS and Makeup* (Crown, 2001), Simmons explains, "So here I come, fresh off the plane, and there's a close-up of a man's face on the screen reading the news. I actually went around behind the furniture to see where the guy was. That was my first impression of television, which later bloomed into a full-fledged love affair."[1]

His life, and the future of rock and roll, would be forever changed on a Sunday night in 1964, when Gene and his mother sat together for their Sunday night ritual of eating dinner and watching Ed Sullivan.

When Sullivan announced that "tonight on our show, we have the Beatles," Simmons explains that for all he knew, it was going to be one of those novelty acts like a flea circus featuring bugs or cockroaches. Then the Fab Four took the stage. His initial reaction was that they looked silly and dressed like girls, but when his mother expressed her disapproval, he changed his tune, saying "No, Mom, I think they look cool." He recalls that as a moment of rebellion; a profound insight. At a time when a sense of rebellion was on the rise among American youth, he discovered and understood the cultural relevance of rock and roll and how it would capture and form a long-lasting grip on a new generation. It would be an insight that he would use to capture his band's place among music fans and in rock-and-roll history.

At a far less cerebral level, something else would catch Gene's attention that night—the hoards of screaming girls, hanging desperately on every note the Beatles sang. Simmons explains, "My first thoughts about pop music were born that night, and they were simple thoughts: If I go and start a band, maybe the girls will scream for me. Don't let anyone tell you any different—that same impulse launched a thousand bands."[2]

Inspired by the impulse almost universal among teenage boys, Gene Klein started a band with two friends. He also learned that being in a band brought him friends that he never previously had—including, yes, some girls. It was these girls who asked him during class, "Hey Gene, will you show us that weird thing you do with your tongue?" Of course, being an obliging kind of guy, he did, and it landed him in the principal's office because it was interpreted as a sexual act. From that time on, regardless of the voice or guitar skills he would develop, it would be his unusually long tongue that would bring him the most recognition. It also eventually became the most recognizable symbol of Gene Simmons,* although it never was

---

*We have chosen not to explain the entire story behind Gene Simmons's famous tongue, nor of the pictures of the 4,600 girls who serve as references for its significance. If you don't want to leave this story to your own imagination, you can read about it in Simmons's autobiography, KISS and Makeup (New York: Crown, 2001).

introduced as a part of the official KISS logo. The Rolling Stones had already done that.

As much attention as he was getting from being in a band, Simmons says that it never occured to him that he could make a living with a band, so he worked at whatever jobs were available. Delivering newspapers, he learned the need for responsibility and hard work as ingredients of success, but his ability to sing and his unusual tongue got him places that most paper carriers never go—in the long run. Beyond earning money, he was a disciplined saver, the importance of which he learned from his mother, who urged him to save and to go to college. Her approval was so important, Simmons states, that he never smoked or drank or got high as a teenager, a value he continues even now—and as the old adage states, "Two out of three ain't bad."

Gene Klein entered Sullivan County Community College in South Fallsberg, New York, and majored in theology. After getting his associate bachelor's degree, he moved back to New York City, lived with his mother, and went to school at Richmond College in Staten Island, where he completed his bachelor's degree and taught eighth grade briefly. All the time, he played on weekends with his band, Bullfrog Beer, eventually recognizing that he really wanted to make it in a rock-and-roll band. He had taught himself to play the bass, mainly because everyone else played guitar. His instinct was to set himself apart from most others, noting that "me too" brands in mass markets are far less likely to succeed than brands that appeal to clearly defined though smaller segments. And let's face it, competition among bass players wasn't as great as that among guitarists. This type of bigger-fish-in-a-smaller-pond mentality would serve as a key strategy in the KISS invasion of rock-and-roll music.

SETTING THEMSELVES APART

By 1970, Gene Klein had hooked up with Paul Stanley (born Stanley Eizen), a guitarist and songwriter who responded to a newspaper ad Kline placed. They concentrated on songwriting and performing, both of which would ultimately fuel their eventual success in the industry. Even at this point in their careers, their stage antics were more important from a branding and positioning standpoint than their original tunes. Like Elvis and Aerosmith, Klein and Stanley *performed* music—not only playing and singing, but jumping up and down while they did it. This was in sharp contrast to most musicians of the time, who sat on a stool strumming a guitar or simply stood on stage in blue jeans, singing songs, reminiscent of Simon and Garfunkle and James Taylor. They made a commotion with showmanship, costumes, and a more theatrical model of rock and roll that pushed the visual aspects of music. The duo understood the importance of entertainment, and decidedly evolved their style of multisensory performance. They also knew they had to develop their music.

Many changes occured in 1972—Klein changed his last name to Simmons (because he liked it better), he and Stanley branched out on their own, and they found a drummer, Peter Criss (born Peter Criscuola), who was willing to dress and act as wildly as they did. Finally, Paul Frehley, who changed his name to Ace to avoid having two Pauls in the band, joined the group as lead guitarist.

The new union needed a new name. Simmons explains that the word *kiss* seemed to sum up a lot about the glamour of rock and roll. It was also perfect for international marketing because it was understood all over the world—it was short and simple, easy to say and remember, it translated into many cultures, and evoked simple emotional responses. And, bottom line, Simmons and Stanley liked the word.

Creating a successful organization of any kind takes a lot more than a good product and a good name. It requires equity, which for cash-poor KISS meant sweat equity. To make ends meet, Simmons, who could type 90 words per minute as a result of his college days, took a job with Kelly Girls (later the Kelly Agency) as a temporary typist. As he relates in *Kiss and Makeup* (Crown, 2001), the pay was good, and because very few men were secretaries, it was a good place to meet women. He also learned to fix office machines, which got him plenty of work, including a six-month position at *Glamour* and *Vogue* as an assistant to the editor. He also worked as a cashier in a deli until 9 or 10 at night, which confined practice time with the band from then until the wee hours of the morning. Stanley drove a cab. His taxi stand was right outside the door of the building where the band rehearsed, so when he took a break, he would run upstairs, practice, and then go on to continue his shift. Both Simmons and Stanley had passion and were willing to work for their dreams, living the old adage, "Don't give up your day job."

Simmons portrays an underlying principle especially relevant to start-ups of either the musical or entrepreneurial breed. It's the difference between firms such as Hewlett-Packard, the archetype of the garage start-ups, and the myriad of dot-coms of the 1990s, which began with millions of IPO dollars available to fund a lot of unnecessary and frivolous expenses. The same principle applies when building brands. Sometimes rich marketing campaigns and product launches make for lazy, unfocused strategy execution. Often the results attained from sweat equity are much more effective than those arising from deep pockets because of the attention to every detail and the heightened sensitivity to expenses and utilization of time and human resources.

CREATING A KICK-ASS EXPERIENCE

Just as it would be wrong to describe Southwest as just another brand of airline, it would be wrong to call the KISS product just another rock-and-roll brand. Admittedly, KISS never set out to be the best musicians the world has ever known. Nor did it set out to change the world with deep social messages and complex lyrics. KISS did set out, however, to give people the best damn show they'd ever seen. And it did set out to change the standard for concerts—focusing on the entire entertainment value of the event the band commandeered each night. The band also set out to connect with fans and make gobs of money along the way.

Band members would make a connection to audiences from the stage, giving the fans something to talk about for weeks and remember for years. Unlike other bands before them, KISS brought fireworks to the stage, along with fire-breathing tricks, simulated blood, and unleashed craziness—tactics that focused more attention on the musicians and the overall concert experience rather than the music itself. Simmons explains in the VH1 interview, "I started spitting fire during [the song] 'Firehouse.' I would come stalking from stage right holding a metallic sword on fire at the handle. My mouth was full of kerosene. At center stage I would pause and hold the sword still. Then I'd rush it within six inches of my face and spray the kerosene at the flame. When the flame met the kerosene it would ignite. The fans saw what looked like a huge fireball shooting out of my mouth."

After all of the pyrotechnics, the stage would be ablaze with fire, smoke, and sometimes brimstone, conjuring up images of another world, especially since band members described themselves as "evil incarnate." Add black costumes and eight-inch platform shoes to already tall band members, and the effect was intimidating—as it was intended to be. You can imagine that not too many bands were keen on having KISS be their warm-up band—literally because the group might set the place on fire and figuratively because it got the crowd so riled up that it was a hard act to follow.

Even more than the fire antics, KISS made its mark with its pseudo-Kabuki makeup. The black-and-white face paint was new to rock and roll and served to set KISS apart from any other band. "The KISS image really was born out of our philosophy that a band should be more than just a bunch of guys who looked like they just rolled out of bed who got on stage and were gonna jam for an hour," explains Stanley. Previously a few bands, like Alice Cooper, which KISS emulated, and the Dolls used makeup to make a statement on stage. But dramatic, consistent makeup was different and became central to the identity of KISS. "We had to find something that truly was ours. The idea of us being a second-rate Dolls was not what we wanted; we wanted to be a first-rate KISS," says Stanley.

"At the end of the day," Simmons adds in the VH1 interview, "we decided that everyone in the band should be his own personality, his own star." Each band member developed his own on-stage persona: Simmons was the Demon and Stanley was Star Child, while Frehley was Space Man and Criss was the Cat. It took each one hours to apply his makeup before a show, but it was a transformation process that prepared the band for showtime.

In the product world, packaging plays an important emotional role as well. It's been said that the package makes the present; it certainly adds personality to even everyday products. Just think of those little Hershey's Kisses. In reality they are just big milk-chocolate versions of the semisweet chocolate morsels our mothers used to bake fresh chocolate-chip cookies. But Kisses are individually wrapped in foil—which in recent years has extended way beyond the traditional silver to include a palette of colors from red and green to pink and blue, released at special times of the year. The packaging has also added personality to the chocolate treat, and created attention around it, prompting the purchase of special colors at Easter, Valentine's Day, or Christmas.

KISS's makeup became an important part of the aura of its brand. The fans started writing the band, believing that the group wore the makeup all the time. They wanted to believe in the fantasy, and out of respect to what fans wanted, explains Simmons, the band decided to keep the makeup on in public—at all times. It became central to the mystique of the brand. The makeup also provided an important relational component to the KISS brand. Not only did it communicate an image from the band to its fans, it gave fans a way to communicate back to the band, participate in the brand, and complete the two-way communication cycle.

"Something definitely was going on between the fans and the band, a kind of you-are-us we-are-you; without you, we are nothing," says Simmons.

Fans loved living the brand; they showed up at concerts in KISS makeup and costumes and conjured up the type of fanatical frenzy reserved for NFL and college football games. For the first time, concertgoers weren't just listening to music; they were seeing it, feeling it, smelling it, and living it. With all senses stimulated, their emotions were heightened as never before, and afterward, they were often left in that awkward state of complete excitement, exhaustion, and shock. After an experience like that, word of mouth and repeat patronage was not a problem.

What KISS brought back to the stage was an element of surprise—a sensory overload kind of surprise. To this day, KISS combines creativity, escapism, and surprise into one action-packed event. The combination leaves audiences temporarily deaf and dumbfounded, but permanently delighted. Creativity and surprise are what some industry insiders say is missing from many musical acts today. Company executives take note—that is also what some corporate insiders say is missing from many shopping and service experiences today.

Pushing the envelope of creativity and generating the unexpected can be risky and may not always work. In the case of KISS, it did. Tina Weymouth, of the Talking Heads points out, "Today, the pressure is to be mainstream—or commercially safe. Celine Dion has a great voice; before her was Barbra Streisand, and there will be someone after her as well. But there isn't a lot of surprise there, something that will stop you and make you say wow." KISS audiences said wow—and still do.

In corporate terms, the element of surprise can help to exceed customer expectations, which impacts fan creation and brand loyalty. For example, Westin Hotels recently developed its new Heavenly Bed, hoping to give customers something more than just a restful night's sleep—an above average sleeping experience. Travelers, especially seasoned ones, expect a nice bed to sleep in, but don't expect a bed befitting a five-star resort. But the Heavenly Bed delivers; hotel guests are treated to a lush bed outfitted with all-white down comforters, extra pillows, and crisp linens on a high-quality padded mattress. Guests are surprised when they see and sleep in the bed—they are left remembering the experience, telling their friends about it, and often inquiring how to buy the beds for their homes.

Adding makeup as a central part of KISS's identity may, in hindsight, seem a simple tactic to create an image, an experience, and fan interactivity. But hindsight is 20/20. What turned out to be a brilliant marketing move could have been an all-out blunder because of how foreign the band's look was. Being too far over the edge can alienate even the most forward-thinking people—even those on the fringes of society. When is something different and intriguing versus just plain weird? Innovators must gauge the risk of alienating customers when they step out of the safety zone of acceptance and into the danger zone of unconventionality. Think of what happened when famed musician Prince changed his name to a symbol. Because no one could speak a symbol, they could only refer to him as "the artist formerly known as Prince." For many people, that transcends the borderline of bizarre. Perhaps the most vivid example is Michael Jackson, whose obsession with plastic surgery, odd social behavior, and childlike existence in a mansion turned amusement park took him from singing genius to all-out weirdo in most people's minds. Not only can few fans relate to him as a person anymore; he has crossed the line of normality to the point that many people don't want to admit they still like some of his new music—and even fewer will admit to still being fans.

THE ART OF KISSING: ROLLING OUT THE STRATEGY

Creating a vast fan base requires more than having the right product and promotional campaign in place; it also requires strategies to induce trial of the product in the right markets. Having released three records in just over one year and with image, concert experience, and brand strategies in place, it was time to roll out the KISS brand—take it to the people.

With all four members living in the back of a station wagon and in cheap motels, they took the KISS experience to rural North America. Their first stop would be South Edmonton in Alberta, Canada, where they appeared as a replacement for another group.

KISS toured and played anyplace someone would listen; however, the members were strategic in choosing the cities they visited. In his book, *Kiss and Sell* (Billboard Books, 1997), Chris Lendt explains the rollout strategy that established KISS's brand. "Performing in out-of-the-way places was a key ingredients to KISS's success. KISS would appear anywhere and take with them their legendary stage show with all of its trappings—the full arsenal of explosions, fire, smoke, flash pots, flame shooters, bombs, props, lights, and sound. No town was too small for KISS to appear at local hall."

From Ashville, Columbia, and Wyandotte to Lethbridge, Kitchener, and Regina, small towns were central to KISS's fan-building strategy. Why? Because KISS could roll in and be the biggest thing to hit Wyandotte—perhaps ever—leaving a lasting impression in its wake. While the band might not make as big a splash or have as great an impact in Los Angeles or Chicago, where concerts by famous performers were commonplace, it could be the most exciting event of the year in towns that big-name bands ignored. This was grassroots marketing, rock-and-roll style.

To build momentum and publicity, KISS courted the press everywhere it went. Frankly, most people found the group so strange that it wasn't hard to get media coverage—though granted, it was often less than flattering. Nevertheless, KISS focused on its impact on its fans. "From the time we started in New York City, our belief was always that we can love other bands. But all's fair in love and rock and roll," says Stanley. "When we hit the stage, our purpose and our mission is to destroy any other band these people have heard before us or will hear after us."

Consequently, announcing a KISS concert in a small, rural American town was like throwing raw meat to hungry dogs. Kids living in these conservative towns were even more drawn to the drama of KISS because the rest of the townspeople were so against what they thought the band stood for. Concertgoers packed fairgrounds and skating rinks to live the KISS experience they'd heard about. Never rude and never turning away kids seeking autographs, KISS built its brand at the grassroots level. Farmers, blue-collar workers, and middle America appreciated KISS coming to their usually neglected towns, where the band stirred up a media frenzy and a whirlwind of buying activity. In addition to traditional advertising, contests, and television and radio interviews, KISS promoted its brand through aggressive merchandising, placing order forms in their albums and selling T-shirts, belt buckles, posters and anything else they could brand KISS at concerts. KISS was a leader in generating merchandise revenue, capitalizing early on what brands like Ralph Lauren, Abercrombie & Fitch, and Hard Rock Café have discovered—the best advertising possible occurs when your fans pay you to wear and to promote your brand.

However, even after a series of sold-out concerts and with legions of fans living the KISS brand, album sales fell dreadfully short of the potential the band and its manager expected.

KISS LISTENS TO ITS BOSS

In many respects, KISS had become one of the most successful rock-and-roll bands in the United States, selling out concert venues wherever it went, but the music industry measured a band's success by the number of records it sold. With poor album sales, expensive shows, and a nearly bankrupted record label, doom loomed dangerously near. But KISS would tackle the problem with two brilliant branding strategies, both of which drew upon the band's intense relationship with its fans.

From a technical perspective, KISS's first three albums were quality productions, following conventional wisdom of laying down tracks in the studio, getting the perfect sound, and mixing the product to the highest quality. Yet their records didn't hit the charts, received little airplay, and failed to create much excitement in the market. The band was baffled.

In what researchers today would call focus groups, the band talked to its fans. "People would come to see us in droves," says Stanley. "And when people would tell us about their feelings about the albums, they would always say, 'it doesn't really sound like you guys.' I think the problem with the first three albums was that they didn't capture what KISS basically was and is—and that's a live experience."

Whereas fans of other bands wanted their heroes to perform songs the way they sounded on the albums, KISS fans wanted their idols to perform the songs on the album the way they sounded on stage. The challenge was capturing the concert experience—energy, explosions, excitement, and all—on a flat piece of vinyl, foregoing the studio-perfect sound of most albums for the raw sound of a live performance.

The only way they thought they could do this would be to record a live album, which producers and label execs insisted never sold well. They didn't understand KISS fans and how they were different from fans of other rock-and-roll bands. KISS's management fought for what the fans wanted, and the result was *Alive,* not a single disc but a double-album compilation of live recordings of concerts in Iowa, New Jersey, and Michigan, where the band's connection with its audiences and fan appeal were strongest. Released in September 1975, immediate success ensued, with the album selling over 4 million copies. "After *Alive* came out, we became the biggest band in the country," says Simmons.

The album featured a song that would forever synonymous with the band. "Rock and Roll All Night," which had been recorded on a previous album, was the brainchild of Neil Bogart, Casablanca Records' president and a staunch believer in the KISS brand. He went to the band with the idea that it needed an anthem (a jingle, if you will) that would represent what its fans believed and what the band stood for. The world of music was devoid of rock-and-roll anthems at that time, and Bogart thought it would become important to the positioning, image, and fan appeal of the band. As Paul Stanley explains, "To me, the essence of rock and roll is celebrating life." The rest of the band and its fans would agree. "Rock and Roll All Night" was not deep, but it was concise and it represented what the band stood for at that point—having a good time.

The live version of "Rock and Roll All Night" got the attention of listeners. The song would go on to become one of the top-500 influential songs in rock-and-roll history, according to the Rock and Roll Hall of Fame. Though it climbed only as high as number 68 on *Billboard*'s pop chart, it emerged as the theme song for a whole generation of kids and young adults who wanted to forget about the pressures of life and the deeper meanings hidden in the lyrics of other songs and just have fun.

CREATING A DYNASTY

Alive established KISS as national superstars. After that, the music industry took notice of live-performance recordings and began to understand their connection with fans. Soon live albums would become commonplace among other musical superstars' recordings. Great commercial success ensued—a hit single "Beth" (a ballad about a girl and the stresses of being part of a rock band on the road, a lifestyle that many of KISS's male fans no doubt fantasized about); an album, *Rock and Roll Over,* which went platinum before it even hit the stores; recognition as the number-one band in America in a 1977 Gallup poll; and the hit single "I Was Made for Lovin' You." The recognition was momentous because KISS had always considered itself to be of the people, by the people, and for the people.

The industry also took notice of KISS because of the power of its brand, which transcended the borders of music to a whole new world merchandising. Soon the market was flooded with KISS lunchboxes, action figures, games, and makeup kits. Fans could also buy pinball machines and KISS comic books. Many of these products are collectors' items today and remind fans from that era of the position KISS achieved in American culture. Responding to criticism for selling out, Gene Simmons poignantly says, "There are no rules, and the idea of selling out, you're damn straight we sell out . . . every night we play."

But too much of a good thing can be bad, especially when it conflicts with the core of the brand and its strategic intent. By the late 1970s, KISS had become too much about the makeup and not enough about the music, going from rock-and-roll band to family entertainment. With children in the audience, the group was compelled to tone things down, leaving a watered-down version of the edginess that once defined the band and the brand. Peter Criss left the band in 1979, followed by Ace Frehley in 1982.

In a bold move and with a big vat of cold cream, the band took off its makeup, appearing on a 1983 MTV special in the flesh. The group played through the 1980s and early 1990s as a plain rock band, releasing a host of albums and videos and maintaining its famed high-energy concerts. The band produced several hits throughout the next decade—"Crazy, Crazy Nights," which reached number four in 1987; "Reason to Love," which broke the top 40; and "Forever," which hit number eight in 1990—surviving a string of lineup changes and changing music preferences. Eventually, Bruce Kulick (guitar) and Eric Singer (drums) seemed to settle into their posts, bringing stability and continuity to the band.

In June 1995, the first official KISS convention was held, giving fans a chance to get up-close and personal with the band. Fans looked at vintage costumes, traded and bought merchandise, performed in copycat bands, and gathered for a KISS performance. Fans still loved the brand. this led to a performance on MTV's *Unplugged* series where KISS played a few songs and then, as a surprise to the crowd, Ace Frehley and Peter Criss joined the other band members and performed with the current lineup. That's when the audience really went crazy, and it was clear that together, the four original members were a special force.

In pure KISS fashion, the band would show up, unannounced and uninvited, at the 1996 Grammy Awards—in full makeup. No one asked them for a ticket; no one stopped them from going anywhere; everyone took their pictures. "It was like the Red Sea parting because Moses had hit the rock," recalls Simmons. The question was, did the people get it? Were they ready? Did they want KISS with makeup and with the original guys?

Unexpectedly, during the live telecast, KISS was brought up on stage as surprise guests. The audience stood. The fans answered the questions—what they saw on stage that night was what they wanted. The reunion tour was announced shortly thereafter, selling out Detroit's Tiger Stadium in 47 minutes. The group's new album, *Psycho Circus,* debuted at number one around the world. Fans were ready to have their band back, and KISS was ready to be back—makeup, flames, platforms, and all.

Today, KISS is everywhere, in nearly every nation and in nearly every medium. Chances are you've seen the group either in the movies, gracing magazine covers, or on *The Simpsons,* and if you watched the closing ceremonies of the 2002 Winter Olympics, you saw the band perform live while famed figure skaters pirouetted around the stage (an odd combination, to say the least).

KISS's formula for establishing its brand is simple. Work hard to create the best product you can; understand your limitations and have realistic expectations; emphasize the entertainment value of your product experience; perform when others in the industry just execute; develop a way to let your fans participate in and live the brand. And, when possible, add a little magic—the surprise factor will bolster word of mouth and loyalty. From examining the success of the KISS brand, we see that every component of the brand builds an image that is unique, dominating, and greater than the sum of its parts.

KISS's strategy allowed it to win its battle for brand dominance before competitors even knew they had been engaged. Wal-Mart approached dominance in much the same manner.

BUILDING THE MOST SUCCESSFUL BRAND IN THE WORLD

KISS and Wal-Mart—similar creatures? Sounds surprising, but it's true. Granted, their values and appearances may be quite different, but many of their success strategies are similar. Both brought a new experience to the heart of America; both penetrated the market through secondary and tertiary markets while remaining relatively unnoticed on competitors' radar screens; both changed the yardstick by which success in their industries was measured; and both sell more merchandise than anyone in their respective industries. And finally, in addition to starting in the same era and appealing to a wide range of age groups, ethnic identities, and geographic regions, Wal-Mart and KISS both deliver their product with attention to detail and a constant eye on their fans.

The most striking similarity between KISS and Wal-Mart, however, is their segmentation-to-mass-market growth strategy—bringing new, exciting, emotional experiences to rural and small-town North America and building on that structure to conquer cities around the world. It is one of the most important foundational strategies Wal-Mart used to confront and beat larger, established competitors at the game of global retail dominance.

GIANT AMONG US

Wal-Mart is the most successful brand in the world today, getting its start just one year before Gene Simmons watched the Beatles on the Ed Sullivan show that fateful night in 1964. Consider these staggering facts:

♫ Approximately 1.3 million people work for Wal-Mart, which equates to 1 in 123 Americans and 1 in 20 retail employees.

♫ It is the largest private employer in the world, with roughly twice the number of employees of the U.S. Postal Service.

♫ With sales already over a quarter-*trillion* dollars, analysts project it will be a *trillion-dollar company* within a decade.

♫ Wal-Mart operates 4,300 stores in nine countries and averages 100 million customers per week.

♫ Wal-Mart's computer network, an important part of its productivity, profitability, and overall success, rivals that of the Pentagon.

♫ Two of its private label brands—Old Roy dog food and Equate vitamins—are *the* top-selling U.S. brands in their categories.

♫ Wal-Mart boasts the largest fleet of corporate airplanes, the largest training program of any corporation, the biggest and most sophisticated logistics and global supply chain in the world, the largest data warehouse of any corporation, and the largest fleet of trucks of any retailer.

♪ Wal-Mart is now the largest grocery retailer in the world, the largest apparel retailer in the world, and the largest jeweler in the world.

These facts, especially when coupled with the company's sales, profits, and growth figures, are impressive, but you might still ask whether a company this large and dominant can really have fans. Though some skeptics might believe that emotional bonds are reserved for smaller, less mainstream brands, we found in a series of focus groups conducted for the International Mass Retail Association (IMRA), that the answer is a robust *yes*. Some people told us they visit their local Wal-Mart as many as three times a day to see and talk to friends they've made in the store. Many customers talked about the excitement they feel when they find a good deal. Many college students told us it was the number-one store they shopped or wished they could shop because it had everything they could possibly want at reasonable prices. But talk is cheap, as they say. Measuring consumers' behavior to determine their loyalty to a brand is even more important than their words, and Wal-Mart's phenomenal sales can attest to consumers' follow-through on their said devotion to the stores.

Creating fans for a fledgling company is challenging, but retaining their connection as the company becomes the largest corporation in the world boils down to maintaining total dedication to the customer, just as KISS did with its fans. Wal-Mart's founder, its culture and values, and its locations support the corporate charge of staying close to the customer. Some might chuckle at the small-town roots of Wal-Mart and the fact that it remains headquartered in Bentonville, Arkansas, but life in this small town is more representative of life in the vast majority of America. Potential disconnections between customer and company culture are minimized because life in Bentonville mirrors more closely the lifestyle of the target Wal-Mart customer than life in New York City. No one represented the Wal-Mart customer better than company founder Sam Walton; he walked, talked, and lived the brand. Analyzing Wal-Mart's success strategies is impossible without first talking about Mr. Sam—the Elvis of retail.

THE MAN FROM MISSOURI

Sam Walton grew up modestly in Columbia, Missouri, where he, like Gene Simmons, was a paper carrier and learned quickly the value of hard work. He would go on to graduate from the University of Missouri, which gave him a solid education, but one devoid of the instant status of a diploma from a prestigious Ivy League institution.

Walton pursued his career working in none other than a Ben Franklin store. Although he was effective as a small-town retail manager, he had ideas for innovating and improving the firm. When management rejected his ideas, he took the entrepreneurial plunge, opening his own store in 1963, in Rogers, Arkansas, at the ripe age of 45. Armed with minimal capital but loads of energy, an array of retail ideas, and a definite vision, Walton opened his first store around the same time that Kmart and Target were launched. Kmart, backed by billions of dollars from Kresge, and Target, backed by the fashion experience and resources of Dayton Hudson, had the resources, experienced managers, and locations that Walton didn't have. But the unpretentious man from Missouri would soon dispel the popular notion that small firms can't compete successfully against large ones. His organization would go on to influence the ultimate bankruptcy of Kmart and to limit the growth of Target by executing, with precision, simple strategies reminiscent to those KISS used to build its dominant brand:

♫ Gain a foothold in markets others don't serve and attack big markets later.

♫ Create a culture and a message to explain to fans and employees who you are and what you stand for.

♫ Create a product and an experience that customers value and prefer over others.

♫ Add a little magic to the value of your product experience.

♫ Listen to and observe customers and change accordingly.

♫ Change your system to fit the wants and needs of customers.

FROM RURAL ROOTS TO URBAN EXPANSION

Wal-Mart's strategy, stated simply, was to enter neglected markets with a store that gave customers a better retail experience than currently existed in those towns. Those who understand the military concept of flanking strategy realize that it's usually fatal to launch a frontal attack at the core of a superior force. Marketers often make this mistake when crafting new branding strategies—they overlook niches and go for the masses in an attempt to attract large numbers of consumers faster. Like KISS, which had decided that starting out as a whale in a pond was better than starting out as a minnow in an ocean, Wal-Mart chose to build its brand and fan base in rural America, segment by segment, foregoing mass markets where it had relatively few differential advantages. By staying away from cities and suburbs, Wal-Mart avoided head-to-head competition with giants Sears and Montgomery Ward, which were entrenched in American culture in the 1960s and 1970s. Rather than compete with Sears, Sam Walton took on the "Harry's Hardwares" of America, winning fans town by town for several decades, gradually amassing scale.

Walton's strategy sounds simple enough, but the key to his success over time was in execution—giving customers better value and better in-store experiences. When Wal-Mart entered a small town in the Midwest or rural South, it brought with it the electricity of a KISS concert. In contrast to the sleepy marketing and inexperienced management that characterized so many of the small stores in these areas, Wal-Mart offered a consistent experience of clean stores, friendly personnel, and a wide array of hard goods and apparel at reasonable prices.

Though Wal-Mart might not have been the most sleek, sophisticated retailer in America, it was the hottest, biggest retail deal to roll into these small towns. And though Wal-Mart didn't set off fireworks and employees didn't march around in strange makeup, Wal-Mart did generate as much buzz and fervor among its fans with its everyday low prices (EDLP) strategy, offering consumers consistent, low prices every day, every time they shopped. Competitors usually employed high-low pricing, in which a particular item acts as a loss leader one day (to entice customers into the store to pay full price for everything else) and is full price the following day. Customers began seeing Wal-Mart as their friend in an environment where most other stores faced rising expenses and tried to pass them on to customers in the form of higher prices. Low prices and value remain an important brand proposition for Wal-Mart, which today uses the phrase "Always Low Prices" in its tagline.

The ultimate goal, however, was to enter larger suburban markets. First circling cities with a ring of stores in surrounding small towns, Wal-Mart would then gradually build newer locations closer and closer to the target city. Incrementally, Wal-Mart grew both in size and in operating efficiency, and by the early 1990s, its total sales were greater than those of the Goliaths who had previously ignored the little David from Bentonville and the markets they deemed too small.

Wal-Mart continues to penetrate further into target markets, marching from conquered suburbs into larger cities. This type of expansion is forcing a new twist—going from stores so large that some customers have requested benches so they can rest during shopping sprees to a smaller, neighborhood market concept with less space and stock-keeping units (SKUs) than in rural and urban locations.

PERFECTING THE WAL-MART EXPERIENCE

When Wal-Mart finally went public in 1970, most of Wall Street didn't get it—and perhaps still doesn't. Not all analysts would see that, town by town, customers were voting with their dollars and their loyalty on which stores and strategies they liked best and that, more often than not, Wal-Mart was winning the retail election. But could a combination of relatively simple strategies really guide the company to become the biggest, most powerful brand in the world? In their desire to figure out what set Wal-Mart apart, few analysts recognized that the Wal-Mart difference was in its sameness. Like McDonald's in its early years, consistency played a key role both in

Wal-Mart's international success and in its adoption into the American culture.

If a trip to Wal-Mart is like going to a KISS concert, then the mix of having what customers want at the price they want to pay is the makeup and the Wal-Mart greeter is the magic. From day one, Sam Walton's vision was to give customers a consistent shopping experience and the best possible prices. In the early days, the combination of friendly service, casual conversation with other customers, and low prices left customers smiling and delighted. Although achieving that personal emotional connection became more difficult as the retail chain morphed to megasize, the basics of creating a positive in-store experience remained the same. Overall customer satisfaction depends on how well the store performs on a host of simple tactics, from clean restrooms and organized stores to signage that is simple and easy to understand. Wal-Mart's success stems from mastering the mundane, the importance of which many stores still underestimate.

Beyond the mundane, however, is the magic of Wal-Mart—its people. As Sam Walton used to say, "Customers are more important than stock." The company understands that every interaction with a customer affects his or her satisfaction with the overall shopping experience. Therefore, management preaches friendly, competent service—to provide accurate answers to customers' questions, find additional help if necessary, and make the in-store experience positive for the customer. Wal-Mart implemented the "10-foot rule," which prompts employees to greet each customer within 10 feet, offer to help them, and take them to the products for which they are looking.

And then there's the Wal-Mart greeter—the likable person stationed inside the front door who gives you a cart, a smile, a friendly word, and occasionally a hug (at least that's what happens on the commercials). Held over from the earliest days of Wal-Mart, the greeter is an ambassador of the Wal-Mart philosophy and culture and a little bit of magic in a sea of hectic moments. As the company continues to expand, hiring the best people and training them in the Wal-Mart way is challenging. And while failures in the employee-training system may be inevitable, speed in correcting problems is part of the culture at Wal-Mart.

The hallmark of the Wal-Mart shopping experience is the organization's ability to offer customers what they want to buy at a price they want to pay. Wal-Mart defines one-stop shopping—customers can buy everything from steak to tires under one roof, and know they're getting quality products at great prices. In fact, Doug Degn, executive vice president of food merchandising at Wal-Mart, says, as others have said before him, "At Wal-Mart, we don't consider ourselves as selling products to customers; we consider ourselves buying agents for our customers."

Ask most vendors, and they would have to agree. Today, the power of Wal-Mart plays a big role in what manufacturers make. For example, Procter & Gamble sold its Crisco shortening and Jif peanut butter brands because it wanted to focus more on Tide and other brands that were more favored by Wal-Mart. Similarly, video-game maker Planet Moon Studios made changes to its game Giants in order to receive a teen rating, which is a requirement for products to be sold in Wal-Mart. Lack of distribution by Wal-Mart was too much of a financial risk.

Because Wal-Mart has delivered on its low-price promise so well over the years, it has contributed to the elevation of customers' expectations in regard to product assortment, quality, availability, and price. This in turn means working even closer with vendors to cut expenses out of their product and delivery costs.

Wal-Mart's guiding strategies remain simple, but the execution has become complex, requiring the most advanced logistics, technology, and supply-chain systems the company could develop. Retail Link (Wal-Mart's electronic data interchange [EDI] technology) and Wal-Mart's satellite communications network (the largest private one in the United States) have revolutionized retail logistics systems and supply-chain strategies. Not only are stores connected to Bentonville via voice, data, or video, but over 30,000 suppliers are linked to dozens of warehouses and can monitor daily sales figures. Wal-Mart's systems help vendors improve inventory positions and reduce costs, thereby making competitors' systems seem hopelessly out of date. The company's investment in technology to analyze inventory, assortment, costs, transportation, and delivery continues to fuel its gains in productivity, profits, and customer satisfaction.

WE CAN ALL BE FIRED

Perhaps even more important than the logistics and operations systems Wal-Mart developed to provide value to its customers are the corporate culture and values system that Sam Walton instilled. From the founding of the company, Walton held Saturday morning meetings in which store managers and company executives met at headquarters to talk about sales performance, marketing and product ideas, and observations about other retailers and about customers. The tradition continues today. The meeting always starts with the Wal-Mart cheer—yes, they have one. In pure high school, rah-rah fashion, the leader yells "Gimme a W!" and the room answers, all the way through the name, to the final question of "Who's number one?" You might consider this an obvious question, but the answer is "The customer!" That is the guiding philosophy of Wal-Mart—it is the company's anthem, as much as "Rock and Roll All Night" is for KISS. It succinctly states what the company is about and represents the interests and sentiments of its fans.

Central to the Wal-Mart culture is an intimate understanding of the customer, which requires talking one-on-one to customers and employees in the stores. Walton was famous for listening to them talk about what they liked and disliked about their Wal-Mart experience and what his competitors were doing better than he was. On the quest for improvement, Walton frequently challenged his employees with two questions:

♪ *What are our competitors doing better than we are?* Walton knew that even the worst competitor probably did something better than he did. Think of the power of that principle in building a brand. If you have examined all of your competitors' strengths, adopted them, and improved on them, your brand can become best of the breed on nearly every attribute in the brand promise.

♪ *What books have you read lately that would help our firm be better managed than our competitors?* Walton knew the need to get the best ideas in the world from the best thinkers in the world. Those ideas are usually found in books, not magazines, and not in the restricted environment that makes up the experience of even the best managers.

WAL-MART WORLD

Though some may not like to admit it, Wal-Mart is part of contemporary American culture because it represents middle America's desire for value in an environment that is nonthreatening and easy to navigate. Its strategies remain entrenched in the simple—it's all about giving customers what they want to buy for the best prices possible and creating a shopping experience that keeps them coming back—but what it takes to execute that strategy continues to intensify. As Wal-Mart fights for the lowest prices possible for consumers, its relationships with vendors become even more important. Wal-Mart is now the biggest customer for many leading companies, including Kraft, Gillette, and Procter & Gamble. For these and 450 other suppliers, the relationship to Wal-Mart is so vital that they have offices in or near Bentonville, with another 800 such branch offices planned to open in the next five years.

Wal-Mart's reach is still expanding. Even though it has already captured 8 percent of all U.S. retail sales (excluding auto dealers and restaurants), it has set its sights on banking, used car sales, travel, and Internet access, and there is no reason to believe its effect in these industries will be any less staggering than in those in which it already operates. In order to support its expected growth, Wal-Mart plans to hire an additional 800,000 workers over the next five years, which in any economy, especially a stalled one, is a positive brand attribute in and of itself.

THE VALUE OF KISSING

The successes of Wal-Mart and KISS demonstrate that the most effective strategies are often simple, but involve brilliant approaches for relating to consumers. When implemented with excellence, winning strategies give advantages competitors cannot readily replicate, and often they succeed before the competitors even know they have been engaged. When a strategy is brilliantly conceived and executed with precision, an organization—whether a musical group or any other organization—dominates with a differential advantage that is difficult to duplicate.

Jerry Garcia, late leader of the Grateful Dead, was once asked how the group became known as the best at what they do. He replied, "Our goal is never to be considered the best at what we do; our goal is to be considered the only one that does what we do." Sam Walton and Gene Simmons would have to agree.

5

THE ROLLING STONES:

BRANDING STRATEGIES BEYOND SATISFACTION

We were very conscious we were in a totally new era. Rock and roll changed the world. It reshaped the way people think. It was like A.D. *and* B.C.
                                                                —KEITH RICHARDS

Sitting in a meeting with phrases like *return on investment, P&L statement, business models,* and *product pricing* flying around the room might make you think you've entered a board meeting for the *Fortune* 500 company of your choice. Now add to that scene a short whisper of a guy, dressed undoubtedly in tight trousers and an anything-but-conservative shirt, who can dance around a stage even better than any CFO can dance around his or her numbers, and you might conjure up an image of a Rolling Stones business meeting. The Rolling Stones organization is a well-oiled, money-making machine, and to say it resembles anything less than a *Fortune* 500 firm would be unjust. In the world of rock and roll, not only would the Rolling Stones likely top the list of legendary bands; they would most likely top the list of rock businesses, as well.

At the helm is CEO Mick Jagger, who attended the London School of Economics, but professes never to have really *studied* business per se. He does, however, have 40 years of industry acumen under his tiny belt, along with a keen intellect, a deep understanding of business models, and a knack for turning a profit.

Fans think of a lot of things when they think of the Rolling Stones. There's the music of course, spanning hits from the 1960s ("Satisfaction" and "Let's Spend the Night Together" jump to mind), 1970s (such as "Jumpin' Jack Flash" and "Honky Tonk Woman"), and 1980s (perhaps "Emotional Rescue" and "She's So Cold"). Generation Xers might think of "Start Me Up," which was used to launch Microsoft's Windows 95—the most successful product introduction of all time—for which the Stones reportedly were paid somewhere between $4 million and $12 million (secrecy in numbers). Twenty-somethings may think of Ford Motor's recent attempt to rev up its car sales with ads featuring "Start Me Up," which appeared during television programs such as the Fiesta Bowl, *The Practice, The Tonight Show, 60 Minutes,* and *The Simpsons.* Some fans may also think of the infamous lips-and-tongue logo that adorns T-shirts and biceps around the world. And all fans think of the energetic, ever-gaunt Mick Jagger and his seemingly sleepy, somewhat chemically preserved counterpart Keith Richards.

Baby boomers who have found themselves inside corporate America, however, may choose to deem the Rolling Stones their business, branding, and marketing heroes. Just as the nation's nerds worship Bill Gates, so too do some business managers worship Mick, Keith, Charlie Watts, and Ronnie Wood. When it comes to brand loyalty and profits, the Rolling Stones can match wits and records with even the best entrepreneurs. Ray Gmeiner, vice president of promotions at Virgin Records, explains, "The Rolling Stones are a unique brand because they've taken the business side of rock and roll to the level that few if any other bands have."

The Rolling Stones, the business, operates like many other large corporations—as a financially driven, global operation based in the Netherlands (because of its more favorable tax laws). The business model focuses on three core revenue-generating areas—album sales, royalties, and touring, each led by a team of competent executives. The corporate executives hold regular meetings to examine the effectiveness of the managers for each product line in generating revenue and controlling expenses. Although the organization is private and secretive, *Fortune* magazine estimates that the Stones' revenue since 1989 totals $1.5 billion (see Table 5.1), eclipsing competitors such as U2, Bruce Springsteen, and Michael Jackson. Keith Richards claims, "It's a mom-and-pop operation. Mick is the mom, and I'm the pop, and then we have these offspring that need feeding."[1]

It's a well run mom-and-pop operation nonetheless, guided by business manager Joe Rascoff and Prince Rupert Zu Lowenstein, a London banker and trusted business advisor for over 30 years. Gmeiner adds, "A lot of the direction of the band comes from Jagger who is not only the front man of the band but the front man of the business. He has been instrumental in adding some of his ideas to the promotions side of the band, from the integration of technology to corporate sponsorships."

Together, management and band work closely to create the Rolling Stones brand, which combines the image of the band, the personalities of its members, and a diverse array of products, including logo merchandise, concert tours, royalties, recordings, videos, books, and corporate endorsements. The band is also a master at delivering a consistently satisfying blend of old and new music (more old than new) in an evolving musical experience. This intense combination helps the Rolling Stones brand infiltrate the culture at many levels and keep fans engaged and wanting more.

The strategies that have created legendary success for Jagger and company can be implemented in any firm looking to build market

TABLE 5.1 Rolling Stones Income

ACTIVITY	REVENUE
Royalties	$ 56.0 million
Album sales	466.4 million
Tour revenue:	
Ticket sales	865.3 million
Merchandise	135.9 million
Sponsorships	21.5 million
TOTAL	$1, 545.1 million

share, maintain customer loyalty, and remain relevant in the culture and among its fans. The Rolling Stones illustrate how to:

♪ Evolve a product over time at a rate that doesn't alienate current fans yet keeps it fresh in the market.

♪ Build product familiarity and cultural acceptance with repetition, repackaging, and recycling.

♪ Harness the buying power of baby boomers to grow profits.

♪ Explore new marketing avenues from corporate alliances to alternative product delivery to maximize market impact and profitability.

♪ Relate to the changing attitudes and lifestyles of customers.

♪ Keep a talented team together for the long run.

The Rolling Stones didn't start out as the slick performers or businesspeople they are today, but the band also didn't fall into the trap that squelches the success of many corporate start-ups—waiting for the perfect product before going to market. It often takes experimentation, mistakes, and some outright flops to perfect a product, and few would claim that the Stones started with a perfect product. Their earliest recordings were mostly hits of others, surrounded by some blues riffs, because they had little original material at that time. They certainly weren't anyone's definition of beautiful (far less cute than the Beatles); in fact, they appeared dark and dangerous to the general public. They prove, however, that just because early prototypes may not be perfect or stunning in appeal, doesn't mean an entrepreneur can't make modifications and improvements while in search of the perfect product.

IT'S ONLY ROCK AND ROLL, BUT BOOMERS LIKE IT

Few bands exceed the staying power and commercial success of the Rolling Stones. In part, it's talent (quality in the world of commerce), hard work, vision, planning, and execution, a basic formula that keeps the band rocking decade after decade, similar to the way brands like Coke and Cadillac keep rolling through the generations. And, in part, it's timing. The Rolling Stones happened to hit the music scene and become part of the collective life soundtrack of the largest demographic segment of our time—the baby boomers. Teenagers of the 1960s listened, made out, danced, smoked, rebelled, and fantasized to Stones music. It was their puberty music, and it was good enough that the kids continued to sing it, and the band evolved enough that the kids continued to follow it for decades.

"When bands connect with fans during their growing-up years, during emotional times, they will feel emotions when they think about them in the future," explains Stephen Swid, founder of *Spin* magazine. "We want to listen to favorites over and over again because they help us remember." The fact that the band and its music are ingrained in the memories of what many marketers consider to be the most important market segment of the twenty-first century helps explain why the Rolling Stones are a relevant American cultural icon today.

But not all in the Stones' formula for success is corporate babble— this is, after all, rock and roll, and therefore sex and excess beg to be mentioned. But, bottom line, after 40 years this group continues to perform the kick-ass, take-no-prisoners brand of music that has earned it the title of "Greatest Rock-and-Roll Brand Ever" in the minds of music fans.

START THEM UP

Music history took an interesting turn one fateful day in 1960 when two teenagers met by chance in a railway station in Dartford, England. Mick Jagger was carrying a few old blues albums under his arm, which may well have sparked recognition in Keith Richards that they had known each other in childhood and shared a mutual love of American blues music. It wasn't long before they were playing in a band called Little Boy Blue and the Blue Boys. Jagger went off to the London School of Economics and Richards to Sidcup Art College. Blues guitarist Brian Jones joined the band, and the trio moved into a dilapidated apartment in Chelsea, playing whatever gigs they could get around London, performing covers of their heroes—blues greats Muddy Waters and Howlin' Wolf. It was Jones who suggested they call themselves the Rolling Stones, after the Muddy Waters tune, "Rollin' Stone Blues," starting what was to become the world's most successful rock-and-roll corporation.

On January 14, 1963, the Rolling Stones (with the addition of Ian Stewart, Bill Wyman, and drummer Charlie Watts) first played together as a group at the Flamingo Club in Soho. With the help of a 19-year-old aspiring business manager named Andrew Oldham, the group signed a contract that June with Decca Records and released its first single, a cover of Chuck Berry's "Come On." It was a hit on British radio stations, as were their next two singles, covers of the Beatles' "I Want to Be Your Man" and Buddy Holly's "Not Fade Away."

After "test marketing" their music, the Stones began an aggressive product rollout, expanding from a limited sales area to wider geographic areas. The band quickly merged its successful singles into an LP—*The Rolling Stones*—released in the United Kingdom on April 16, 1964. It included blues-oriented versions of songs people already knew, such as Bobby Troop's "I Get My Kicks on Route 66" and Sam Cooke's "Honest I Do." That year marked many milestones for the Stones. They recorded a second album, *12 × 5,* and began their first U.S. tour, allowing them to tap the largest market in the world (much the same way as successful European and Japanese firms do). Ed Sullivan debuted the Stones on his show on October 25, 1964, experiencing some of the same audience reaction as when he debuted Elvis and the Beatles. On a roll, the Stones hit it hard in 1965 and released four albums, *Rolling Stones No. 2, The Rolling Stones Now, Out of Our Heads,* and *December Children.*

The Rolling Stones' early days would not be without trouble, however. In fact, they could be described as "Good Times, Bad Times," the name of one of the songs on the band's second album. The good came from the fans—they were buying records and attending concerts. The bad, however, came from the critics and columnists who described them as "five, shaggy-as-Shetland-pony lads," "long and scruffy." One critic would go so far as to say "one of them looks as if he had a feather duster in his head." Although it didn't inspire a new hair fashion, fans apparently didn't mind the feather-duster look. Also in the bad column were the newspaper accounts of the mayhem the Stones created everywhere they went—riots, the tearing off of teenage girls' clothing, enough booing to sometimes drive the Stones from the stage, and police barricades being attacked by thousands of teenagers. There were reports of fire hoses turned on fans at concerts, fines for "insulting behavior," and questions from the establishment about whether the Stones made music or noise.

Though fraught with controversy, the Rolling Stones concert tours evoked strong emotions and created an experience no fan was likely to forget. There were giant lotus-flower-shaped stages, a giant, inflatable phallus ridden by Mick Jagger that sometimes would rise from the stage, and unofficial protection from a swarm of Hell's Angels. Their stages became combinations of futuristic technology blended with ancient superstition and inflatable figures so large that the Federal Aviation Administration required installation of aircraft warning lights.

Newspapers all over the world ran front-page stories about the chaos that occurred at Stones' concerts. Some critics even wrote about disappointing vocals and poor sound quality, which did push the band to work harder on its product. Though the news was negative, it meant global exposure for the band. Parents were shocked. Teens were intrigued. Worship ensued. The band proved that an intense relationship with fans can outweigh the impact of critics and bad press on overall success.

PRODUCT STRATEGY: ONE GOOD SONG DESERVES ANOTHER

In the 1970s, the Boston Consulting Group published research showing that firms that expand capacity so fast that competitors fall behind often end up dominating an industry. The Rolling Stones' masterful and aggressive approach to creating product follows this principle. Throughout the 1970s, the Stones released an album every year until 1979. Some years it was one album, often two, sometimes three, and occasionally four. Many went to number one on the U.S. or U.K. sales charts, and often on both.

Acting on the idea that one good turn deserves another, the Stones put some of their best songs on multiple albums. The albums they released in 1965, for example, contained some songs from the past, such as "Route 66" from their 1964 album and the classic blues song "Little Red Rooster," which they recorded during their first stop in the United States. With this recycling and repackaging approach, the Stones could release four new albums of new and existing material instead of just two albums of all new material. They continued this practice on album after album. For example, "Time Is on My Side" first appeared on *The Rolling Stones 12 × 5* in 1964. That song would go on to appear on *Rolling Stones No. 2* in 1965 and *High Tide & Green Grass* and *Got Live If You Want It* in 1966.

Repeating songs on multiple albums has helped ingrain Rolling Stones music in the minds and hearts of baby boomers across socio-economic and geographic segments. In addition to the publicity and promotion that accompanies the release of a record, each product introduction gives the band a chance to strengthen the relationship with current fans and creates an opportunity to reach new fans. Creating and releasing albums at such a rapid rate also generates an aura of demand, popularity, and success with which people want to associate. An aggressive product release implies that the previous products are hits and that the band must be hot or it wouldn't be releasing another album. For new customers, the fact that a song has already appeared on a previous album may go all but unnoticed. Among devoted fans, a song they already know just makes the new material more familiar, an important principle in the theory of how people learn to like something.

SLOW CHANGE

One of the secrets to the Rolling Stones' long-term success has been the band's ability to change and evolve at a rate that doesn't alienate its greatest fans yet keeps the band relevant in the market. How have they done it? With a strategy built upon the psychological theory of generalization and discrimination, which illustrates that the more similar something is to the past, the more likely people are to learn it.

The Rolling Stones practiced the theory of generalization, in the context that the more a new song sounds like one from the past, the more likely people are to learn it, accept it, and like it. But if something is perceived as being the same as something else, it usually doesn't warrant purchase or adoption. Therefore, marketers must build something new into a product for it to be perceived as different and worth buying. The Rolling Stones could repeat songs on albums because the old songs were surrounded by new ones, making the albums quite different from one another. However, throughout the years, the band didn't really change its music very much, choosing to stick with the blues roots and overall sound that brought it to the forefront of rock and roll.

Gradual evolution has served all of the legendary bands featured in this book well; in fact, some of the problematic times for star brands occur when they stray too far from what their fans expect and have rewarded with loyalty in the past. Success in the market can usually be attributed to specific brand strengths, and completely abandoning those traits rarely results in greater acceptance or sales. Whereas U2, Bruce Springsteen, and Sting have improved and embellished on their musical strengths to increase their popularity over the years, Garth Brooks almost brought his career to an abrupt halt with a bizarre twist on total reinvention.

Brooks almost single-handedly led the migration of country music into mainstream culture. Wearing a cowboy hat, western jeans, and a country-boy grin, he combined the electricity of a KISS concert with the beat of the Rolling Stones' or AC/DC's music to create a new genre of music that struck a deep, rousing chord with Americans from a vast array of socioeconomic and demographic backgrounds. Some called it crossover, some called it country rock, but nearly everyone called it sensational. It crossed the wide chasm that had traditionally divided rock and country audiences. But even beloved stars can go too far in pushing the envelope of originality.

After several platinum albums, numerous Grammy awards, and a string of sold-out stadium concerts, Brooks assumed the identity of Chris Gaines, a fictitious character he created to allow himself to explore different artistic channels without alienating or diminishing the Garth Brooks band. Then people were told that Gaines was really Brooks. Try as he might to explain to his fans and the media why he suddenly looked like someone in the witness protection program, many thought he had lost his marbles and didn't buy the new album.

It wasn't long before the blonde, hard-rock version of Brooks disappeared and the good old country boy reemerged. Since then, however, Brooks has failed to hit the level of popularity he claimed in the early to mid-1990s.

Marketers sometimes underestimate the time required for innovative new products to diffuse through the population because of failure to understand generalization. Products that require a substantial change in behavior are classified as discontinuous innovations; they take more time to diffuse and be accepted than products that consumers perceive as similar to what they've used in the past. Microsoft Windows dominates the market in part because of the evolutionary nature of its product. Rather than create a new system every few years that requires that consumers abandon what they know and learn something new. Windows offers upgrades that consumers can adopt quickly, easily, and voluntarily—or they can choose to pass and wait until the difference is great enough to warrant a change.

Just as Microsoft Windows had the focus to become the operating system of the masses (not just the opinion leaders as in the case of Apple), the Rolling Stones did whatever it took to grow their fan base and be adopted by the masses. The Ed Sullivan show was important enough in reaching the U.S. mass market that the Stones modified their product to fit the culture in which they found themselves—accepting the cultural boundaries of America. When they appeared on Sullivan's show in 1967, Jagger changed the words of "Let's Spend the Night Together" to "Let's Spend Some Time Together." Foregoing a purist view of their art form, the Stones were realistic and pragmatic about how to get the product out and accepted by potential fans.

The psychological theory of generalization and discrimination also applies to the success of the Rolling Stones' string of record-breaking concert tours. Though he knows that a majority of the fans come to hear a retrospective of Rolling Stones' classic hits, Jagger is dedicated to updating the concerts, not just to make them new, exciting, and relevant to fans, but to reflect changes in society and in fans' expectation levels. This prompted the Stones to perform the first live rock-and-roll concert on the Internet back in 1994.

Ray Gmeiner explains, "Jagger interjected his own personal interest in the high-tech side of things into their 1997–1998 world tour. During opening night at Soldiers Field, they projected up on a screen a giant main page and cursor. They tried to tie into what was at that time an emerging interest in the Internet and interactivity by letting their fans decide which songs would be played on tour. Fans were able to select, via the Web site, the songs that the band would play—a.k.a., go to www.whatever and submit your song choices."

In the early stages of the tour, Jagger would actually stop the show, project onto the screen the number of votes for a particular song, and explain that that was why they were playing "Jumpin' Jack Flash," for example, that night. The problem was that it slowed down the momentum of the show too much, so the concept was abandoned. "It was a good attempt, however, to stay up-to-date and relevant in a changing society—perhaps a little ahead of what people were ready to do," adds Gmeiner. "In the end, the Rolling Stones weren't willing to sacrifice quality of the show—the number-one product and concern of the band."

The technology theme did, however, get press, and whether some fans experienced it on stage or not, they were aware of the efforts of the band to be timely and creative. The Stones tried to take the new Web-based, interactive world people were beginning to explore at that time to a rock-and-roll audience, reaching out to a younger crowed or a with-it boomer crowd. It didn't go unnoticed.

Neither did the unprecedented success of the *Forty Licks* tour, which coincided with the release of the greatest hits album of the same name. Although the Rolling Stones adopted a heavy product focus, it was never at the peril of failing to focus on the audience. The *Forty Licks* tour provides a masterful lesson in product development, band loyalty, merchandising, and marketing. A closer look reveals insights for brand managers about how to develop and manage a complex integrated marketing communication (IMC) campaign. Mind-boggling in scale and market dominance, this world tour conveyed the Stones' primary brand message with a comprehensive, multimedia attack on several market segments.

FORTY YEARS, FORTY LICKS

After a 40-year run of hard-hitting rock-and-roll hits, you might expect the Rolling Stones' "senior executives" to trade in their T-shirts and leather for wool cardigans, collect Social Security, and spend their days on the golf course and their nights in front of the telly. But Jagger, Richards, Wood, and Watts are not your stereotypical AARP members. They haven't settled for the passive life; they are still creating, performing, and innovating. Mick Jagger's sixtieth birthday did not bring retirement; instead, it brought the *Forty Licks* 2002–2003 world tour, the band's most ambitious to date, which would go on to reach 1 million fans (willing to shell out over $200 million), as it played 32 dates throughout the United States, Canada, Europe and the Far East.

Touring has always been good for the Stones, selling out arenas since their 1972 *Through the Past Brightly* appearances, which attracted everyone from screaming fans to celebrities such as Truman Capote. During the past decade, their concerts grossed over $750 million, with their stadium tours becoming the three largest selling concert tours of all time. *VooDoo Lounge* (1994) remains the top-grossing North American tour, raking in $121.2 million; *No Security* (1998–1999) made $337 million, attracting 5.6 million people worldwide. That works out to a hefty chunk of change per performance—an average of $2.3 million for a night's work in the case of the *No Security* tour.

The Rolling Stones are able to create sellout megaconcert tours because of who they are—because of the brand they have created over time and all of the hoopla that goes along with it. They will attract fans who go to at least one performance of each tour, friends who attend a few concerts over time, and customers who just want to see the legendary band once while it is still performing. These groups of concertgoers vary in the degree of relationship they have and want to maintain with the band. Whereas customers want to engage in a piece of music history, fans want to add to their *repertoire* of personal experiences with the band.

Regardless of the degree of fanaticism, audience members are attracted to the core Rolling Stones product, which is Mick Jagger on vocals, Keith Richards on guitar, Charlie Watts on drums, and Ronnie Wood on guitar. The classic product is augmented on tour with the dazzling keyboards of Chuck Leavell and bass playing of Darryl Jones. While the fans appreciate variation between tours and perhaps even in how the songs are performed, they want the original Stones performing Stones music.

They also want the trademark energy of Jagger, who trains for months to prepare to go out on tour. In a *60 Minutes* interview, Ed Bradley asked Keith Richards how he prepares for a tour. The weathered Richards just looked at him and laughed. "Oh Ed, I just turn up . . . there's no secret. People ask me if I work out and I say, are you kidding, I play guitar with the Rolling Stones. You try that. That's enough of a workout for anybody."[2]

THE SINGLE: FROM PRODUCT TO MARKETING TOOL

In gearing up for the *Forty Licks* tour, the Rolling Stones looked to a combination of marketing and promotion methods to announce the concerts and generate buzz. The key would be to hit traditional fans and a newer generation of fans through channels and with partners that were relevant to them.

The presale of *Forty Licks* tickets received an overwhelming response from fans. It provided the perfect platform to launch Clear Channel Entertainment's (CCE's) new membership program, called GetAccess. It teamed up with album retail chain Sam Goody for the Stones' promotional program, which granted people who bought a $60 GetAccess membership the right to buy two tickets to the concert of their choice. Because demand for tickets was expected to be very high, the urgency to secure them was high among fans, many of whom would have paid even more than $60 to get tickets to the concert of their choice. Sam Goody promoted the GetAccess program throughout its 900 stores with in-store signage, bag stuffers, and radio and online advertising, and the program was also marketed to nearly 2 million members of Replay, Musicland's customer-loyalty rewards program.

CCE's Access Group has seen the number of its customers buying tickets online skyrocket from about 10 percent to almost half in the past several years. Combine that with the fact that it marketed 28,000 shows and sold 68 million tickets last year, and marketers understand the GetAccess potential. The Stones presale was the perfect way to generate buzz for both GetAccess and the *Forty Licks* tour.

Just as they and most bands have done in the past, the Stones prepared to release the new *Forty Licks* single, "Don't Stop," to jumpstart the tour's campaign. However, the release would push beyond the traditional release of a single to radio stations, by including partnerships in new media, technology, and advertising. Together they created the desired blitz in the market.

The first partner was AOL. "Leading up to the *Forty Licks* tour, the Rolling Stones gave AOL an exclusive of the first single, "Don't Stop," before we [Virgin] were allowed to give it to radio. AOL had a five-day advance before it hit the traditional airwaves," explains Gmeiner. Fans could log on and hear the song before it hit radio stations and music stores. "It was an attempt to reach out to the masses, to the larger audience than the current fan base with a newer technology and to go beyond the traditional ways to promoting a record."

The Internet release strategy attracted a lot of attention, which got the word out about the song and, more important, about the tour. It also positioned the band as current and forward-thinking among a new generation of fans. In addition to partnering with AOL, the Stones partnered with the NBA to increase exposure of the single "Don't Stop," which was used in television spots to kick off and promote the NBA's 2002–2003 season. This came right after the release of the single to radio stations, in the early stages of album release to retail, and before the tour promotions started. The goal of this release strategy was to increase visibility for albums in stores and for the tour and to increase ticket sales.

Using a new song in advertising and in commercial tie-ins is a trend that has recently taken off. It can create word of mouth and visibility for the song as well as position the product being advertised as up-to-date. It can increase familiarity with the product among those who know the song and increase familiarity with the new song among those who know the product. That's what happened with the collaboration between Nissan Pathfinder and singer Lenny Kravitz.

" 'Fly Away' had already been established on the radio, but using the song in the ad was a huge help in increasing popularity of the song by making it more familiar with people who heard it on the radio and those who didn't," says Gmeiner. "That strategy played an important part in making that song bigger than it already was, and perhaps bigger than it otherwise would have been."

The Rolling Stones used the release of "Don't Stop" in an interesting way. In the past, promotion of the single would focus on pushing the record—the success of which was determined by sales of the single. But if you examine the role of "Don't Stop" in the overall promotion of *Forty Licks,* the sales and performance of the single on the charts seems quite secondary compared to the marketing value of its release. What used to be the "product" of a band may now very well have become the give-away promotional item that helps build brand equity for the band and generate awareness for what really makes the money—concerts and merchandise. Granted, no band wants its album to flop; a hit enhances credibility and perceived relevance while a miss can damage the image of the band. However, does it really matter if it doesn't hit the top 10? Not really—especially if your focus is more oriented toward selling merchandise than albums.

Attend a Rolling Stones concert and you'll notice that the band does not sell CDs at the venue as other bands do. Rather than use the concert to peddle CDs, the Stones use it to push other merchandise that carries significantly higher profit margins. Other artists usually bring in Sound Scan to capture sales data that will be given credit toward official sales figures. At this point in their careers, however, the Stones don't need to push albums. Fans will buy them online or in stores if they want them, and many of them do. The Stones would prefer that fans spend the limited funds they bring to a concert on T-shirts, hats, and other higher-profit items.

In the grand scheme of the Rolling Stones organization, the album really serves as a marketing tool. But the Stones have never really been about record-breaking album sales. "The Rolling Stones never had huge sales of an individual album at the time of its release," explains Gmeiner. "Look at Peter Frampton, who sold 60 million albums at one time, and compare that to the Rolling Stones, whose biggest sales in current lifespan of an album is 2.5 million copies, which I think *Forty Licks* will surpass."

YOU CAN SOMETIMES GET WHAT YOU WANT

The Rolling Stones understand the complexities and opportunities that arise from having a fan base that encompasses both ends of the socioeconomic spectrum. In the vein of classic product differentiation and discriminatory pricing strategies, the *Forty Licks* world tour played in three different types of venues—stadiums, arenas, and select small-venue theatres—with the goal of selling out each concert regardless of venue size. Marketing research identified which cities had fan support strong enough to warrant large stadium appearances and which were more likely to sell out midsized arenas. Some cities were better suited for smaller, more intimate theatres and ballrooms, which not only gave the most dedicated Stones fans a special experience but added to the aura of the brand. Seven cities, however, proved to contain enough demand that the band played all three types of venues with multiple appearance dates.

The geographic market and retail outlet selections for *Forty Licks* comprised only half of the strategy required to reach all types of Stones fans; executing the strategy successfully meant offering unique experiences to different types of fans willing and able to fork over varying amounts of cash. Therefore, Jagger and company would create three different shows, with three different musical and physical sets. Michael Cohl, the Stones' longtime tour promoter, said, "Only the Rolling Stones would dare to come up with a concept so ambitious—three dramatically different shows in three different venues . . . a spectacular musical event."[3] This also of course, permits a variety of prices—from mass-market tickets at $75 to $90 to some "Gold Circle" tickets at up to $350. This is where those economic concepts—such as maximizing the revenue under the demand curve, with multiple price points attracting multiple segments of the market—taught at the London School of Economics come in handy.

People's perceptions of value, however, play an important role in the overall perception of the brand. Performing in a select number of small venues (at much higher ticket prices) adds to the aura of the Rolling Stones brand among those who can't see them in intimate settings, and the rarity of such performances enhances the value to those paying top ticket prices because they are buying an experience few others will have. Similarly, Nike does sell $170 shoes to a select number of customers willing and able to pay the price. While marketing strategy contributes to the sale of the high-priced shoes, Nike sells far more shoes in $70 range. From a branding standpoint, the expensive shoes give an overall perceived lift to the Nike brand and add to its aura in the marketplace.

CORPORATE SPONSORSHIP

Mick Jagger and the Rolling Stones have never been shy about corporate sponsorships. In the early years, the band made little money from its touring activities because there really was no proven model of how to generate profits. The structure consisted of a hired tour manager, who would contact local promoters in each tour city to plan each show, then collect varying amounts of money from them afterward. Jagger got firsthand experience with this side of the business, personally negotiating with some of the local promoters in specific markets and countries.

Canadian rock promoter Michael Cohl began managing the band's shows with *Steel Wheels* and created the structure that would allow the band to recognize the real money-making potential of this side of the business. The Rolling Stone's tour model would consist of Cohl working directly with local venues and booking the entire tour without the use of local promoters. He generated additional revenue with sky-boxes, bus tours, television appearances, and expanded merchandising efforts. Corporate sponsors—from Volkswagen and Tommy Hilfiger to Anheuser-Busch and E*Trade—were added to the formula along with a heavy dose of cross-promotion between all of the elements to integrate all of the marketing activities. The *Steel Wheels* tour earned $260 million worldwide, which was a record at the time for any rock concert tour.

Since *Steel Wheels,* the band has grossed over $1 billion on the road with the same basic formula—although it continues to tweak the operations side of the equation. It is the biggest revenue generator of the Rolling Stones organization.

Key to the success of *Forty Licks* was e-commerce financial giant E*Trade, which sponsored and promoted the tour on its web site. From the band's perspective, this let Jagger further his continued personal interest in and support of technology—similar to the giant home-page screen in the *No Security* tour—and made the band relevant among a variety of consumers. E*Trade grabbed the attention of a substantial portion of the Stones' target audience, which varied by age but had common financial and net-worth characteristics. Not only do E*Trade customers have enough money to be stock market investors, they have enough income to be concert ticket buyers. Sponsoring *Forty Licks* gave E*Trade the opportunity to connect with current and would-be customers at an emotional level and in an entertaining way, telling them "We understand who you are and what you like, and if you like the Rolling Stones, E*Trade is for you." It also allowed the company to position itself by aligning itself with the Rolling Stones image—classic yet contemporary, cool but not trendy, relevant to twenty- to sixty-somethings (a far cry from the fly-by-night images associated with Internet companies of the past). The *Forty Licks* sponsorship matched companies and market targets extremely well. For E*Trade, the synergy was great enough to withdraw from advertising during the Super Bowl, which had delivered good market demographics but probably not as much bang for the buck as the Stones alignment.

The end result of the *Forty Licks* tour can be measured in quantifiable means—from ticket sales and albums sold, not to mention the millions of dollars of merchandise that was sold. Just as important, however, might be the success achieved in nonquantifiable terms. These include strengthening the bond between the band and its fans, creating new generations of fans, and reestablishing the Rolling Stones brand in the market. Not only does this translate into more merchandise and album sales and greater demand for the next tour, it also increases the value of the band's music to advertisers and sponsors looking to create an emotional connection with baby boomers by riding on the coattails of the music they love.

UNDER THE THUMB OF THE BABY-BOOMER MARKET

At the heart of the Rolling Stones' entrenchment in our society is the band's deep connection with baby boomers. In the early years, authorities accused the Stones of decadence, undue influence on teenagers, and anarchy. Whereas sociologists called that cultural conflict, it could also be described as creating a relationship with emerging elements of a new culture. The Beatles had made a significant connection with baby boomers, but they opened the door for the Stones to capture an important part of the baby-boomer life soundtrack when they stopped touring and split. Once inside the door, the Stones spent the next four decades creating and nurturing an extrasensory connection with the largest demographic segment of the population.

Branding, when done well, generates profits from consumers' willingness to buy the brand (often at premium prices) and increased repeat purchases. Therefore, from a branding perspective, the significance lies in the sheer size of the market—76 million people, with varying needs, wants, and problems and differing degrees of ability, willingness, and authority to buy. Yet psychographic similarities—shared interests, opinions, and activities—tie these segments together to form the largest base of purchasing power in the U.S. market. One commonality among the group's members is that they grew up on a diet of classic rock; it is part of them. Understanding the significance of this market helps explain why legendary rock bands are, for the most part, satisfied with staying relevant to their core market and don't feel the need to position themselves too heavily to today's teens. Their focus is on remaining a part of the cultural fabric of baby boomers everywhere, a sentiment shared by many great brands, from Coca-Cola to Cadillac.

The Rolling Stones have remained relevant to the baby-boomer market by adapting to changes within it. This begins with a thorough understanding of the boomers—their market power, lifestyles, attitudes, fears, realities, and dreams—which for many classic rock bands is made easier because they are of that generation themselves. Just as retail executives need to put themselves into the shoes of their customers by mystery-shopping their stores, brand managers need to study baby boomers' childhoods and life dilemmas. Demographics determine about two-thirds of everything—what problems people face, what products they buy, and frequently how and where they buy. Understanding demographics thoroughly increases the likelihood of creating successful brands and crafting strategies to connect with them.

SHOW ME THE PEOPLE!

The year 1957 was a good year for babies; an unprecedented 4.3 million of them were born in the United States, a peak not attained since.

After the war, beginning in 1946, the nation went on a re-creation spree, resulting in over 4 million births per year until 1965, when the number dropped to 3.7 million. The baby-boom fertility rates would give birth to the most significant generation marketers would have to appease for the next 80-plus years.

Baby boomers get attention because of their concentration, at one time 40 percent of the total U.S. population. As a result, the smaller number of consumers born later, about 41 million between 1968 and 1979, were to some degree forgotten—labeled Generation X. Those born in the 1980s and 1990s followed suit and were called Generation Y.

The baby-boomer population explosion moves through markets like a pig that's been swallowed by a python, inviting marketers to satisfy the needs, wants, and fantasies of 76 million people. Add to that the fact that many of them are still the primary purchasers, or at least primary payers, for a lot of children and grandchildren, and you begin to understand the need to connect with them. They not only *affect* the economy; they *are* the economy, representing the greatest share of the workforce, the greatest share of income, and the greatest share of voting power and political influence.

For public corporations, it's not just profits that are important, but growth in revenues and profits. According to U.S. Census projections, the number of boomers age 45 to 54 is projected to increase 14 percent between 2001 and 2010, while the number of 55- to 64-year-olds will grow by a whopping 44 percent. During the same decade, the number of consumers in the 25- to 34- and 35- to 44-year-old groups are projected to *decline.* Public corporations faced with analysts who determine their P/E ratios by forecasting their growth potential can point to the baby-boomer market for opportunities if they have the right mix of brands, services, and prices. The problem is that competitive firms have figured this out as well—hence the race to find *something* to connect with this vital market. Brands that evoke emotion (from nostalgia to sheer exuberance) may hold the key to customer loyalty in this market, assuming they deliver in the areas of quality, functionality, design, and value. Using classic rock in commercials aimed at boomers makes sense, as does using musical acts from the 1970s and 1980s to entertain at corporate events.

SHOW ME THE MONEY!

Baby boomers have discretionary income that vastly exceeds that of any other cohort of customers, explaining the popularity of *Forty Licks* and other classic rock bands and tours, including the Eagles and Chicago. Marketers have followed the baby boomers and their money for decades—from their turbulent teens and twenties, in which they were dubbed hippies, to their thirties and forties, in which they settled into good-paying careers and had families. At this juncture they were considered *yuppies*—young urban professionals—and they bought homes (and everything for them), clothing, food, and cars at record levels, and spurred cultural changes reflected in everything from television programming (remember *thirtysomething*?) to fashion and beauty products. Today, those baby boomers have become *muppies*—middle-aged urban professionals—whose changing needs today and over the next several decades will create dramatic effects on the sales and profit levels of the brands they've supported in the past. As they move through different stages in their lives, they will continue to support the brands with which they have an emotional connection, and their sheer volume will be a moving driver of consumer product sales.

Baby boomers delayed getting married and having children longer than any previous generation, but eventually they entered the trap and brought with them a permanent propensity to consume. They earned a lot of income during the 1980s and 1990s but they spent more than they made, buying products that past generations considered luxuries, such as consumer electronics, cable TV, cellular phones, second homes, and household services. They drove the minivan market in the 1980s and the SUV market in the 1990s, and they will drive the resurrection of the sporty convertible in the 2000s. They will also drive overall spending rates. Understanding the spending trends of boomers helps explain which sponsorships make sense for concert tours—such as E*Trade and VISA's alliance with Elton John in the 1990s.

BRANDING TO BOOMERS

Brands are gaining importance among boomers' product choices. If you examine boomers' spending patterns, you can begin to predict demand for various consumer and industrial goods. For example, when people are between the ages of 25 and 44, nearly everything they buy classifies as a *necessity*, because they need everything to build and run a household. In these markets, brands guide the *choice* between which food, cars, clothing, and household options *will* be bought, not whether the products *should* be bought. Although younger baby boomers and Generation Xers have definite brand preferences, their purchases are driven by such strong immediate need that they may not have the opportunity to exercise much *brand insistence*. If the household is empty, it needs to be supplied with furniture, food, and a car suited for commuting and carting kids to soccer practice; price often plays a more important role than brand during this life stage.

The baby-boom buying frenzy of the 1980s and 1990s, characterized as the *Need Economy*, put retailers on Easy Street to growth and profits. Today, however, the Need Economy is giving way to the *Want Economy*, which ticks upward every seven or eight seconds, as another baby boomer someplace in the United States turns 50! Often, these peers of Mick Jagger are at the height of their careers and earning power, have low or no mortgages to pay, and have generally reduced family responsibilities.* Yet, as they reach age 50, their need to buy things to build a household is decreased, unless they have to furnish a second home due to divorce. For the most part, as they become empty nesters—with children out of the house and later out of college—they find themselves with too much stuff. They are in the unique position of having the ability to buy what they want but without the immediate need.

Boomers have *freedom* both to spend and withhold spending. Because they already have enough housing, cars, and clothing, they not only have the freedom to spend on what they want; they have the freedom to withhold until they find exactly what they want, whether that's a Jaguar, a Hummer, or a Cadillac. This elevates the importance of brands in reaching growing, profitable market segments. If brand managers can create fans among aging baby boomers, the likelihood of converting interest into a sale is greater, because the boomers can

---

*However, Mick Jagger himself seems each year to discover another new family responsibility, if you follow the paternity suits filed in various places.

probably afford to buy it. That's a major difference in their lifestyle compared to a decade ago.

Aging baby boomers become fans of brands that fulfill certain expectations—quality products that are aesthetically pleasing, personally satisfying, natural, convenient, easy to use, and, if possible, noncaloric. Expect empty-nester boomers to indulge in luxury travel, restaurants, and the theater, which often means they need more fashionable clothing, jewelry, and the designer brands found in department and specialty stores. They watch their waistlines and diets and are good prospects for spas, health clubs, skin care products and cosmetics, beauty parlors, and healthier foods. As they approach retirement, they purchase condominiums and begin to take more frequent but perhaps value-oriented vacations, often purchased online. They need financial planners with financial products oriented toward asset accumulation and retirement income—perhaps even stocks that pay dividends.

Baby boomers also want to buy experiences, youth, and memories, and they look for ways to remind the rest of the world that they are not your stereotypical 50-year-olds. They are younger in mind, body, and spirit than generations before them, and the picture of rocking back and forth in a rocking chair is something they reserve for people in their eighties. These midlifers remember Woodstock (or at least have some evidence that they were there) and have kept classic rock as part of their lives. It explains why the Rolling Stones, Elton John, and Neil Diamond thrive on tour.

CONNECTING WITH BOOMERS

Nothing establishes an extrasensory connection with baby boomers more effectively than the songs and bands they loved during puberty and early adulthood. "Music defines a generation, and who could better represent or influence boomers than rock stars who are mostly baby boomers themselves, like the Rolling Stones and the Eagles," says Stephen Swid. Some people still get the urge to gulp a Coke when they hear "I'd Like to Teach the World to Sing." What defines them as a generation defines them as a market to advertising, marketing, and brand managers.

Sheer size, spending power, and accessibility make the baby-boomer market extremely attractive to all kinds of marketers, even those who previously sold products to a different generation of consumers. Penetrating a new market, however, means brand rejuvenation and repositioning, even if the brand is, arguably, one of the best known of the previous century. We refer, of course, to Cadillac, the brand that went from status symbol to age identifier—becoming known as the wheels of choice for oldsters around the country. Similar to the Rolling Stones, Cadillac faces the challenges of:

♪ Evolving its product at a rate that doesn't alienate current fans but positions it as fresh among baby-boomer markets

♪ Creating an emotional connection with and harnessing the buying power of baby boomers to grow profits

♪ Relating to the changing attitudes and lifestyles of its customers

Since the inception of the Cadillac brand, culture and mass-market values have changed, due in part to the likes of Elvis and the Rolling Stones. Conventional behaviors, attitudes, and style of sixty-somethings indicate that Jagger, Richards, Watts, and Wood should be sporting cardigans and taking quiet walks with grandchildren. Whereas the Rolling Stones shattered the traditional image of what it means to be 60, Cadillac's brand only furthered it. The more people adopted a youthful mind-set, the greater the disconnection between Cadillac and the baby-boomer market became. To bolster sales, create a new generation of fans, and increase profits, Cadillac would have to position itself as a lot more Rolling Stones and a lot less rocking chair.

REINVIGORATING CULTURALLY RELEVANT BRANDS

Few brands represent American culture as well as those created, owned, and marketed by General Motors. Under famed chairman Alfred Sloan, GM not only pioneered many management processes for large, centralized corporations; it built powerful consumer brands, such as Chevrolet and Cadillac, and industrial brands, such as Delco and Detroit Diesel. Today, however, GM faces the same challenges as other firms—the need to represent, relate to, and influence the culture in which it operates.

Years ago, brand managers at Chevrolet evaluated America's core culture to guide marketing and advertising themes. They determined that hot dogs and apple pie were the culture's comfort foods, and baseball its national pastime. The resulting musical slogan—hot dogs, baseball, apple pie, and Chevrolet—connected brilliantly with Americans in the post–World War II era, as did the boat-sized cars GM produced. Chevy represented and connected with the culture, eventually influencing the mass-market psyche of an entire generation. Rather than focus on smaller customer segments, Chevy and most GM divisions targeted the mass market. The jingles, products, and images weren't cutting edge or fashion forward—but then, neither were most of the division's customers.

As America emerged into more segmented markets, so did Chevrolet. One constant in the past decade has been its "Like a Rock" campaign, which uses the Bob Seger classic hit to represent and communicate with customers and drive home the brand promise that Chevy trucks are built rock-tough. The theme and the music are highly relevant to both the work and leisure values of a core market segment, whose members are often young or rural, or both. More recently, Chevrolet commercials have included the music of Smash Mouth reaching for newer, younger market targets. But music has its limitations. Though it makes the brand memorable, cultural relevance makes the brand enduring. To reinvigorate some of its brands, GM would have to enter reinvent mode, starting at the top of the line.

THE CADILLAC OF BRANDS

During the latter half of the twentieth century, firms strived to be called the Cadillacs of their industries and people strived to own a Cadillac Fleetwood, *the* status symbol of the 1960s and 1970s.* Hollywood and the glitz and glamour it represents furthered Cadillac's

---

*Not to be confused with legendary rock band Fleetwood Mac, which didn't have a formal connection to the car, but may have benefited from name association with the brand. The band was actually named for drummer Mick Fleetwood and bassist John McVie, members of a band dating back to 1967.

crème de la crème positioning. Each time a movie star, ambassador, or other famous person arrived at an important event in a Cadillac, the brand made a greater foothold in American culture. Similar to the Rolling Stones, Cadillac had a knack for being at the center of the action, always surrounded by onlookers. The Elvis connection also helped—he bought Cadillacs as frequently as he did jelly doughnuts, gave them away to adoring fans (both of him and the car), and went to his final resting place in a funeral procession lead by 12 white Cadillac limousines.* At the height of its popularity, GM's nameplate icon accounted for 8 out of 10 luxury car sales in the United States, helping GM become the most profitable and valuable firm on the planet.

As with many successful brands, Cadillac gave in to the temptations of laziness and status quo mentality. The Cadillac brand fell from its lofty position to playing second fiddle to Mercedes, Lexus, Jaguar, and even Lincoln. For years, Cadillac survived, but it failed to represent changes in the market and failed to evolve. By 2000, Cadillac's market share had fallen from nearly 80 percent in the 1950s to about 10 percent. However, while market share plummeted, the average age of its new customers soared to 66 by 2001, nearly 10 years older than those of competitors such as Lexus, BMW, and Audi.[4] Cadillac still had fans, but unfortunately, the number of future purchases they would make was no doubt limited.

The company recognized that without change, a slow death was likely. The challenge became how to change the product and positioning enough to attract new, younger consumers without alienating loyal, older ones. The Rolling Stones turned to their affinity for technology to update their relevance and connection to the baby-boomer market. Cadillac did something similar with its rebranding efforts by reengineering the car itself to reflect better the changing attitudes and lifestyles of its desired customers.

Cadillac introduced the CTS, a sleeker, entry-level luxury sedan designed to appeal to baby boomers in their late forties and fifties

---

*Yes, we acknowledge that many fans do not accept that Elvis has yet gone to his final resting place and that some even report he has been spotted locally only recently.

currently driving a BMW or a Lexus. Its introduction resembled the release of a new Rolling Stones album, combining the best of the old with new features likely to entice target customers, such as cupholders and a standard Bose 200-watt, seven-speaker system with CD player. The right mix of design and function resulted in an edgier look—influenced by stealth fighters and Bang & Olufsen electronics products—and higher performance, with a 220-horsepower Twin Cam V6 engine that lets it do 0 to 60 in 6.9 seconds with a five-speed manual transmission. Although some 60-year-olds might still prefer the more traditional Cadillac style, their choice wasn't removed from the line, just updated a bit as well.

IT'S BEEN A LONG TIME SINCE I ROCKED AND ROLLED

The key for Cadillac would be grabbing the attention of these baby boomers long enough to get them to even consider a Cadillac, let alone take a test drive. In order to cut through the clutter of contemporary advertising, reinvent the brand's personality, and form an emotional connection with potential customers, Cadillac turned to rock and roll—the conduit to puberty, family, love, and other emotion-evoking times and moments for its target market.

Its 2002 Super Bowl ads featured anything but the refined and hushed voices that traditionally characterized Cadillac television ads during Sunday golf tournaments. Instead, viewers heard Robert Plant's screamy voice singing the Led Zeppelin classic, "Been a Long Time."

Cadillac General Manager Mark LaNeve explains, "Cadillac's resurgence in the luxury marketplace is the result of incredible new products, combined with a new contemporary, pop culture attitude. The 'Break Through' advertising campaign, with the use of legendary music from an iconic band, has certainly helped to change Cadillac's image with a new generation of luxury car enthusiasts."

The Escalade is everywhere cool people and cultural influencers are and everywhere people who aspire to be cool want to be. At the 2003 Super Bowl, an event in which classic rock-and-roll songs dominated every time-out on the field, Escalades—usually black—were everywhere, along with the CTS and other Cadillac models. The brand is recapturing the position Cadillac occupied with the Hollywood set of the 1950s and 1960s. Today, the Escalade dominates product placement in music videos and is the new vehicle of choice for rap and rock musicians. In an urban school in a large Midwestern city, teenagers were asked by their teacher what car they would choose as their dream car. The answer was unanimous—the Escalade.

The new Cadillac brands scream vitality to potential buyers. Their electricity borders on that felt at an AC/DC concert, while their energy is reminiscent of what Mick Jagger exudes during one of his marathon concerts. And while the Stones update themselves, they never do it at the peril of alienating current fans; Cadillac has also done this well. Neither organization can afford to ignore some of its fans, even if they don't represent a majority of future potential growth, as they do represent significant current sales, and both Cadillac and the Stones have made a commitment to continue to keep them engaged. For Cadillac, fulfilling its brand promise will ultimately determine how successful the company's efforts to reinvigorate its classic brand will be. As of today, Cadillac is rolling again.

ROCKERS OF THE CENTURIES

The Rolling Stones exemplify how to change your brand to stay relevant in the market without abandoning core strengths. Their efforts to update themselves are not so much about attracting new fans as about staying relevant to the baby-boomer market. Being of the boomer generation themselves, they embody the market they are vying for; rather than follow the lead of many product marketers today, who embark on the continual search for youth, keeping their collective eyes mostly on what's new, what's novel, and the hottest new trend, the Stones have focused on the significant buying power and evolving nature of their loyal fans. There's nothing wrong with focusing on the young and their innovative interests as an indicator of the changing culture, of course, unless it causes marketers to focus on the minutia of the market instead of the mass.

In 1989, the band's drive toward the perfect product was recognized as the Stones themselves were inducted into the Rock and Roll

Hall of Fame, with Mick Jagger, Keith Richards, Ron Wood, and Mick Taylor present at the ceremony at the Waldorf-Astoria Hotel in New York. Pete Townshend of the Who helped induct the Stones, telling them, "Guys, whatever you do, don't try to grow old gracefully. It wouldn't suit you." Jagger responded, "After a lifetime of bad behavior, it's slightly ironic that tonight you see us on our best behavior."

Best or worst behavior aside, the Rolling Stones have changed the way people look at rock and roll, from the strategy and business savvy that goes into keeping a brand relevant to a culture to how people think of age, how they dress, and what they sing. They've forged the way for corporate sponsorships and bands as multimillion dollar corporations. They set the standard for longevity and vitality in the market and for live entertainment value. They represent continual product improvement and quality control. They are masters of fan creation and fan loyalty. They are, in short, the one and only Rolling Stones.

6

AEROSMITH:
REINVENTING A
ROCK-AND-ROLL BRAND

All the big bands started as little bands with a vision.

—STEVEN TYLER

It's the spring of 2001, and DJs around the country are previewing the hottest summer concerts scheduled to visit their respective cities. In the majority of the top markets, an old familiar group is coming to town, selling out venues from Cincinnati to Sin City (Las Vegas, of course). Aerosmith's *Just Push Play* tour is going into full bloom.

When fans arrive at the concert, they immediately fit in with the crowd. Every possible socioeconomic, demographic, and psychographic profile is in attendance—from the scantly clad, surgically enhanced twenty-something girls to the black-T-shirt-wearing 60-year-old guys who might recently have either fixed your plumbing or given your car a lube job. Look closer and you might see your boss or coworker, decked out in Dockers and button-down shirt.

Suddenly the speakers rumble, an eerily sexual pulse coming from an unidentified instrument somewhere on the darkened stage. Bimbos, aged hippies, kids, grandparents, and yuppies alike unite in one enthusiastic cheer as Steven Tyler, the stick-insect-like lead singer, traverses the stage. From that moment on, and for the next three hours, the band and the crowd become one ball of rock-and-rolling energy, as each feeds off of the other's passion.

Expect lots of high-pitched screaming when guitarist Joe Perry and Tyler pair off together on stage during instrumental interludes, flexing their muscles and showing off physiques that should only be found on men half their age. But looking beyond their chiseled bodies, even former critics and skeptics have to admit that their sound is top-shelf. Tyler hits every note and infamous scream with perfection; Perry's guitars are slave to his magical touch; Tom Hamilton and Brad Whitford flawlessly conjure up all of the intense sound the other two don't make; and Joey Kramer beats the drums like nobody's business.

As with other classic rock bands, Aerosmith blasts audiences with its repertoire of 30-plus years of hits. "Sweet Emotion," "Dream On," and "Toys in the Attic" feed the nostalgic side of the older crowd, while "Crazy," "Livin' on the Edge," and "I Don't Want to Miss a Thing" satisfy those who were in high school in the 1990s. Sprinkled in between are the new songs of 2001—"Jaded," "Fly Away," and "Sunshine." What makes this classic rock concert different is that the band has the current number-one rock song in the country. In fact, "Jaded" even grabbed the Teen Choice Award honors for best rock song that summer, beating out much younger bands to define cool among American teens.

By the end of the night, fans feel emotionally charged and physically exhausted—from dancing around and watching the band exude a level of energy most of us lost sometime during puberty. As they leave the theater, many will rehash the evening's events with respect and devotion in their voices.

Ask die-hard fans who have followed the band since 1970, and they'll tell you that Aerosmith has earned that respect. Most rock-and-roll bands have roller-coaster careers. Oftentimes the band splits either for good or until enough time for a reunion tour has passed. But sometimes, though rarely, the band reunites—for the better. What makes the reunion of this megaband so unique is that the reformed version of Aerosmith became stronger and more successful than the original version. On its horizon would be the ups and downs that plague bands—and brands—that achieve popularity, cope with fame, and struggle to stay on top. It gives great insights into:

♪ How to court fans and involve them in the creation of a successful brand

♪ The role of reflecting your market to increase cultural adoption

♪ How to reenter the marketplace after brand failure

♪ How to reinvent a brand with quality improvement, evolvement, and fan involvement

♪ How to create reverse customer intimacy

♪ The role of energy and passion in branding

One of Aerosmith's primary brand strategies is *evolution.* Some brands are holdover brands, labeled as popular with a specific group of customer or a specific generation. Neil Diamond falls into this category. Oldsmobile even tried to fight that categorization with the "This is not your father's Oldsmobile" campaign. Other brands are crossover brands, making a connection generation after generation because of how they evolve. Sony has done this well over the years, making a splash with the Walkman and then moving on to the Discman and now plasma-screen television sets. Aerosmith has used new technology, physical fitness, cutting-edge fashion trends, and new sounds to court new generations of fans, making the Aerosmith saga a cross-branding story that's part epic drama and part business plan.

WHAT IT TAKES

Unlikely as it might seem, Sunapee, New Hampshire, was fertile breeding ground for musical talent in the 1960s and early 1970s. Families from nearby cities would descend upon the town to spend the summer away from the hustle and bustle of regular life. Among them were Steven Tallarico and his family.

Steven's ambition and knack for making an impression began early, before you could classify his musical muses as a true career. A chronically skinny kid with large lips that begged for banter from other kids, Steven went against the grain from day one. When students in school wore baggy pants, his were tailored and pegged. He befriended the kids others made fun of, grew his hair long, was hated by teachers, and joined a "club" (the 1950s version of a gang) to stop others from beating him up. This club would go on to become his first band and first set of real friends.

By the age of 12, the kid who mostly kept to himself became passionate about listening to, learning, and performing music. He came by his love for music honestly—his father was a classical pianist, and he would go on to play the drums for his father's band, Vic Tallarico's Orchestra, a few years later. Steven's attuned musical ear, work ethic, and obsession with perfection made him the likely leader and soul of any group with which he would play, attributes that should not go unnoticed by entrepreneurs hoping to be CEOs of industry-changing businesses.

Tyler would invest much time and energy in developing many music skills that would make him a real asset to any band. His first group, the Strangeurs, a clean-cut, Beatles-like band, played gigs from proms to birthday parties, giving Tyler experience as a drummer; but his showmanship made stepping out from behind the drums inevitable. "The truth was I had to get out front," admits Tyler in *Walk This Way: The Autobiography of Aerosmith* (Avon, 1999). "I was after total immortality. I couldn't sleep nights, thinking about how famous I could be. I was terrified I would die before I made my mark on the world."

IGNORING RULES

In March 1966, the Strangeurs got the job of opening for the Byrds at Westchester County Center. At the time the Byrds had the hit record "Eight Miles High," making them one of the hottest bands in the country. But ticket sales were slow in White Plains, and Peter Agosta, a Shopwell supermarket manager turned Strangeurs manager, promised the promoter a sellout if he put the Strangeurs on the bill. Within a few days of the posters going up around town, the following the band had cultivated came through, and the concert sold out.

The group salted the front rows with some girls they knew and told them to start screaming when the Strangeurs began playing—it would be the first time Tyler would involve his fans in his band's step up to the next level. The band had been instructed not to play any Byrds songs—so, of course, Steven took the stage and opened with "Eight Miles High." And the girls started screaming, but the shills had been joined by hundreds of other screaming girls. Although they were supposed to do only two songs, Tyler and crew did six numbers because the kids kept yelling for more. Jim McGuinn and David Crosby were so impressed, they hired the Strangeurs to open for them in Asbury Park the next night. Another lesson learned: Breaking the rules is sometimes okay, especially when executed well. When the result is positive, forgiveness is often granted.

Even with such early successes, Tyler would return to Sunapee for the summer, each year with a greater following, creating a bigger ruckus. Kids packed the now-infamous bring-your-own-bottle dance club, the Barn, to watch Tyler. His on-stage persona was derivative of his natural personality traits—constant energy, quirky coolness, and all around "notice me" attitude. He signaled early on that he would set the tone and personality of any band he would eventually lead.

Tyler attended a performance by another local group, the Jam Band, and saw Joe Perry create magic with his guitar on stage. He sensed that if they got together they could find their place in rock-and-roll history. Fast-forward to 1970. Tyler, without a band, and Perry, looking to build his dream team, joined forces and created a union that would go on to span four decades. Fresh out of high school, Tom Hamilton would play bass, and Ray Tabano would play guitar. After the band moved to Boston, Joey Kramer was recruited to play drums, and Brad Whitford replaced Tabano on guitar.

DO-IT-YOURSELF MARKETING

It wasn't long before Aerosmith's members became grassroots marketers, personally promoting and selling their shows, renting local town halls, and dropping posters around town. They played high schools, colleges, and anywhere there were people who would listen. Though they didn't care *where* they played, they obsessed about *what* they played. While other bands were making $1,000 per week playing popular songs penned by various artists, Aerosmith played for $300, passing up instant gratification for what the bandmates believed would be an eventual greater reward from writing its own songs. They felt that anything less would trap them into a life of chasing gigs, devoid of fame and brand identity. So, the band existed on little more than ambition and passion in those early years, sharing cramped quarters, driving to and from gigs in Tyler's black Volkswagen Beetle, struggling to save enough money to eat, and occasionally swiping when they couldn't buy food. But they had vision.

After a few years of solidifying its sound, creating music, and playing lots of concerts, the band signed with Columbia Records in 1972. *Aerosmith* was released in January 1973 to little fanfare. In fact, other than a few company executives and the band's inner circle, no one really noticed that the music world had just published the first record from what would become one of America's top rock-and-roll bands ever. There were no interviews, no reviews, no airplay, no parties—nothing more than the physical record the group could hold up as a testament to its art.

Until that point, Columbia really hadn't had much success with a hard rock band, and after listening to the album, managers felt it contained no single. No single meant a slim chance of airplay; no airplay meant no distribution; and no distribution meant no sales. Instead, Columbia seemed to be very excited about the release of a first album by a new singer from New Jersey named Bruce Springsteen. "For every dollar they put into Aerosmith, they put a hundred into Springsteen because he fit into the folksier CBS essence," says David Krebs, Aerosmith's manager at that time, in *Walk This Way.* "So Aerosmith was a band that, in the early stages, happened despite Columbia."

Aerosmith recognized quickly the difficulty of getting the attention of the people inside Columbia, let alone the DJs and fans who generated demand and sales. And while the band was elated to have its first record out, it was equally frustrated by having to sell a product that couldn't be found in stores. Without the marketing machine that supports many of today's new artists, the band had to make it happen the good old-fashioned way—blood, sweat, tears, and do-it-yourself marketing. Entrepreneurs understand the frustration of trying to get a product on retailers' shelves—it usually doesn't happen just because the new product is so obviously better than existing ones or because of a PR agency's efforts. Successful products usually succeed through the entrepreneur's or CEO's personal marketing efforts. Aerosmith's solution was to create groundswell by touring from city to city. The key was getting the fans involved, motivating them to call radio stations, request songs, and go to stores looking for the album, all designed to pull the album through the system. The strategy was simple in design, but exhausting in implementation.

"Aerosmith became like the Marines, having to challenge every city, beachhead by beachhead, play live, command respect, play live again, create word of mouth, play live, get people to buy the record and turn the radio on. It was Aerosmith going in and creating excitement as a brilliant, magic live entity," says Krebs.[1]

After a spree of hitting clubs and colleges around the Northeast, WBCN in Boston began to play some Aerosmith songs, thanks to Maxanne Sartori, a rebel DJ at WVBF in Framingham, who played music other on-air personalities wouldn't. She saw Aerosmith as the band that would represent the next generation of high school kids and began playing "Dream On" and "Mama Kin," much to the delight of the kids, who lit up the station's phone lines. This led to the appearance of Aerosmith at the station's Battle of the Bands. The group's opponent was the J. Geils Band. Aerosmith entered the ring in tip-top fighting condition, reinforced by legions of fans the band had mobilized. The fans would go on to cheer the band to a big upset.

That night, Aerosmith discovered the power of its fans.

The band continued to carry out its touring formula—hit a town, make a splash, and return three weeks later to do it again. Aerosmith blanketed the Midwest, cultivating fans who would bombard radio stations with requests, and finally got airplay, city by city.

Although Aerosmith cultivated fans superbly, it found another route for growing its fan base en masse—*fan inheritance*. The band became more strategic about with whom it shared the stage. After opening for acts that had very different audiences from the hard-rocking, working-class fans Aerosmith easily attracted, Krebs began to tie Aerosmith to bands that were just beyond its pinnacle of success—bands that might be heading downward and whose audience its wanted to inherit. Targeting bands that could still draw a significant audience—but ones that Aerosmith could outperform—led to a bait-and-switch type of fan inheritance. Aerosmith counted on the big-name band to bring fans to the concert, then played to inherit their loyalty.

After months of generating pull through the channel, "Dream On" went on the *Cashbox* singles chart in October 1973, reaching number 43 during an 11-week run. The album finally got on the charts 10 months after its release, but it only climbed to number 166. Though disappointing for the ambitious Tyler and Perry, it was a moral victory for the group—one which would tell Columbia and the industry that Aerosmith had created brand recognition and band loyalty with its rock-and-roll genre of grassroots marketing.

COURTING ANGEL FANS

Even though the early days were tough for the group, Aerosmith began developing one of its most important assets—*angel fans,* a term we use to describe fans who discover bands and brands before they become stars. Similar to angel investors who discover fledgling entrepreneurial ventures and swoop in with funds to help them grow and become viable market players, angel fans invest time and money by following a band from venue to venue, forging an emotional bond with the group. Ultimately, they have an altruistic interest in its success, recognizing that although they may not be able to become rock stars, they can be involved with someone who can.

Angel fans enthusiastically cheer on their favorite bands from obscurity to fame, giving them the chance to tell their once-skeptical friends "I told you so" and boast, "I first saw them when they couldn't sell out Ben's Bar and Bowl-O-Rama." It is similar to how people like to talk about the stock they bought for $2 and sold for $65, giving them bragging rights on picking a winner early in the game. It's the equivalent of following a high school star through the ranks of professional ball in sports. For consumers, it may be discovering a little-known brand, buying from a store before others even know it exists, or pioneering a new way of shopping. The rewards for the faithful include being the first to experience or own something and capturing a reputation for being ahead of their time.

Aerosmith's angel fans have followed the group since its Sunapee days—spreading the word about the band, attending every show they could, and hounding record stores until they stocked Aerosmith records. In return, they got bragging rights and accumulated an interesting scrapbook of great stories. To this day, they take pride in the success of their band. Many of them talk in chat rooms about the concerts they attend and tattoo Aerosmith logos on their bodies.

AN AFFINITY FOR ANGEL FANS

The loyalty showered on Aerosmith is due in part to its understanding its fans in a way that CRM programs can't duplicate and perhaps only corporate culture can. From the time they united, Aerosmith's members well represented the collective voice of the kids of their generation, which made them different from most of the rock groups around during their early years and fostered a better connection to the wants of the market. They had an inherent marketing orientation and affinity for their angel fans.

Aerosmith's members always dressed in funky clothes they found in little boutiques: hippie garb with an attitude—a little granola, a lot of cool. They all wore their hair too long; Tyler painted his nails; Perry dyed a blonde streak in his black mane. The group created a look that was difficult for others to emulate, let alone carry off without setting off a tidal wave of snickering. While they were different enough to get noticed, they were so representative of their audience that it made adoption of the band into their fans' lives easy. The kids got it—and at a certain level, they were Aerosmith, and Aerosmith was them.

Stu Werbin was an associate editor at *Rolling Stone*'s New York office when he was asked to write liner notes for Aerosmith's first album. He saw the group perform at Boston University, where he was treated to a passionate display of vintage street-band rock and roll. The students danced, the band jammed, and the cynical critic was won over. He'd found a band of young punks that the music establishment would initially hate but would eventually have to accept because Aerosmith was its own audience.

Aerosmith became the voice of the mills and the malls—working class suburban kids who had grown up on English rock.[2] The bandmates resembled the English musicians enough in sound and appearance to appeal to the fans of the Rolling Stones, yet they understood American kids and their way of life. Today, their music continues to reach the mills and the malls and well beyond, appealing to America's working class as well as the hoards of white-collar types who grew up on classic rock. They have fans spanning the ages of 12 to 70—from the teens who support their latest musical endeavors to the grandparents who include "Dream On" and "Sweet Emotion" on their personal favorites lists.

As Aerosmith demonstrates, brands are more likely to capture angel fans when they well represent the audience they are targeting. This was true for Apple computer. Positioned as the computer of choice among antiestablishment, nonconformist types, Apple countered the traditional suit and white shirt image of the market leader, IBM. Even its most famous television ad, which aired during the Super Bowl, showed a woman heaving a javelin at large-screen images of Big Brother, literally shattering the traditional image of computing. Apple's angel fans were quirky by nature. So was Apple, in its interface and attitude. Many of these fans became graphic designers, creative directors, and advertising executives, and Apple retained their loyalty with an evolved positioning that stayed connected to that group. Both were still quirky, just more grown up. Apple continued its off-the-beaten-path positioning by bringing out a line of brightly colored computers in 1998, which delighted its fans and allowed them to express their individuality and pride in being different.

EBAY ANGELS

Both Aerosmith's and Apple's angel fans invested time and energy in supporting their passion, and in turn, claimed partial responsibility for its success—and that's what happened at eBay, as well. Call them fanatical, innovative, or just plain weird, eBay's angel fans, known as the eBay Army, are a faithful bunch who live and breathe eBay, so much so that 5,500 of them showed up at the first company convention, held in June 2002.[3] There they met people they had traded with online, got autographs from CEO and idol Meg Whitman, and communed with other devoted eBay fans, telling stories of their virgin eBay trades and staking their own claims on the overall success of the company.

But not all was sweetness and light at the convention. As the company pushed to increase large corporate sales, courting giants such as Sears and IBM to sell their wares through the eBay channel, some mom-and-pop sellers felt a bit betrayed. eBay's angel fans—the early collectors and traders who helped build the company from day one—wanted their role in the early success of the company to be recognized and valued. They not only watched the company go from $7.1 million net income in 1997 to $90.4 million in 2001, they traded on, talked about, and cheered for the company along the way. In this instance, the first-mover advantage belongs not only to the unique company, but to the avid fans who were there from the beginning and have enjoyed the ride to corporate stardom.

However, as eBay expands beyond a community of collectors and small traders, some angel fans are beginning to develop a love/hate relationship with the company, similar to the way some music fans feel if their bands create songs designed to be commercially successful rather than artistically superior. Often this is labeled *selling out.*

Aerosmith and eBay alike feel the solution to keeping fans happy is showing loyalty toward them; they've come to learn that faithful fans expect loyalty in return for their zealous support. Just as the band allows fan club members to buy tickets before they go on public sale and makes great seats available to them, eBay shows its appreciation to its angel fans by offering special perks. Most recently, the company began offering its Powersellers—those who sell more than $1,000 per month on the site—group health insurance.

Overall, the eBay Army continues its support of the company and its leader wholeheartedly, preaching the eBay gospel and acting as an unofficial sales arm of the company. With every convention and new transaction that occurs, eBay fans continue to add new chapters to their eBay storybooks, just as Aerosmith fans do with the release of each new album or announcement of a new tour. Though the Aerosmith hit "Angel" wouldn't come until 1987, its lyrics and tone could easily be dedicated to the fans who have made the band the superstar that it is today. It is a declaration of needing someone who holds your happiness in his or her hands—the ultimate definition of a fan.

LIVIN' ON THE EDGE AND FALLIN' OFF

After years of writing, recording, touring and selling, the band had reached what to most would be the pinnacle of success. In a 1979 article, *Rolling Stone* had this to say about Aerosmith:

> Aerosmith is a dinosaur among bands, the last of a generation of rock 'n' rollers being edged out by more streamlined competition like Boston, Foreigner, and Fleetwood Mac. What keeps Aerosmith rocking is their ability to relate to their loyal, largely male audience. Night after night, the band's success or failure hinges on something that's hard to package; they have to tap into a little of the teenage insanity that lures you to rock 'n' roll in the first place."[4]

Aerosmith had completed a grueling tour schedule in 1978—selling out 50,000- to 60,000-seat stadium venues and playing with other giants such as Ted Nugent, Cheap Trick, Santana, and Heart. But the union of the band was worse for its wear. Drug abuse led to fights, infidelity, and physical problems (no matter how good you are, it's difficult to perform when you're passed out backstage).

Tyler and Perry, known as the Toxic Twins because they would do any drug put in front of them, had an intense love-hate relationship; it was a kindred-spirit, brotherly thing one minute and an ego-trip personality clash the next. For years the band did whatever it took to put on a good show for the fans, but the fighting between Tyler and Perry eventually found its way on stage at the sacrifice of great performances.

After the release of *Night in the Ruts* in November 1979, Joe Perry officially left Aerosmith and formed the Joe Perry Project. By mid-December the band was selling out smaller venues and getting rave reviews from the media. About the time the Joe Perry Project had been declared hot, Aerosmith was declared *not*, and its *Nights in the Rut* arena tour was cancelled.

For a few years, Perry worked on his band, and Whitford even backed him up on occasion. Aerosmith continued, filling the gaps in the band with other talented musicians. But neither the Project nor

Aerosmith had the power, dazzle, or impact that the five bad boys from Boston had when they were together. The power came from their union—that magical something that happens when bodies, souls, minds, and energies meld to form an entity that is much stronger than the mere sum of its parts.

Rising from the ashes of burned bridges, bruised egos, and thousands of shared joints came the new Aerosmith, one that would experience more success—both financial and personal—than the original band. Getting clean and sober was key in restructuring the band, especially since all of the original members were back on board. Today, as the band approaches 15 years of sobriety, each member is quick to say that life is more rewarding and focused than ever before.

NOT THE SAME OLD SONG AND DANCE: REINTRODUCING THE AEROSMITH BRAND

Reentering the rock arena meant reintroducing the Aerosmith brand to a market that had changed during its absence. Hard rock had given way to the hair bands* and new-wave punk sounds of the 1980s, and music had taken on a new visual dimension with the invasion of MTV. To complicate things further, Aerosmith hadn't left the music scene with a good reputation because the band's performances had suffered fiercely due to the members' abuse of drugs. Many labeled them washed-up has-beens—victims of the excesses of success.

REINVENTION WITH BRAND DISCIPLINE

Formulating Aerosmith's comeback was challenging at best. What would be the right combination of *newness* that would make the band relevant in the music scene and *familiarity* that would enhance the

---

*Not to be confused with hairballs, *hair bands* consisted of well-coiffed, long-haired young men who belted out rock songs that were big on sound and small on substance. Some bands, such as Bon Jovi, proved later that they were about more than their teased 'dos and snazzy outfits, but many remain permanently entombed in the video archives of the 1980s.

loyalty of its current fans? Brand managers advising Aerosmith might have counseled the group on the importance of brand discipline—remaining true to a brand's personality and image. Did that mean changing the look and dress of the band, its sound or genre of music, or the personalities of its members? Did it mean adapting to the new medium or playing to Aerosmith's strengths of the past? Did it mean collaborating with a hot new band to grab attention in the new music arena?

Brand discipline dictated that Aerosmith examine the changes occurring in the music landscape, many of which were due primarily to a disruptive innovation, the music video. MTV forced rock and rollers from Christopher Cross and Bruce Springsteen to the Kinks and Foreigner to explore the visual side of their music. Some stars would rise to the occasion while others faded into oblivion—not because their music wasn't good, but because they didn't look the part of the 1980s rock-and-roll star—proving all's fair in love and marketing.

Once MTV fans made it clear that music videos were not a passing fad, rock and rollers like Aerosmith hoping to stay popular in the market would have to adapt or die. It was a scary thought for an aging band. Reinvention could bring success or failure—or, even worse, indifference. The potential benefits that music videos brought to the Aerosmith equation were enormous because of Steven Tyler's sex appeal, Joe Perry's flare for the dramatic, and the nature of their music. Aerosmith embraced technology, which it continues to do today, and used it to make a big splash during its rebirth.

RAP THIS WAY

In addition to examining changes in the environment, brand discipline meant identifying projects that could build rather than undermine the brand equity Aerosmith had built over the years. One potential avenue for reintroducing Aerosmith was collaborating on a remake of "Walk This Way."

As Aerosmith prepared its reinvention, rap music was beginning to emerge from its confined urban market. One group that was getting a lot of attention was Run-DMC, comprised of Joseph "Run"

Simmons, Darryl "D.M.C." McDaniels, and DJ Jason "Jam Master Jay" Mizell. They became the first rap act to have an album go gold in 1984 and built further on their status in this growing market with ferocious touring. Run-DMC and Aerosmith explored the possibility of making a rap version of "Walk This Way," singing together on the record and performing together on the video. Why "Walk This Way?" One could argue it was the first rap song to ever hit the charts. Listen to the style and you'll recognize that Tyler rapped those lyrics in the original 1970s version, before Run, D.M.C., and Jay could spell *rap* or *hip-hop*. And the lyrics, to this day, are classics.*

The remake defines diversity—part urban rap, part rock and roll; young emerging artists, older stalled stars; black and white. Strategic questions over the potential pairing ensued: Would the danger of alienating angel fans be worth the temporary flash of attention? Would it position Aerosmith as up to date or out of place? Would it muddy the group's rock-and-roll image? Depending on how it was executed, the union could be either the most brilliant or the most stupid move the band had ever made.

At first glance, one might think that a step *toward* rap would be a step *away from* the traditional Aerosmith brand. Fans had come to expect several things from Aerosmith—rock and roll and an attitude that celebrated the unexpected. Fan's expectations were grounded in the band's personality as much as in its music. They expected Aerosmith to evolve and push the envelope of musical creativity without abandoning the basic sounds and familiar tones they'd come to love.

Aerosmith and its management decided that the urban rap version of "Walk This Way" made sense. It had the potential of attracting new fans—in terms of age, ethnicity, and musical preference—while striking a chord of familiarity with angel fans, who had been singing the song for over a decade. But Aerosmith would have to hold up its end of the creative and musical bargain to avoid coming off as the oldsters

---

*Most people have admitted, however, to reading the album liner notes to figure out what Tyler is chanting throughout the song. Even reading along with the song doesn't necessarily explain exactly what the words mean. The authors feel that sometimes it is best not to know all of the sordid details; for you, this might be one of those times.

who originally sang the song but now rode on the coattails of a newer, hipper group. It would be brand reinvention at its finest.

In May 1986 the Aerosmith/Run-DMC collaboration hit television and radio, and climbed to number four on the charts. The video depicts Aerosmith in one room with Run-DMC in another, divided only by a wall. Aerosmith is trying to sing and play its music, but the noise coming from the adjacent room is so loud that the band can't perform. So, Tyler and crew break down the wall and sing the chorus of "Walk This Way" through the shattered plaster and into the world of rap. The video continues with the unified band performing and prancing Tyler-style across the stage together.

Trends That Trickle Up   Similar to the way Elvis helped R&B trickle upward from black culture to mainstream culture, Aerosmith acted as a conduit for the passage of rap music from the urban market to suburban America. Dr. Dre, who played a vital role in rap's evolution, explains, "They [Aerosmith] were responsible for getting hip-hop played on MTV."

Aerosmith wagered its comeback on the future acceptance of rap and hip-hop by mainstream markets and the impact rap would have on the music industry. It was a smart bet with a big payoff. Rap has captured a huge part of the market for contemporary music, with rappers and urban artists from Eminem to Nelly becoming favorites among wide portions of the population.

Is the trickle-up theory of cultural adoption at work in the marketplace today? Just look at what happened to the Tommy Hilfiger brand during the 1990s. The label, which at one time consisted primarily of conservative clothing, began taking its fashion cues from urban neighborhoods. Enter the superbaggy, waistline-below-the-underwear look. Teens thought they looked hot, and parents of the suburban kids who wanted to sport this look paid big bucks for designer versions of urban clothing donned by gangs.

The Tommy logo was everywhere as it pushed the urban look upward to suburban markets. The brand and its dominant red, white, and blue Tommy logo were even big inside urban neighborhoods, the realities of which had inspired the fashions themselves. In the 'hood, one way a young male gains manhood is to do time—once he is out, he is a man. But what is one of the first things that happens to a man when he goes to prison? The police take his belt, and his pants droop below his waist, a look that became popular back on the street.

However, after helping urban fashions trickle up to mainstream markets and profiting from them, Tommy is being passed over by urban constituencies for labels they see as more authentic, such as Fubu, Phat Farm, and Sean John. Today, Tommy Hilfiger is changing its branding tune, going back to some of the more conservative styles of its past—where perhaps more of its authenticity resides.

Because of trickle-up consumer trends, marketers that scour urban settings to monitor changes in fashion, language, behavior, and attitudes can identify some trends that will eventually hit the suburbs. Hilfiger is just one example of a label that took an urban look to the masses with great market acceptance. The Cliffs Notes version of monitoring trends in real urban markets is monitoring trends in popular music. Successful artists portray well what is happening in urban settings and what is likely to take off in mainstream markets.

Fixing the Machine   To this day, the "Walk This Way" video is included in the top 10 on both the VH1 and MTV most influential video lists, primarily because of the effect the video had on breaking down the real barriers between rap and rock, between black and white kids, and between generations. Aerosmith broke into music television the day the video aired and hasn't looked back, reinforcing the personality of the band and the strength of the brand. It also crushed any notion that this middle-aged rock band couldn't be accepted by a new generation of fans.

For Aerosmith, the rebirth of the band was the relaunch of its brand, but it would have to prove it wasn't just a reincarnated one-hit wonder. Pressure mounted for the band to release a stellar album, but it couldn't afford to generate attention, start a tour, or release an album without being ready physically, professionally, and personally. The band members entered rehab, got themselves clean, and rededicated their lives to their families, their art, and eventually themselves. The new version of Aerosmith was healthy and energetic, and would go on to write and perform its most critically acclaimed music to date on its comeback album, *Permanent Vacation.*

Just as a major band can fall from the pinnacle of success to the floor of despair and then reincarnate itself to rise to top the charts again, so too can a firm willing to change more than its marketing message and image. The reinvention of the Kmart brand in the 1990s started out with a bang, in part because it put most of its marketing eggs in the Martha Stewart basket. Unlike Aerosmith, however, Kmart failed to fix the problems in its operations, stores, and personnel as the band did when its members entered rehab and rededicated themselves to personal and artistic discipline as well as physical fitness. Wanting to be better is not enough; a firm has to fix its operations if it expects to reinvent a once-great but currently downtrodden brand.

Successful brand reinvention is uncommon, business history reveals, but there is one case in particular that reads almost like a modern-day application of Aerosmith's principles. Like most rock-and-roll bands, few brands recover. One that did was Volkswagen.

DRIVE THIS WAY

Admit it. When you see one, you smile. It calls to you, with its bulging eyes and defiant little grin, making the kid in all of us want to run up and hug it. If you drive one down the street, people smile at you and occasionally wave. It attracts attention with an approachable tone, soliciting Aww!s and Oh!s that until its introduction were reserved only for puppies and cooing babies.

Ah yes, the VW Bug—the icon of teens and young adults of the 1960s and 1970s. The flower-power generation adopted the Volkswagen Beetle (also known as the Bug) as part of its culture, inviting the car into its garages, families, and lifestyles and plastering its image on notebooks, lunch boxes, and T-shirts. Beetle fan clubs formed around the country, giving owners a chance to meet, exchange maintenance advice, and create a special kinship through a *soiree* of Bug lovefests.

The Beetle filled a specific transportation need in the U.S. car market that the typical large American car didn't meet in the late 1950s and 1960s. In addition to being countercultural in its appeal and, to some, simply adorable, the car was known for its low price, reliability, unique design, and good gas mileage. Volkswagen intentionally kept the car design the same for many years, changing the car only under the skin so that parts remained readily available and fix-ups were easy.[5] The car appealed to independent-minded people, often centered in university-oriented locales, who frequently found themselves explaining why they bought a VW. But devotees rather enjoyed talking about their cars—as fans usually do—taking pride in their ability to pay less without sacrificing quality.

The U.S. car market changed in the 1970s, when Japanese automakers entered the market during the energy crunch with several low-priced, efficient, compact cars. Volkswagen was left going head-to-head against a new array of formidable competitors who seemed to steal the spotlight from the familiar Bug.

Although VW kept upgrading the car, it was the collective footsteps of its new competitors and its parent company that would eventually squash the Bug. Volkswagen decided to phase out the Beetle and replaced it with the Rabbit in 1975. The Rabbit was Beetlesque in its quirky looks, fun colors, and great gas mileage, but the similarities basically stopped there. The Rabbit had many quality issues—from cold-start problems and noisiness to faulty electrical systems and high oil consumption—which would tarnish the reputation of the company. Quality problems, a lackluster array of cars (remember the Scirocco, the Dasher, and the Thing?), increased competition, and dissension within the company about strategic direction created a sales and image meltdown for VW. Management's slowness to correct the problems that plagued its U.S. operations became the "drug" that poisoned the brand in the minds of industry insiders, consumers, and even devotees, just as surely as chemical drugs had poisoned the members of Aerosmith.

The proverbial sink-or-swim moment had arrived for Volkswagen. The company had some success with Passats, GTIs, and Cabrios imported from Germany, but reliability problems were rampant with the Golf and the Jetta—the entry-point cars for VW's customers. The company was down to "selling only to die-hard VW fans, the ones who would buy the cars if they came in boxes and had to be assembled in their driveways."[6] Without a complete revival of its manufacturing, operations, and marketing, it couldn't survive in the U.S. market.

Assuming it could fix these problems, the big question loomed—how to regain trust and revive the emotional connection with its lost or disheartened customers.

The make-or-break moment for Volkswagen in the U.S. market had arrived. After years of living as an endangered species, VW was reborn with the reintroduction of the Bug in 1997. To the delight of VW, the Bug had never really died in the hearts of its fans, many of whom had kept and restored their 1960s or 1970s models for nostalgic reasons.

The new Bug was VW's "Walk This Way" remake—the car and the song were just the opening paragraphs of the rest of the story for each entity's branding saga. Just as Aerosmith had to fix the addiction and relationship problems of the band's members before releasing its next album and attracting new fans, so did VW have to fix its brand before unleashing a new advertising campaign and attracting new customers. Fixing the brand meant solving product quality and reliability issues that had alienated customers in the late 1970s and 1980s. If there is something wrong with the brand or the product, the worst thing a marketer can do is create a great advertising campaign that attracts customers. Why? Because their trust is tough to gain the first time, let alone the second time, after they've been disappointed. Good advertising only accelerates the demise of poor products, brands, or companies. Volkswagen had been there, done that, and, frankly, didn't want to do it again.

Instead, it got support from the dealerships and delivered quality standards consumers expected, understanding that a fundamental principle of taking brands from good to great is exceeding, not just meeting, customer expectations. All in all, the rebirth of Volkswagen was a triumph in marketing, branding, and engineering.

REVERSE CUSTOMER INTIMACY

Customer relationship management (CRM) has received much attention from marketing and branding executives in recent years, with the goal being to learn more about customers in order to connect better with them and at a deeper level. This in turn allows firms to tailor offerings to specific customers or stock items certain customers prefer, all in the name of building brand loyalty.

In the CRM vein, Aerosmith monitors its fans' behaviors during concerts, understanding that the right balance between classics, contemporary favorites, and new releases is important in keeping fans engaged during a three-hour show.* Legendary bands do that better than most fledgling bands because of the depth of material they can play. In notes published on the web site of AeroForce One (Aerosmith's official fan club), talking about their experiences on the road, Tom Hamilton admits to watching audiences from the stage, especially when performing new songs. When the crowd starts singing songs from a new album, they know they have been adopted by fans, giving the band guidance as to which songs to keep performing during the tour, which ones to add to the next tour, and perhaps when to add another new track to the set list. On that web page, fans are encouraged to learn the words to new songs, so they can sing along at the concert and participate in the experience.

Aerosmith, however, puts an interesting spin on the concept of customer intimacy. Whereas much of corporate America focuses on strategies for knowing and understanding customers better, Aerosmith focuses on ways for *fans* to get to know the *band* better. Fans may be more likely to connect emotionally with a brand after having a personal experience with it, especially one that allows them to get to know the brand or company better than others do.

Aerosmith allows customers to get to know the band more intimately with remote staging, special tours, travel packages, and good old-fashioned meet-and-greets. As a result, fans feel that they have a special relationship with the band, becoming more emotionally tied to the band and its success.

------

*It is known among concertgoers that the worst time to get food or a drink is during a song from the new album the band is promoting—unless of course it is in fact a big hit single—because that is when the lines are longest. When a legendary rock band plays one of its classics, however, no one leaves their seats. Not even Elton John is immune from this phenomenon—when he announced during his recent concert tour that the next few songs would be from his new album, customers and friends alike headed for the john, en masse.

HOW TO TREAT YOUR FANS

At the heart of bands' interaction with fans is Steven Tyler's understanding of what it means to be a fan. In the early days, Tyler spent as much time and money as he could going to rock shows. He was, admittedly, starstruck, and reveled in being close to stars. An interesting exercise for brand managers charged with creating brands with fan appeal is to become one yourself.

Tyler recalls how he worshipped the Rolling Stones during the mid-1960s. People kept telling him that he looked like Mick Jagger (with his big lips), and Keith Richards *was* the music he loved the most. When the Stones came to play a concert in New York in May 1965, Tyler and his friends schemed to get close to the band, waiting outside the hotel for the limo to pull up. When it did, Bill Jones, Mick Jagger, and Bill Wyman emerged. A friend aimed his Polaroid camera as Tyler tried to get close to Jagger. Girls started screaming and people started shoving, but the Rolling Stones stopped to sign a few autographs in the midst of the chaos. Tyler recalls in Aerosmith's autobiography, "We hung around for a while, buzzing, like crazy just because we got to touch them!"

Today, the members of Aerosmith are the ones dealing with screaming fans when they pull up to their hotels. Tyler remembers what it was like to be a fan and treats his fans accordingly, signing autographs when asked and taking the time to talk to people he meets.

LETTING CUSTOMERS GET CLOSE TO YOU

Aerosmith values its relationship with fans and looks for ways to let them get closer to the band. But that's easier said than sung. In addition to making the web site sing with stories from the concert road, insights on band members, photos that can be downloaded, and fan-club-only information, Aerosmith finds ways to get close to fans physically. When fans make contact, they spread stories like wildfire and generate even more interest in the band.

Lyndon Johnson may have made pressing the flesh—meeting people and shaking hands—commonplace, but in the rock-and-roll world, Aerosmith is one of the bands that has perfected it. When other bands of its stature choose not to deal with fans one-on-one, Aerosmith still does old-fashioned meet-and-greets. The fans who are lucky enough to get backstage, usually by winning a radio contest, get their pictures taken with the band and have the chance to get something autographed, from album covers to various body parts. But the band members don't sit stoically behind desks as fans parade by with posters and Sharpies; they mingle in an open room with dozens of fans. Tyler takes time with his fans, looking each one in the eye as he speaks to them, making them feel as if they were the only person in the room at that moment. Fans realize quickly that the awkwardly sexy Tyler is even more attracting once they've met him; he is someone fans want to be with. Fans leave the experience more exuberant than before because of the willingness of the band members to acknowledge and be nice to them.

During its *Just Push Play* tour, the band devised another way to get close to its fans—a second stage positioned among the lawn seats of outdoor venues. In the middle of the concert, Tyler announces from the stage, "Okay, we're coming out to you." On cue, someone begins a deep-thumping drum march, and the band leaves the stage and moves through the crowd, flanked by security. But even a tightly constructed caravan can't prevent the gropefest the band must endure to get to its hard-core fans. The band then takes to the B-stage, giving fans in the cheap seats, from which the band usually looks like a bunch of ants, a chance to be in the front row for four or five songs. The fans appreciate the gesture; they feel important, valued, and connected.

But the band's attunement to fan relationships doesn't stop there. Aerosmith began offering special backstage experiences to fan club members. For about $595, AeroForce One members can buy the Velvet Rope package that includes concert tickets in the first five rows, Aerosmith garb, and a guided backstage tour that explains the inner workings of the stage and crew. While management can't guarantee that groups of fans will get to meet the band, they often do. Finally, Velvet Ropers often get to stand at stage edge during the concert, poised perfectly for Tyler to sing to and for the cameras to capture and project onto the Jumbotron to the rest of the crowd.

What Aerosmith demonstrates is the power of intimacy in creating loyalty. But it also shows that band loyalty is not just about the band knowing its fans (the focus of most literature on customer loyalty); it's about the fans knowing the band on a different level of intimacy than casual listeners. That's where the emotional connection—the feeling that "I can relate to these guys"—comes into play, and every marketer knows that emotions last longer than slogans.

Reverse customer intimacy is at work in corporate America as well. Some firms achieve it by putting a personal face on the company or the brand, as Wendy's did with founder Dave Thomas. For 12 years, he starred in a series of television ads that showed him doing everything from gardening to driving a motorcycle. Customers developed such a liking for the genuine, everyday guy, they felt that they knew him, and through him they got to know the brand better. When Thomas died in 2002, restaurant managers reported that fans all over the country stopped that day to have a Wendy's—in honor of Dave.

Reverse customer intimacy is also at work at Starbucks when customers get to know the people who take their orders. While the relationship is initially formed by the employee who recognizes customers and remembers their orders, it is internalized when the customer feels comfortable enough to initiate conversation with the employee. Regulars feel that they know the brand better than other customers because they have closer personal ties to it.

Crate & Barrel accomplishes reverse customer intimacy with outstanding product signage in its stores. Customers attracted to a display of glass vases can read about them in detail—where they are made, how they were discovered, whether they are handmade, and the like. The information acts as a mechanism to further the customer's relationship to the brand.

OH YEAH!

After three decades of making music, Aerosmith has become a cultural icon—adopted by and welcomed into the lives of millions around the globe. It has evolved the Aerosmith brand and built band loyalty by reflecting changes in society and remaining relevant in today's culture. Its story is one of brand reinvention and what it takes to create a brand that is better than the original version.

One of its key success factors has been achieving and maintaining sobriety—fixing the machine. The band members are as dedicated to staying drug and alcohol free as they are to creating great music, perhaps more so now than ever. Their addictive tendencies are still present; they just channel them into working out, eating healthy, and working hard. Tyler, the group elder, turned 55 in 2003, but to see him perform you'd never guess his age. The sheer energy and electricity he, Joe Perry, and the rest of the group exude during a concert are impressive at any age, let alone an age our parents told us meant retirement, arthritis, and comfortable shoes. But vitality takes hard work. There are the grueling workouts and hours on the treadmill. Tyler, especially, is also known for his strict diet—opting for carrot juice rather than the beer he used to chug. How ironic it is that people who used to abuse their bodies can now serve as poster children for physical fitness; that is total brand reinvention.

Another key to Aerosmith's success has been fan involvement. Its angel fans supported the band during its early days, followed its members during their ascent up the ladder of rock-and-roll success, stuck by them as they tumbled back down, and cheered their band's reinvention and rise back to the top. The key for brands and bands is to keep the attention and loyalty of those initial fans who might have been attracted to the newness of their discoveries by involving them in the process and maintaining intimacy. For Aerosmith fans who have held on and enjoyed the somewhat stereotypical rock-and-roller-coaster ride, their reward lies in the atypical, surprise ending that the band continues to craft.

The greatest testament to Aerosmith's reformulation strategies is the fact that its greatest accomplishments have come postreinvention. Mass popularity followed a string of hit songs and award-winning videos, including "Dude Looks Like a Lady," "Love in an Elevator," "Angel," "Crazy," "Livin' on the Edge," "What it Takes," and "Sunshine." It wasn't until 1997 that Aerosmith would have a *Billboard* number-one hit. "I Don't Want to Miss A Thing," the theme song for the movie *Armaggedon*, which starred Liv Tyler (Steven's daughter), finally gave Aerosmith the spot it so rightly deserved.

Since its reinvention, the group has also won fashion awards, teen music awards, and Grammys, proving that some new, improved products are actually new and improved. In 2001 alone, the band headlined the Super Bowl halftime show, played the American Music Awards, hit number one with "Jaded," won an award for best teen rock song, and was inducted into the Rock and Roll Hall of Fame. The band was everywhere, making fans salivate at the chance to see them live, which fueled ticket sales for the *Just Push Play* tour.

In *Walk This Way,* the band's autobiography, Tom Hamilton explains, "We know we're not the new groovy cool band that's coming out. We have to really give people a reason to keep listening to us." The Aerosmith concert experience is reason enough for many. It creates an emotional connection with the audience that makes the fans feel that they know the band better than they did a few hours earlier and much better than those who weren't there.

Aerosmith continues to connect with new and old fans alike. The year 2002 brought about Aerosmith's two-CD set of greatest hits, *Oh Yeah!* Its release prompted another concert tour—and the wheel of marketing and music required to keep a legendary band at the top of its game continues spinning. At the axis is the vision, zealous pursuit of perfection, and dedication of Steven Tyler, which started when he was a boy.

"Immortality. It's not much to ask for, is it?" says Tyler. "I wanted to sing on a record so after I died I'd still be singing. That way I could live forever." And live on, Aerosmith will. In fact, when asked how long they planned to keep on rocking the house, Tyler replied, "Until we have to rename the song 'Walkers This Way.' " Oh yeah.

7

MADONNA AND NEIL DIAMOND:
THE RELEVANCE OF SEX IN BRANDING

Soul is a constant. It's cultural. It's always going to be there, in different flavors and degrees. —ARETHA FRANKLIN

If it's true that sex sells, Madonna should be a multibillionaire. Born on August 16, 1958, in Rochester, Michigan, Madonna Louise Veronica Ciccone is sexy, sexual, sensual, stylish, energetic, sometimes outrageous, always provocative, and usually controversial. Even though these descriptors apply to hoards of rock-and-roll stars, Madonna stands out among them as someone who can command fan, media, and general interest like few others in the world. More than Tina Turner, Aretha Franklin, Cher, or any of rock's female superstars, Madonna was the first female pop star to take complete control of her music and her image, in a way that redefines shaking up the status quo.

Madonna is a musical superstar—one whose personality usually overshadows her musical product. Whether by design or by happenstance (and it's hard to believe that anything she does isn't by design), Madonna's product is as much about Madonna as it is about her music. In her video *Truth or Dare,* she says, "I know I'm not the best singer, and I know I'm not the best dancer. But I'm not interested in that. I'm interested in pushing people's buttons, in being provocative." And push buttons she has, managing to capture mass attention from fans and the media based on how she lives even more than on how she sings. Even people who didn't like her during her bubble-gum pop days of the early 1980s and have been asking themselves when she will go away? have come to realize that she's not going to. She has eclipsed the commercial accomplishments of many other more talented musicians because of the overall package she has created—one that focuses on experiences, events, and extravaganzas, and one that reaps the rewards of the publicity they create.

Two recent biographies—*Madonna,* by Andrew Morton (St. Martin's Press, 2001) and *Goddess,* by Barbara Victor (HarperCollins, 2001)—chronicle the lifestyle that grabs headlines and entices people to engage in her performances in a wide variety of media. Both books, Ann Oldenburg wrote in *USA Today,* "portray a driven, ambitious woman who had star quality from childhood and a sassy, brassy star who falls in love easily, only to become insecure and needy in her relationships. Both books paint a picture of a disciplined creature who prizes organization and being in control and who has put her quest for stardom before just about anything else."

Stardom doesn't come easy for anyone, including Madonna, who has thrived primarily due to her raw ambition rather than raw talent. Her discipline serves as a reminder to even the most experienced marketers that laziness can lead to obsolescence, diminished awareness, and a tarnished position among competitive brands. Competitiveness, diligence, and brilliant execution, on the other hand, lead to staying power. And Madonna definitely has proven that she has that.

One of Madonna's most lethal weapons in the war to remain relevant has been continual brand reinvention. The changes she undertakes to redefine herself every five years or so go beyond the gradual evolution many other bands undergo. Madonna's brand sustenance is complicated by the fact that one of her brand promises is to be on the cutting edge of newness in the areas of fashion, expression, exercise, and other lifestyle trends. Because of this positioning, a gradual evolutionary approach to change, which fans of many other bands prefer, would disappoint Madonna's fans; they expect her to change the way she looks, sounds, and lives. Joel Denver, founder of AllAccess.com, one of the industry's leading sources on music trends and information, has watched performers rise to and fall from stardom for decades. Madonna, he says, is a master at reinvention. "She zigs when you expect her to zag," he says. "She taps the direction of society and relects that in her music, concerts, visuals, and appearance—in her overall brand."

Madonna has mastered a chameleon-like approach to staying true to the foundation of her brand. She doesn't walk away from a brand promise based on sex and sexuality; she just redefines sexy according to her current life stage. In her words, "I've grown. I've discovered things I had no idea of when I was in my twenties." Among them is the value of inner peace, and the fact that fashion trend setting is best left to those with more youthful blonde ambition, according to a 2003 *People* description of Madonna.[1] Her experiences as a master marketer reveal insights and lessons on:

♪ Harnessing the power of controversy

♪ The power of sex, sexuality, and sexiness in gaining consumer attention

♪ The role of brand authenticity—being the real thing—in connecting with fans

♪ The risks of going too far in sexual branding and alienating customers

♪ How to evolve and remake brands over time

Madonna is the shining example that sex sells. Even after years of hard work by women's organizations to further women's rights and squelch the degradation of women, society can't deny that sex still intrigues customers. Initially, one might see using sex to sell a brand as easy and by some standards a cop-out to formulating a more substantive branding strategy.

Achieving significant long-term sales and keeping fans interested in a brand with a sex-oriented sales pitch is *not* easy, however. First off, maintaining a sexy image becomes more difficult as a brand ages—

especially if that brand is a person. But even for products, what is sexy and cool one moment becomes average and humdrum the next. Second, sex can sell on a limited basis, but product and experience quality build loyalty over time. The classic example of the sizzle selling the steak is true—but there needs to be a steak, and it has to taste good in order for someone to order it a second time. As Denver points out, "Something has to connect with fans to move a record from passive, where fans enjoy listening to the song on the radio, to active, where they go buy the CD or attend the concert. It takes more than just sizzle to do that, but Madonna's image and positioning over the years has been pretty good sizzle."

A brand message that features a sex angle needs to fit the natural characteristics of the brand. After revamping its line of shampoo and conditioners, Herbal Essences was unleashed on the market in the late 1990s. The sexually charged television ads grabbed peoples' attention. The series featured a woman washing her hair and becoming excited by the scent and feeling of the Herbal Essence experience to the point that she moans and groans the words "Yes, yes, yes." A final sigh and shake of the head leads to the tagline, "Herbal Essences, a totally organic experience."

Calvin Klein, fashion brand extraordinaire, has attracted attention and fans over the years with its sexy positioning. Who can forget the steamy Obsession television ads that heated up many a living room or the Calvin Klein underwear ads featuring chiseled young men that grace billboards around the United States? They got as much word of mouth as they did paid display time. Tom Murry, president of Calvin Klein, explains, "Creating a sexy campaign that's successful requires a balance of risk-taking, good judgment, and genuine connection to the product. You can't do sexy for the sake of being sexy. That usually falls flat—fast. For a sexy campaign to be effective it has to feel real to the consumer; it has to emote authenticity."

AUTHENTIC SEX

Brands are judged by their authenticity—how real they are in terms of their promises, attributes, and positioning in the eyes of consumers. If the positioning and image are too contrived, the brand often fails to connect with fans, who chalk up a fabricated image as a blatant marketing scheme to sell them something. This is very apparent in urban markets, where rappers are judged based on their real-world experiences with urban strife and violence. Just as the new in-your-face gangsta rap artist 50 Cent has been deemed an authentic brand, partially because the lead singer is a former crack dealer who has been shot nine times, so too can Madonna be judged as highly authentic regarding the sexual attributes of her product.

According to her biographies, Madonna lost her virginity at age 15, has had hundreds of affairs (some with women), and has posed for erotic magazines, released an over-the-top book of erotica, and shot a video which bordered on pornographic. Once married to actor Sean Penn, she admits that she tried to seduce Michael Jackson after they appeared together at the Oscars in 1991, but failed to arouse his interest. She's also reported to have told friends that John F. Kennedy Jr. was "interested" in her but too nervous to click with her sexually. Then there were the jocks in her life, preferring men who dribble basketballs for a profession, with the most controversial of them being Dennis Rodman.

But sexuality evolves, even for Madonna, who at the age of 45 now appears to have been matured by marriage to current husband Guy Ritchie and motherhood of her two children. Although they may be like any other married couple—she criticizes the way he chews his food and he makes fun of her hairpieces—no one could dispute that Madonna exhibits authenticity as a sexual goddess. In fact, in talking to people about the pop diva, many find her sexier at forty-something than at twenty-something because of her confidence and authenticity.

Madonna has been revered as a trend guru. If Madonna jogs, so do her fans, and when she takes up yoga, so do those looking to have a body like hers. Her ability to set trends in fashion, exercise, beauty, expression, dance, spirituality, and lifestyle stems from identifying something occurring on the fringe of society that is likely to catch on in mainstream culture—and she becomes the conduit for its introduction and acceptance. She is an authentic brand that takes the lead and invites others to follow her, not a fabricated brand that adopts the latest look and says "Can I join you?"

MATERIAL GIRL

Madonna was a cheerleader and good student during her high school days in Detroit. Her father rewarded her with 25 cents for every A she received, so she focused and did well academically as well as in dance and theater. Though she describes herself as an outcast, her classmates describe her as popular, funny, and a bit of a show-off. She received a scholarship for dance and attended the University of Michigan for a few semesters but left for the allure of New York City and the fame and fortune that it offered. Her intellect served her well throughout her career, giving her a foundation to formulate her own image and her own future. Like many starving artists before her and after, she did whatever it took to get noticed and get a break.

That break came when star DJ Mark Kamins created a hit on the club scene with one of her demo singles, "Everybody," in 1982, followed by "Physical Attraction" in 1983. Many of Madonna's subsequent hits would encompass the sounds, rhythm, and beat of her dance club heritage, which kept her earliest fans connected to her music through the next several decades. Her first album, titled simply *Madonna,* was released in 1983, and its first single, "Holiday," reached the top 40 within one month, eventually reaching the top 20 in the United States and the top 10 in Europe. *Madonna*'s second single release, "Borderline," spurred a string of 17 consecutive top-10 hits, including "Papa Don't Preach," "Like a Prayer," "Dress You Up," "Justify My Love," "Rescue Me," "Express Yourself," "Like a Virgin," and "Material Girl."

These singles were released in the MTV heyday—if any medium had ever been created for a performer, the music video was created for Madonna. Fueled by the visuals in her videos, Madonna quickly became a household name, not just because teens, college students, and twenty-somethings were singing her songs, but because they dressed, looked, and danced like her. Soon, girls were ripping their sweatshirts to hang over one shoulder, tying big bows on top of their heads, and wearing stacks of rubber bracelets and big earrings. The hair was fairly long and big, as were the layered skirts that were worn over tights. The makeup was bright and noticeable. The girls were labeled "Madonna wannabes," and some continue to dress in vintage Madonna to this day (after work, of course).

Madonna's second album, *Like a Virgin* (1984), propelled her popularity to even greater heights, with the single of the same name becoming her first number-one hit. Who can forget the "Like A Virgin" music video or footage of Madonna performing the song during a concert? Rolling around seductively on stage in a wedding gown, she embodied the juxtaposition of virginity and sluttiness—the fantasy of what every girl wanted to be and what every boy wanted to find. While "Material Girl" and "Crazy for You" sat at the top of the charts, *Playboy* and *Penthouse* magazines containing the nude photos Madonna posed for in 1977 resided under the beds of lots of teenage boys and curious men.

Those who couldn't get enough Madonna on radio, album, or MTV could see her in several aweless movies, from *Shanghai Surprise* to *Body of Evidence*. Critics panned her performances and branded her a less-than-stellar actress; however, they were only watching her performances on the big screen. Her greatest acting accomplishments, in retrospect, have been in playing Madonna—cultural icon and superbrand. Her comfort in the role stems from total involvement with her brand image, personality, and promise, all of which she controls and changes as *she* sees fit. This may be why her first movie, *Desperately Seeking Susan*, in which she plays a sharp-tongued character similar to the Madonna persona of that time, remains a standout performance. It even did fairly well at the box office.

Madonna had established her brand: It stood for self-expression; it begged for breaking the rules; it screamed sex. She established herself as a trendsetter who kept one pace ahead of what her fans would adopt shortly after she debuted it. Fans expected her to push the envelope of acceptability, sexuality, and creative freedom, and they expected her to keep evolving and guiding them on fashion and lifestyle trends. She might be controversial and criticized by many, but she sparked a flame not only among the boys, but also thousands of teenage girls who adopted her sexy styles.

LIKE A PRAYER

The defining musical product for Madonna was her 1989 album *Like a Prayer*, with four tracks hitting number one and setting up her 1990 year-long *Blonde Ambition* tour. In this album she bared her soul emotionally as much as she had bared her body elsewhere, with songs appealing to human feelings and emotions about family, death, and divorce, much as the album *Elton John* had done nearly two decades earlier. "Promise to Try" reflected Madonna's reactions to her mother's death at age six, and "Oh Father" focused on her difficult relationship with her father, while "Till Death Do Us Part" reflected her own failed marriage with Sean Penn. It was "Express Yourself," however, that would become an anthem for personal empowerment among women and establish Madonna as a premier role model for women looking to take control of their circumstances and relationships. This song revealed Madonna's true position on sex; while critics saw her blatant sexuality as something that degraded women and set the women's movement back 20 years, she saw it as something that could empower them in a male-oriented world.

It was the title song "Like a Prayer," however, that created the greatest buzz among fans, marketers, and casual observers alike. In a bold step toward marketing and branding innovation, Pepsi-Cola became the first company to debut a hit song and video on a television commercial. It signed a one-year $5 million contract with Madonna to use the song in its commercial and sponsor the *Blonde Ambition* tour. This new formula of corporate sponsorship and pop music seemed to be a natural win-win marketing strategy. Pepsi could ride on the coattails of the emotional connection Madonna had with her fans; Madonna could debut her music and reach a larger base of fans—the Pepsi Generation.

The two-minute commercial aired on March 2, 1989, amid a buzz of hype and anticipation as viewers turned on their sets just to see the commercial. It opened with Madonna innocently watching a childhood birthday party, drinking Pepsi, and remembering it as the same Pepsi she drank at birthday parties when she was a child. The gospel-infused song and the production served up just the right music-picture image and positioning for Pepsi's core market. The song and the ad were the topic around office watercoolers and high school water fountains the next morning.

Unfortunately for Pepsi, MTV released Madonna's "Like a Prayer" video the next day, and all hell broke loose. The visual extravaganza slapped the face of conventional acceptability, featuring scenes of her

witnessing the murder of a white girl, defending a black man wrong-
fully accused, kissing a black saint in church, and dancing in front of
a burning cross. It had a happy ending, which brought the actors
together as if it had all been a theater production. It appeased her
fans, who cheered on her ability and willingness to go where others
wouldn't, and it attracted so much attention that both the song and
the video were catapulted to number one. It was nominated for Best
Video of the Year and captured the Viewer's Choice Award at the
1989 MTV Video Music Awards.

Pepsi, on the other hand, didn't fare so well with its fans. The positive energy Madonna created with the song was completely zapped
by the negative reaction mainstream America had to her video. The
Catholic Church was outraged—offended by Madonna using signs of
stigmata (her bleeding hands) and "having an orgasm on the altar."
Pepsi drinkers protested and organized boycotts, and Pepsi cancelled
the commercial after only two showings.

Pepsi did go on to collaborate with other, less controversial rock
stars, including Michael Jackson (whose hair caught on fire during
filming) and Britney Spears (a young woman of controversy in and
of herself). And other firms have gone on to debut new songs in their
commercials, such as Mitsubishi with "Days Go By" by the new
group Dirty Vegas, which went on to top the pop charts. The rewards
to marketers when they cobrand with the right musical artists can be
huge, from massive publicity and awareness to making extrasensory
connections with fans via the band's musical conduit to memories
and emotions. However, as the Pepsi–Madonna marriage demonstrates, huge risks stand silently in the wings for marketers who fail to
consider completely and control the activities likely to accompany
celebrity endorsements. But Pepsi didn't control Madonna; Madonna controlled Madonna.

Marketers looking to partner with other entities—be they celebrities, spokespersons, other companies, or even nonprofit organizations—for promotional collaborations need to understand that
entity's real brand, including image, promise, and reputation. Partnering with a nonprofit organization often provides many opportunities
for goodwill among consumers, but if the organization becomes controversial (such as People for the Ethical Treatment of Animals

[PETA]), then the partnership can tarnish a brand's reputation as well. In terms of a musical endorser, there are more attributes to weigh than just the type of music he or she creates. Madonna's brand is not just about a visual image or a type of music; it is about the promise to shock and fly in the face of conventional thinking and conventional values, which was probably not the best match for the Pepsi brand. Marketers also need to understand the band's fan base and how their customer base overlaps it in terms of lifestyle characteristics and values. A musical corporate sponsorship needs to be classified as a cobranding strategy, with residual effects on both brands from the association with each other.

COURTING CONTROVERSY

After her Pepsi episode, it was business as usual for Madonna, which meant sex, advancing countercultural thinking, and more sex. In 1992, she advanced the Madonna brand with a multichannel PR and marketing assault on mainstream music. She released her most provocative album, *Erotica,* which contained an ultrasexual S&M title song, as well as "When Life Begins," about oral sex, and "In This Life," a tribute to a friend who died of AIDS. With *Erotica,* Madonna broke the barriers of what could be said and sung in mass-market music, unusual for a female performer at that time. For example, she dealt with homosexuality so explicitly in the album that she even offended many gay fans. In one of her rare cover songs, she also sang "Fever," raising the temperature a little from Peggy Lee's 1950s version, but enlarging the demographic age base.

The sexual web Madonna had woven with *Erotica* was reinforced by the movie *Body of Evidence* and the book entitled *Sex,* a soft-core porn publication that transformed the term *coffee table book* to *bedside table book.* Expensively packaged in an aluminum cover with a steel-core binding, it sold over 500,000 copies at $50 and hit the cover of *Time* magazine. Today, expect to pay $100 or more for it on eBay. It featured hundreds of erotic photographs of Madonna and a host of celebrities including Isabella Rossellini, Big Daddy Kane, Naomi Campbell, and Vanilla Ice. *Sex* received enormous amounts of publicity—most of it negative—and scathing reviews from critics, but it helped sell over

2 million copies of the *Erotica* album. Though that multiplatinum number may sound impressive, it was actually one of her worst-selling albums, capturing only a fraction of the sales of her other best-selling albums, such as *Like a Virgin*.

These three products thrust Madonna's image from racy and on the edge of acceptability to raunchy and over the edge. Hard-core fans loved the album and probably the book; they remained loyal because they expected her to challenge the status quo. But she pushed beyond mass-market appeal and turned off a lot of friends, which can be dangerous territory for even well-established brands like Calvin Klein. Tom Murry explains, "There's a fine line between being sexy and going too far. You have to sense where your target audience is at a given moment—and how far you can take them without turning them off; without losing them."

And Madonna did lose some fans. In many instances, however, fans saw her expression of sexual fantasies as a step toward equal rights for men and women, taking on the double standard that it was okay for men to produce erotica but not women. However, Madonna did change the standards for what is acceptable in the media with her innovative approach to positioning, opening the way for artists of the future to take off their clothes to sell records.

CHAMELEON CHARACTER

From dancing to yoga, trampy rags to haute couture, material girl to mystic mom, Madonna changes her image nearly as often as she changes her hair color, which has gone from dirty blonde to platinum to black to whatever it is today. Just when fans think they've figured her out, she transforms again, keeping them intrigued, involved, and guessing what could possibly be next. That is her greatest brand promise—reinvention.

By 1995, Madonna began a new era in her career and personal life. Her theatrical aspirations had found outlets before as a dramatic actress on Broadway in *Speed the Plow,* on the London stage, and in a costarring role with Warren Beatty in the movie *Dick Tracy.* In 1996, Madonna went on to star in the movie version of *Evita,* for which she won a Golden Globe for Best Actress. The soundtrack sold well, with

"Don't Cry for Me Argentina" and "You Must Love Me" topping radio station play lists. More important, the movie aided her evolution from sexual being to upscale sophisticate, reaching mature, more upscale segments of the market. It also coincided with the birth of her daughter Lourdes, in 1996, fostering her new image of modern mother, and confirming it with the birth of her son Rocco, in 2000.

Madonna remains sexy—she has just redefined sexiness according to her life stage. Today, Madonna's image boasts shades of June Cleaver or someone that Mr. Rogers, if he were still alive, might ask to serve milk and cookies to kids in the neighborhood. She even appeared on CNN's *Larry King Live* with her husband, answering questions on parenting and expressing fairly traditional views on the differences between boys (they love cars) and girls (they love dolls and dressing up with makeup) and the need for children to have disciplined, organized lives. She doesn't let her children watch television—books are better. In fact, she recently completed a deal to write five children's books for Penguin.

Although raised as a Catholic, even her spirituality has evolved. Now she is a proponent of Kabbalah, a form of Jewish mysticism incorporating the Old Testament and the foundational concepts of Jesus, the rabbi. When King asked her about her spiritual evolution, Madonna explained, "I was looking for something. I mean, I'd begun practicing yoga and, you know, I was looking for the answers to life. Why am I here? What am I doing here? What is my purpose? How do I fit into the big picture? I know there's more to life than making lots of money and being successful and even getting married and having a family. . . . What is the point of my journey and everybody else's journey . . . what does it all mean?"[2] Many observers of current cultural trends see spirituality as a mainstream event occurring in American and other cultures. And, as usual, Madonna is on top of that trend, evolving from material girl to spiritual girl.

DIAMONDS ARE FOR EVERYONE

Although a sexual positioning similar to Madonna's might be appealing to some fans and work for brands such as Victoria's Secret, Calvin

Klein, and Herbal Essences, others shy away from explicit sexiness. Not everyone chose to follow Madonna as she took the lead in pop music in the early 1980s—some because they didn't like her music and others because they didn't agree with the values she represented. Consumer product brands can suffer the same rejection and even consumer backlash when they cross the line of moral acceptability. Marketers sometimes point to the passion and emotion that using sex to sell can create among consumers. Others demonstrate the effectiveness of brand personalities and positioning strategies that produce the same passion and emotional connection, but in a way that appeals to the values of the masses. Enter Neil Diamond.

DIAMONDS ARE FOREVER

If Madonna is about sexual explicitness, continual reinvention, and shaking up the status quo, Neil Diamond is the anti-Madonna. Occasionally sporting simple black outfits but eternally radiating a 1970s look and feel, Diamond has captured a place in the heart of America by peddling nostalgia. Singing an array of his 60-plus hits during his concert performances, Diamond lets his audiences relive a time in which things were a little less hectic, a bit more patriotic, and much more innocent. This combination of crooner and rock star excites fans from ages 18 to 80—with more of them representing the 55-plus crowd. In fact, you might be a Neil Diamond fan, having to suppress humming and toe tapping when you recall "Sweet Caroline," "I Am I Said," and "Cherry, Cherry." But you might also choose not to scream your adoration from the rooftops, because he doesn't represent the kind of cool other rock stars do.

The music industry may not get very excited about Diamond, but his fans do. When it comes to concerts, fans snatch up tickets with lightning speed; consequently, he outpaces and outsells many of his younger, hipper, and sexier counterparts. Some industry trade publications report that Diamond was the biggest solo touring act of the 1990s, due in part to an appeal that cuts a wide demographic swath of ages and musical tastes. His 2002 tour generated $52 million in 68 cities, making it the fourth-largest tour of the year. From his first hit, "Cherry, Cherry," in the 1960s to his most recent, "Three Chord

Opera," fans have rewarded him with 60 hits, 38 of them in the top 40. He even inspires Neil Diamond imitators—both black and white versions—in numbers that rival those of Elvis. Tribute bands, the musical equivalent of supermarket private labels, are found across the country, playing and singing Diamond songs in venues including Las Vegas, Nevada, and Branson, Missouri.

Attend a Neil Diamond concert and you may think you've walked into an aerobics class for 60-year-olds. But amid a sea of gray hair are plenty of young people, often a bevy of young ladies in the first row, singing along and shouting their adoration. Don't tell these women Diamond isn't sexy—to them he's very sexy, but in a conservative, wholesome, safe, non-Madonna-like way. Men and women alike enjoy singing the songs they've come to love, swaying to romantic ballads, clapping to patriotic tunes, and gyrating to 1970s-style pop classics. From the stage, the 62-year-old songster holds his fans in his hands, getting the respect that a career spanning four decades deserves. Though he may be far less sexual than Madonna, his stage presence, talent, and values make him just as sexy to masses of consumers. One could argue that Madonna and Diamond are two sides of the same coin.

Examining the brilliance of Diamond's career uncovers some of the same values and marketing strategies that some of the world's most enduring brands have used to stay profitable for decades. Those lessons include:

♪ Connecting with a market segment and moving with it

♪ Creating and maintaining emotional connections based on nostalgia and the comfort of familiarity

♪ Understanding how values affect product, marketing, and management decisions.

The Neil Diamond product and marketing approach creates a musical brand that mirrors several successful consumer product brands. One in particular comes to mind—Neil Diamond is the Velveeta cheese of the world of rock and roll. And before all of you Diamond fans get your feathers too ruffled, let us explain. Upon announcing a tour, Diamond doesn't need to rely on mass advertising to get the word out and sell tickets; word of mouth among fans does the trick. When you attend one of his concerts, you know what to expect; unlike KISS, there won't be a lot of surprises, pyrotechnics, or fire-breathing. There's only one Neil Diamond, and people know his brand well. His new albums are likely to sound like those of the past, which is pleasing to most of his fans, yet he does release new material occasionally to keep in touch with them and keep them engaged. While we know legions of devotees exist, you might be hard-pressed to find many who'll fess up to being die-hard Diamond fans. For most of the 50-and-under group, such admittance seems a bit too schmaltzy, classifying Diamond more as someone their parents should like. Yet, when his tour hits their vicinity, these boomers will go—and, more important, they'll love every minute they are there.

Now, compare that to Velveeta. Kraft certainly doesn't have to do a lot of advertising for this product. It has its place in Americana, and it coasts merrily along on that sea of repeat purchases. When it comes time to replenish the Velveeta supply, what do consumers write on their shopping lists—processed cheese loaf or Velveeta? There really is no substitute. Its popularity is partially about consistency, but occasionally Kraft will shake it up a bit with innovations like Picante Velveeta, which, like Diamond's new releases, is the same basic product consumers love but with a little kick. It's a fact that Kraft sells tons of Velveeta, but Velveeta fans tend to be of the closet variety rather than an in-your-face breed.

Closet fans can be challenging to marketers. Their tendency is to be loyal but not to evangelize—a major benefit to companies that create fans. Hormel's blockbuster brand, Spam, had a similar positioning. Thousands of people ate it, but not many wanted to admit it. But with a tongue-in-cheek approach, the company launched a marketing and branding campaign that let people laugh at the product and the fact that they liked it. In essence, the company made Spam cool—or at least as cool as canned, processed meat can be. Now there are Spam cook-offs, Spam recipes, Spam hats and T-shirts, and Spam fans, who not only are out of the closet but are proud to shout their adoration for the stuff in the blue can.

Diamond established himself as part of the mainstream. Like

Velveeta, he has capitalized on his place in American culture, reaping the financial rewards of doing something well and sticking with it.

CREATING THE SPARKLE

Neil Leslie Diamond (yes, that's his real name) was born on a cold Brooklyn night on January 24, 1941. His cultural roots stemmed from Russia and Poland, birthplaces of his maternal and paternal grandparents. Young Neil grew up with American core values and the discipline of a father who served in the U.S. Army. A New Yorker through and through, he moved to Cheyenne, Wyoming, in 1945, where his father was stationed in the Army, exposing him to the rest of America. After military service, the family opened a dry goods store in Flatbush, eventually moving the business and the family home to Brooklyn's Brighton Beach. Diamond learned in his early years about patriotism, a disciplined approach to delivering a quality product, family values, and a practical understanding of business, all of which he arguably brings to his music career.

His musical journey began with the guitar he got for his sixteenth birthday and continued through singing with his high school's choral group. In 1958 he wrote his first song, "Hear Them Bells," as a tribute to the girl he later married in 1963. Perhaps his discipline and stage presence were affected by his acumen in the sport of fencing, which earned him a fencing scholarship at New York University, where he enrolled as a premed student. But his love for songwriting, and his lack of love for organic chemistry, lured him to leave college 10 credits short of graduation to take a job as a songwriter with a publishing company. Diamond says he never regretted that decision.

Like many singer-songwriters, he struggled in the early years. He first appeared in 1960, while still attending NYU, at the Little Neck Country Club on Long Island, but it took until 1965 for Diamond's reign in rock and roll to begin. The string of hits that ensued read like a modern-day musical timeline (feel free to whistle along as we recap just a few). In 1965, Diamond the songwriter penned the hit "I'm a Believer" for the Monkees, and Diamond the performer released his own top-10 hit, "Cherry, Cherry." Incorporating gospel and country sounds to give his music more emotional content, he overwhelmed his fans, and in turn they gave Diamond two million-selling records, "Sweet Caroline" and "Holly, Holy." "Cracklin' Rosie" was his first number-one hit, followed in 1972 by another number-one smash, "Song Sung Blue." In 1973, he signed with Columbia Records, releasing *Jonathan Livingston Seagull,* which became his number-two all-time best seller and earned him Grammy and Golden Globe awards. Toward the latter part of the decade, he wrote and recorded "You Don't Bring Me Flowers," which Barbra Streisand recorded separately. A bold DJ spliced the two records together and listeners loved it, prompting Diamond and Streisand to rerecord the song as a duet, which became an all-time best seller for both stars.

Diamond expanded his reach in 1980, starring alongside Sir Laurence Olivier in the film *The Jazz Singer.* (He also appeared in another movie in 2001, *Saving Silverman.*) While Diamond's thespian abilities didn't threaten the careers of other actors, his musical career was reinforced by the soundtrack's massive sales and appeal. He released numerous hits throughout the 1970s and 1980s, from "Forever in Blue Jeans" to "Heartlight," which was inspired by the blockbuster movie *E.T.,* but he occasionally disappeared from the recording scene. He explained to reporters, "I wanted to spend time with my family." While of late this has become a euphemism in the business world for "I feel I've failed," or "I'm completely burned out," in the case of Neil Diamond, it's actually very believable.

THE TOUR MASTER

Diamond's continued success stems from his brilliance in the touring game. Clad in sequins and black slacks while his fans are "Forever in Blue Jeans," his concerts have evolved to deliver what his fans expect—a blast-from-the-past sense of nostalgia, great quality music, and a string of sing-along songs packaged in a Vegas-like production. Though many members of his band have been with him over 25 years, the digital equipment and technology used to deliver the high-quality staging and sound are state-of-the-art.

As at an Elvis show, you can't be in a bad mood while jamming at a Neil Diamond concert. There's the innocence of his music, his infectious passion and energy, and the communal emotional ride taken with thousands of fans. Emotions ran high during his *Three Chord Opera* world tour, which began on September 28, 2001, in Columbus, Ohio, soon after the September 11 attacks, and traveled to 90 cities in 16 months. Following the tragedy, many performers canceled performances out of respect for the victims and their families. Some bands, however, decided to continue their tours, recognizing that many people felt the need to bond together, explaining in part the popularity of this Diamond tour. The Irish rock band U2 in fact, decided not only to keep its *Elevation* tour on track, it actually added nine shows to its lineup. Ask fans today, and they'll tell you that U2's decision to play to heal the nation made them even greater fans of the band.

Neil Diamond took a similar approach. His values are American values personified, evidenced in particular by a special tribute to New York City firefighters and police (with a moving rendition of "He Ain't Heavy, He's My Brother") and the unfurling of an American flag to the rousing refrain of his hit "America." He captured the mood of the country, and audiences responded with tears of patriotism, sorrow, and pride. In Canada, he added two Canadian flags to the stage and talked about "neighbors joined at the border." Diamond tells reporters that people want to get out and away from the television set and the dire news that constantly confronts them. "That's why I'm still on tour," he says. "It's more than playing music for people and having a good time. There's an emptiness out there, and I believe I can do something about easing that pain."

THE ANTI-MADONNA

Diamond and Madonna address branding in very different ways. Whereas Madonna focuses on constant evolution and change, Diamond's brand promise is *not* to change. Not one to follow the latest trend, instead he defines what *Time* magazine calls the "Bandmaster of the Mainstream." Chalk it up to the familiarity of his voice and music and the simplicity of his lyrics and style, he provides an emotional safe haven for many generations of fans, especially in times of uncertainty and unrest.

Simplicity is a key concept in understanding Diamond's mass

appeal; it also is a primary reason some products are propelled to mass acceptance and others are not. Research indicates that the more complicated a new product or marketing message, the less likely consumers are to adopt it. Complexity intimidates customers, often keeping them from trying something new. In addition to fearing that they will not understand it and will therefore feel stupid, they also don't want to invest the time they perceive it will take to understand and use the product. In a nation in which half of the VCR clocks still flash 12:00, simplicity rules have affected the acceptance of technology options from microwave ovens to quadraphonic sound. The same holds true for branding and marketing messages. Ease or difficulty in understanding the basic benefit of a product and its relative advantage over competing options is the single most important determinant of new product success. Add complexity, research indicates, and the probability of failure increases dramatically. Simplicity sells to mass markets, whether the brand is a musician or a cheese.

Diamond and Madonna each sing to a generation, connecting the values of their fans with their own values. Both sing about love and relationships (don't they all), but they approach them from different perspectives—Madonna sings from a contemporary, tough, female-powered, "I'm in charge" point of view, and Diamond in a sensitive, old-fashioned, "I'm in love" tone. Their values appear in the lyrics and mood of their songs. Listen to Diamond's hit single "America" and you can feel the emotion with which he sings about immigrants, like his grandparents, arriving on our shores via boats and planes to find "freedom's light, burning warm." Madonna's *Life in America* album is anything but patriotic, causing fans and audiences to protest the original version of the video, in which a grenade blows up a George W. Bush look-alike. Whereas Madonna seems to seek out controversy, Diamond shuns it, living and performing in ways that spotlight mainstream values.

Believe it or not, the underlying commonality between these two performers is sex—more specifically, their sex appeal among fans. Though you hear more people use the words sex and Madonna in the same sentence, watch the reactions of the women at Diamond concerts, and you'll find that sexiness or sexuality is at the top of their collective minds. Diamond's sex appeal is different from Madonna's, but it exists nonetheless, and just as passionately for the women who share his definition of sexiness. Both performers demonstrate that sex sells, at any age. Just ask the folks who regularly bring sex to your mailbox—Victoria's Secret.

THE WORLD'S WORST-KEPT SECRET

If Madonna and Neil Diamond were to spawn a business, it might very well resemble lingerie superstar Victoria's Secret. Combining the brand DNAs of Madonna (sexiness, shock value, controversy, and brand evolution) and Diamond (consistency, simplicity, holistic values, and perfecting what you do well) could result in a product brand similar to Victoria's Secret and a corporate brand and values system mirroring Limited Brands, Inc.

Victoria's Secret peddles sexiness to consumers around the globe to the tune of about $2.5 billion a year. With 900 lingerie stores and nearly 500 beauty stores in America, Victoria's Secret also reaches customers 24/7 with the 350 million catalogues it sends out annually and on its fast-growing web site. Famed for its tastefully risqué catalog, Victoria's Secret is one of the most powerful, sexy brands in the world, ranking as high as the ninth most recognized brand worldwide, even though it has no stores outside the United States.

Just as Madonna's fans expect her to challenge conventional definitions of acceptability, sexuality, and creative freedom, so its fans have come to expect the same from Victoria's Secret, looking for guidance on fashion and lifestyle trends. In addition to bras, panties, and teddies, Victoria's Secret products include swimsuits, loungewear, hosiery, and footwear. Whether it's underwear or underwater, Victoria's Secret (barely) covers American women with a brand that probably leaves Madonna saying, "Why didn't I think of creating that company?"

Yet among a sea of fans exists a pool of critics, who look at the skimpy panties and see-through teddies and snipe at what they perceive as attempts to exploit women. But Victoria's Secret is not about setting the women's movement back 30 years; it is about empowering women, giving them the choice to feel sexy, look great, and express their sexuality, not just to please others, but to please themselves. It reminds women that their bodies are beautiful and they have the freedom to express their beauty, similar to the message Madonna has sent fans through her music, lyrics, and actions.

LIMITED BRANDS

Victoria's Secret is just one piece of the corporate pie called Limited Brands, formerly known as The Limited, Inc. In a move to demonstrate its fervent belief in the importance of brands, the company changed its name and fortified its mission to develop each of the brands within its portfolio of companies, which includes Victoria's Secret, The Limited, Bath and Body Works, Express, Express for Men, Lerner New York/New York & Company, White Barn Candle Company, Aura Science, and Henri Bendel.

Few brands, even Madonna and Aerosmith, provide a better blueprint for brand evolution than Limited Brands. Front man and leader of the Limited Brands band is Leslie Wexner, who opened the first Limited store in 1963 with a $5,000 loan from his aunt. His strategy was based on segmentation—pick a segment of customers, understand those customers, and give them what they want. Don't try to be everything to everyone; be vital and relevant to a select few. As Limited's target market matured, so did its offerings, leaving the need for a second concept to appeal to emerging younger markets. That brand was Express. By 1993, the company had 13 businesses including Abercrombie & Fitch, Lane Bryant, Structure, Galyans, and Limited Too, all of which were grown and spun off.

With an uncanny ability to buy minuscule chains consisting of only a few stores (like Victoria's Secret and Abercrombie & Fitch) and build them into billion-dollar businesses, Wexner reinvents himself and Limited Brands every decade or so based on changes in his customers' wants and lifestyles. New additions to Limited Brands' portfolio include Victoria's Secret Direct and Victoria's Secret Beauty, a sister division of Victoria's Secret stores, which develops and markets fragrances, color cosmetics, skin-care products, and personal accessories. It's a concept that exploded from a corner of Victoria's Secret stores into separate stores dedicated to beauty products. Two of its fragrances are among the ten best-selling fragrances in the United States, earning four prestigious FiFi awards for new fragrances.

Observing Wexner as he leads the $8-billion business is kind of like watching Neil Diamond perform. The direction is clear, the execution precise, the performance consistent, the business strategies sound and proven, and the values noncontroversial. But a Madonna-like sense of control and evolution lingers throughout the corporation, keeping Limited Brands fresh and sexy in its quest for increased profits and market share. Examining Victoria's Secret, arguably its most recognized brand, reveals insights into:

♪ The use of controversy in capitalizing on a brand

♪ The use of sexuality and sexiness in selling positioning, and promoting brands

♪ The role of brand authenticity in connecting with fans

♪ The role of logistics and operations in executing a brand promise

Wexner changed the nature of retail branding by creating stores that *are* brands, instead of stores *of* brands that are controlled by manufacturers. Victoria's Secret is the store; Victoria's Secret is the brand; Victoria's Secret is the experience.

THIS AIN'T YOUR GRANDMA'S UNDERWEAR

The Victoria's Secret brand embodies *sex*. Its catalog has achieved iconic status in American culture, constantly mentioned on television sitcoms and by Hollywood stars. It draws megadoses of media attention. It causes chaos when it arrives in households, as brothers duke it out for first viewing rights. Reactions from raving fans have made the catalog and the brand *the* standard of sexiness in mainstream America.

Taking underwear from the "unmentionables" category to the "talked-about" category and thereby redefining the lingerie market, Victoria's Secret represents true brand authenticity among its fans. Its authenticity is bolstered by a diverse portfolio of models from Claudia Schiffer (the German classic blonde) and Tyra Banks (African-American) to Yasmeen Ghari (Canadian, Pakistani, and German all in one) and Karolina Kurkova (the latest tall, blonde Czech). Individually, they represent many personalities and definitions of beauty. Collectively, they give the Victoria's Secret brand a culturally diverse but global personality of sexiness, sophistication, and beauty.

Victoria's Secret's brand authenticity allows it to evolve without alienating its fans. Similar to the challenges Madonna faces in maintaining a sexy image, Victoria's Secret battles against consumers' changing tastes and perceptions of what is cool or sexy. New colors, fabrics, styles, scents, and visuals need to continually redefine sexiness, because what is hot today may be humdrum tomorrow. Sexiness can also mean cotton briefs, boxers, flannel nighties, and boxy pajamas, all of which have been incorporated into the line in recent years. Victoria's Secret knows that selling sex works only on a limited basis; it may intrigue customers enough to try a product once, but if the product isn't world class or falls below expectations, chances are repeat purchases and loyalty won't ensue. Therefore, its products need to feel good, look great, pleasure the wearer, and hold up to wear, tear, and washing. In the stores, customers need to feel comfortable selecting and buying intimate apparel, an uncomfortable experience for many people.

The steward of the Victoria's Secret brand is Victoria herself. This fictitious creature wanders the halls and collective minds of the Victoria's Secret home office, representing the guiding force of what the brand needs to be to connect with customers. Victoria represents the lifestyles, dreams, and aspirations of her customers. And she is ever present among associates as they design lingerie, buy products throughout the world, and plan stores in locations where she would want to shop. Everyone involved in brand management can always return to the question, "What would Victoria do? What would she like?"

TOUCHING FANS WITH THE BRAND

The Victoria's Secret brand is a 360-degree experience, creating an extrasensory connection with customers at many levels. Under the leadership of Ed Razek, president of marketing and creative services, Victoria's Secret has fashioned an "octopus" approach to branding, in which it sends the same brand message to customers through its catalog, web site, and stores. The tentacles of the octopus include extensive television advertising, online fashion shows and information, television appearances for the supermodels, stylish in-store signage and high-impact visuals, and dramatic catalog layouts, all coordinated to consummate in-store and online sales.

A few years ago, in a bold move, the intimate images of the Victoria's Secret catalog leapt from its pages to the small screen, where the supermodels appeared in television ads featuring skin, an occasional hint of satin and lace, and more skin. A throaty female voice with a British accent spoke over the soft music, inviting one and all to the Victoria's Secret bra and panty sale. Most would say the ads rocked; they surely have come a long way since Jane Russell modeled the 18-hour bra outside her sweater. In a slight advertising twist, the 2003 ads used the Bob Dylan tune "Love Sick" from his 1997 album *Time Out of Mind,* proving that classic rock musicians have even invaded the lingerie business.

An unusually strong tentacle of the Victoria's Secret brand is Victoria's Secret Direct—its web site is the premier example of a retail firm adding e-commerce to its multichannel arsenal for reaching and serving customers. VictoriasSecret.com allows browsers to see the models in action, create a wish list, view runway shows, and, of course, buy the products. While Bloomingdale's and other retailers are retreating from their disappointing e-commerce ventures, Victoria's Secret grows with an achievement few can match—profitability from the start. Even though Victoria's Secret's online venture performs head-and-shoulders above other retail sites, its stores still generate a majority of corporate sales and profits. It's analogous to album releases for the Rolling Stones and Neil Diamond: Albums generate awareness and some profits, but their primary role is to generate buzz and support concerts—the *real* money-makers.

Total customer experience drives the Victoria's Secret retail formula. Not only does management want the store atmosphere to make people feel welcome, comfortable, and eager; it wants the clothing to make women feel sexy, desirable, and good about themselves. Nowhere is Victoria's Secret's brand better executed than at its new, two-story flagship store in New York City's Herald Square, a

25,000-square-foot stage of sexy images of silky lingerie and enticing colors, luscious fragrances and scents, and romantic music that courts fans and titillates media.

As with Madonna and Neil Diamond, Victoria's Secret's brand is as much about how it makes others feel about themselves as it is about itself. Fans leave a Diamond concert uplifted and thrilled with what they've experienced. Getting this reaction from customers shopping for something that could make even the most macho of men blush is not always easy. This is painfully evident around Valentine's Day (the firm's second-biggest holiday), when gaggles of men enter Victoria's Secret stores wearing a collective deer-in-the-headlights look of panic. That's when the associates enter the theatre's stage. At that moment the brand experience rests completely in their hands. How they interact with customers is guided by Limited Brands' Diamond-like values of honesty, integrity, openness, respect, fairness, and inclusion. The ability of associates to exude passion for the product, make customers feel comfortable, and create a glamorous, intimate, and indulgent experience for customers determines overall satisfaction with the total Victoria's Secret brand. Never discount the value of the associates, because they execute the look, feel, and image that marketing and branding strategies create among customers.

The Victoria's Secret brand is about more than sexy images and supermodels, however. The functional component of the brand is paramount in creating and maintaining fans. Just as Neil Diamond's concerts depend on high-end equipment, competent crew, and experienced band members, Victoria's Secret depends on the Product Quality group at corporate headquarters to execute the brand experience seamlessly, from new product development through sourcing to production. Supply-chain issues, from inventory control to delivery, fall under the realm of Limited Logistics Service (LLS), which makes sure that the right products are delivered at the right time, in the right condition, in the right quantities, at the right price, when consumers want them. Rather than relying on vendors to deliver quality goods on time to stores as most department stores do, Victoria's Secret exercises Madonna-like control of its own logistics systems.

Unlike many other firms that view logistics as little more than an operations function, Limited Brands incorporates logistics excellence into its brand strategy and strength. Nick LaHowchic, president and CEO of LLS, explains the role of logistics to a brand. "We're always asking ourselves, 'How do we add value to our brand initiatives? How do we use the supply chain as a competitive weapon? How can we take cycle time out of the process? How can we become more agile?' " These considerations determine how well the brand promise is delivered at the customer level. If products are out of stock, or if size and color assortments don't match consumer demand, or product quality falls below expectations, the entire brand is tarnished—and even ardent fans retreat.

ANGELS IN THE ARCHITECTURE

Victoria's Secret has arguably created the fashion show to stop all fashion shows. A standard in fashion circles, the runway show traditionally was primarily directed toward industry insiders who gathered to look at upcoming styles and lines. As the retail industry changed, the runway show evolved from its roots in the buying arena to focus on media and consumer attention. The bigger the brand personality, the more celebrities attend (and vice versa), and the greater the media coverage and brand exposure.

Victoria's Secret, however, one-ups all other fashion shows, hands down. Rather than turning the heads of industry insiders, it shamelessly courts fans by broadcasting an hour-long skinfest that highlights the hottest, barely there fashions of the season. Originally developed as a live Internet event, the 2000 show in Cannes, France, broke all records for attracting eyeballs, to the point that volume eclipsed capacity and the webcast shut down. The subsequent publicity buzzed about the show itself, its high consumer draw, and the Web crash, eventually reaching an estimated 1.5 billion people worldwide. From a revenue standpoint, it stimulated sales in May—a typically slow period for retail sales.

In 2002, the Victoria's Secret fashion show jumped from computer screen to prime-time television screen, reaching an even broader audience than the Internet alone could deliver. Broadcast in November, it also connected with people primed to shop for the holidays. *Victoria's Secret Fashion Show* was hosted by supermodel Heidi Klum and singer

Mark McGrath and featured the runway show in addition to backstage sneak peeks at the models and the chaos of a fashion show. Add to that performances by pop-salsa superstar Marc Anthony, Destiny's Child (one of the best-selling female groups in the world), and singer-songwriter Phil Collins (who has sold over 100 million solo albums worldwide), and the hour-long event was more variety show entertainment than fashion show. The event culminated with the "Dream Angels" runway pass, in which the Angels float in the air above the runway and one supermodel—who has literally competed for the right to wear the Angel wings—struts her stuff and stops the show.

CARESSING CONTROVERSY

Any company that is perceived to sell sex should expect plenty of critics waiting in the wings to attack any marketing move that can be perceived as risqué. Complaints that used to focus on the images within the catalog now revolve around Victoria's Secret's advertising and most recently its fashion shows. The $7-million production created many times that investment in publicity for the brand—some of it bad, *all* of it good.

With the right spin and among fans, even controversial events can cast positive shadows. For example, activists with PETA interrupted the 2002 Victoria's Secret fashion show as Gisele Bundchen strutted down the runway. The protesters were taken away, the lights went down, and the segment was redone, with a composed Bundchen who strode out the second time to thunderous applause. In the end, most of the mainstream culture thought of PETA as unethical and Bundchen as the hero. Similarly, Concerned Women for America, the National Organization for Women, and the Parents Television Council asked CBS not to air the show, calling it degrading to women. CBS spokesperson Chris Ender responded, describing it as a one-hour fashion show mixed with musical performances and comedy segments. "Does it push the envelope?" Ender said. "Sure, but everyone knows what the Victoria's Secret fashion show is. With the advance publicity and the content advisory, every viewer will be armed with information to make their own choice." Like headlines about the off-stage activities of rock stars, headlines about the controversies around the fashion show attract audiences and extend awareness of the brand.

Much of the controversy surrounding the Victoria's Secret brand has to do with the influence people feel it has on culture—pushing the envelope of what is acceptable in the areas of sexuality, exposure, and even body image. What the average person doesn't see and the media chooses to ignore is Limited Brands' commitment to influencing the culture in which it operates in a very different way. One of the values at Limited Brands focuses on giving back to the community. Following in the personal footsteps of Wexner, Limited Brands topped the list of specialty retailers in *Fortune* magazine's list of 2003 World's Most Admired Companies, due in part to its intense focus on social responsibility. One such initiative is an outgrowth of Governor Taft's Ohio Reads initiative. Hundreds of company associates volunteer one hour per week in a classroom for one school year, teaching on company time, with the company underwriting all program expenses. Each associate tutors two children for half an hour each week, with another associate duplicating that with the same two students on another day. It's a practical example of how to manage a Madonna-type brand with Diamond-type values.

ORCHESTRATING THE PERFECT BRAND CONCERT

Victoria's Secret boasts a growing base of fans that evangelizes others; it embodies an image like no other; it exemplifies functional excellence to execute brand promises. It's a brand that rocks, generating as much buzz among its shareholders as the supermodels do among fans and media. The lesson for everyone is that brand strength, market share, and profitability arise from Limited Brands' strict commitment to three major initiatives:

♪ Maintaining its brand dominance through constant innovation in products with integrated brand marketing in a wide variety of media.

♪ Increasing the presence of its brands through stores, catalogues, e-commerce, and international supply chain excellence, and the delivery of consistently superior in-store and e-commerce experiences.

♪ Constantly focusing its business units on dominant brands. This includes growing some brands (as with Limited Stores, Express, and more recently Victoria's Secret) and spinning off others (as with Lane Bryant and Limited Too) to maintain a portfolio that is relevant and attracts fans.

Leslie Wexner is a brand leader who not only understands innovation and how to reinvent brands; he knows how to communicate his vision to others and assemble teams to coordinate and execute brand strategy. He expresses succinctly the strengths of the firm he founded over 40 years ago; "Clearly, brands win and we have some of the most compelling brands in retailing. Well planned. Well bought. Well coordinated. Well displayed. Well marketed. Well done." Well said, Mr. Wexner; well said.

DIE ANOTHER DAY

Many attributes unite Madonna, Neil Diamond, and Victoria's Secret, and many attributes distinguish them from one another. Eminem sings in his song "This looks like a job for me, so everybody just follow me, 'cause we need a little controversy, 'cause it feels so empty without me." As his lyrics reflect, doomsday certainly doesn't always precede controversy. Madonna and Victoria's Secret have proven that. And while Eminem might believe the cultural scene would be empty without him, so might it be barren without the likes of Madonna and Victoria's Secret.

Not everyone, however, wants to follow brands that challenge the status quo. Neil Diamond's sustained popularity and degree of impact prove that controversy isn't necessary to achieve cultlike fame; in fact, there are legions of fans looking to worship someone with traditional values. One need just look to the popularity of Christian singer Bill Gather, who sells out arenas wherever he performs, and to the phenomenal growth of Branson, Missouri—a *mecca* of good, old-fashioned, family-oriented entertainment (including the revival of *The Lawrence Welk Show*).*

Madonna is innovation, change, and evolution personified. But not all of her moves are smooth, like her appearance in the movie fiasco *Swept Away* (directed by husband Guy Ritchie), which even her kindest critics and audience members panned. Robert Summer, former president of Sony Music International, says, "The challenge she faces now in terms of finding another cat's life is exponentially greater than anything she's faced previously. She handles the matter of relevance masterfully, but more immediate is the issue of *Swept Away*. When you hit the floor that hard, it's really tough to bounce back."

Madonna presents a tantalizing study of how to craft a brand that interprets, relates to, and influences the values of its fans. The next episode in her saga will be how she rebounds from her most recent setback—her controversial album *American Life*, with an antipatriotic video, causing even some fan backlash. But that was last week. Her spin control is already repairing damage. Anticipating her next move keeps us on the edge of our seats to see what she's going to do next and, in times of adversity, how she's going to get herself out of another fine mess. Stay tuned!

The similarities between and juxtaposition of Madonna and Neil Diamond give insight on how two brands can take different approaches to positioning based on the same attribute. Each brand authenticity in the area of sex is real, though very different based on their life stages, values, and fans. And as different as they are, they share fans, who work out or dance to "Ray of Light" and other peppy Madonna tunes and listen to old Diamond favorites over a candlelight dinner. Of different generations, different styles, and different values, they are different sides of the same coin.

---

*If you are child of the 1960s, we know you've seen at least one episode of the original television show. For a real study in how television and culture have changed, try to catch a rebroadcast on your local PBS station. Most likely, you'll recognize some of the music and some of the songsters—at the very least you'll remember sitting around the television with your family, trying to imitate Welk's accent.

8

LESSONS FROM THE LEGENDS OF ROCK AND ROLL

I can explain everything better through music. You hypnotize people to where they go right back to their natural state and when you get people at their weakest point, you can preach into their subconscious what we want to say.
—JIMI HENDRIX

A book on music and branding wouldn't seem complete, somehow, without a mention of Old Blue Eyes himself. Frank Sinatra's music has touched millions of fans over the years, with classics like "Fly Me to the Moon," "Luck Be a Lady," and "My Way." During his legendary concerts, audience members would take a collective trip down memory lane with each song he belted out, reminiscing about good times and tough times, taking solace in the tunes they heard. Some evoked tears; some promoted smiles; all drew applause. But few songs inspired fans to sing along as much as "New York, New York" with its famous lyrics, "If I can make it there, I'll make it anywhere."

That's the world of rock and roll—the New York City of competitive marketplaces. It is hard to imagine a more fickle industry; one minute a song is hot, the next it's passé. A rock star can go from in to out in the time it takes many corporations to agree on which advertising agency to hire to promote a new product. What it takes to make it in this rapidly evolving, fan-driven industry applies to most any fledgling brand or company trying to establish itself.

As you've seen throughout this book, the stereotypical rock-and-roll rags-to-riches story begins with a group of social oddballs joining forces, working hard to create their sound, touring an endless array of dive bars, and selling their souls to the managers and record label executives who "discover" them. Those who survive the music industry's brutal initiation with body, mind, and soul somewhat intact go on to promote the albums they sweat to create inside cramped recording studios. Promoting means touring—usually small venues a few steps up from the dives of earlier days—which means many months on the road, devoid of home life and stability but filled with excess, attention, and temptations that few are strong enough to ignore.

If people like the fledgling band, tell others about it, buy tickets to concerts, and purchase albums, the record labels take a chance on them hitting pay dirt. If the band is a flop, the labels just tell them to hit the dirt.

That's the world or rock-and-roll bands. That's also the world of money-making brands.

FANFARE

In today's competitive arena, retailers, manufacturers, and service organizations alike strategize for new ways to attract and retain customers. Frequent buyer programs, special service offerings, improved customer service centers, and product reiterations sometimes lead to success for the many firms vying for customers' attention and spending. And while a consistent combination of these and other programs may make significant strides in the race for long-term loyalty, few firms achieve an emotional connection with their customers.

As KISS, the Rolling Stones, and Elton John reveal, emotional connections foster devotion among customers. In the music world, these customers are known as *fans*—a group of zealots that bands can count on to buy their latest albums, attend their concerts, and demand that their music stay on the radio. They also represent a baseline of sales for new records, concerts, merchandise, or projects the band produces. For bands, a strong fan base represents a major step toward longevity, sustained relevance, and a place in culture. Though this category of customer is not exclusive to the world of rock and roll, it is far more prevalent there than in the world of commerce.

So what does creating fans mean for businesses? At Starbucks, it means people willing to pay top dollar for a cup of coffee nearly every morning—and a decade of 20 percent annual growth rates, even in 2002 when the rest of the economy was sputtering. At eBay, it translates into people who have developed side businesses of buying and selling online, somewhat addicted to the thrill of a treasure hunt. At Victoria's Secret, it results in intense public interest fueling free television coverage of its fashion shows on *Entertainment Tonight* and other programs. In all of these instances, fans evangelize for the brands they love, help recruit other customers, give little regard to special promotions of competitive brands, and ultimately provide higher profit margins for the companies they follow.

Though fans sometimes exist in the corporate branding world, they run rampant in the world of classic rock. Why? Primarily because of the emotional connection that binds fan to band. The ability to evoke an emotional response—"Wow, that's the brand for me!"—is critically important for marketers looking to create loyalty among customers. Studying legendary rock bands reveals tactical lessons on how to create lasting brands, including:

♪ Forge and foster an emotional connection with fans.

♪ Develop ways for your fans to incorporate the brand into their lifestyles.

♪ Develop what your brand communicates to fans in terms of information and emotion.

♪ Retain fans by continually improving the brand at a rate that doesn't distract from the overall positioning of the brand.

♪ Stay fresh in the market, but true to your core sound or strength.

♫ Create realistic expectations among customers and understand that their expectations will increase over time.

♫ Reposition and update the brand by cobranding with brands that have appeal in the markets you are targeting.

♫ Develop talent continuously, package it well, and relate it through multiple mediums.

♫ Monitor brand adoption and customer behavior to drive brand adaptation.

♫ Resist the temptation of overexposure—fans like to feel like they are part of something special.

♫ Empower your fans to help your brand become and stay successful in the market.

If the stereotypical classic rock band were reincarnated as a portfolio of consumer brands, it would be Kraft Foods—an enduring example of how lessons described throughout this book apply to product brands. A little bit Rolling Stones and a whole lot of Neil Diamond, Kraft's brand umbrella embodies what it takes to get onto retail shelves and stay there for decades. Its string of number-one hits rivals that of Elton John, just as the qualities and personality of its products rival his professional persona.

Kraft is perhaps less hip than many of the brands cast in the marketing media spotlight, but it is sexy because of the profits it generates. Not as glamorous as Victoria's Secret or as funky as JetBlue, Kraft's success results from masterful marketing of the mundane. It proves, however, that the principles pulled from the world of rock and roll apply to just about any product, including cheese, lunch meat, and frozen dessert topping.

KRAFTING WINNING BRANDS

Kraft's portfolio of brands rocks. If you've read this book, that proclamation shouldn't shock you. Just think of the equity the company has built over the past several decades with its household-name brands, including Jell-O, Cool Whip, Grey Poupon, and Maxwell House. It boasts leading brand names in categories mainstream America can't live without—what would we do without Miracle Whip, Velveeta, Shake 'n Bake, and Kool-Aid? Generations of kids have been raised on those four staples alone.

What makes Kraft so cool is the long-term dominance its brands have commanded in the marketplace, their effect on overall financial return, and their role in driving long-term strategy for the company. Kraft's brand focus exemplifies our conclusion that the most valuable assets on a balance sheet often don't even appear on the balance sheet—a company's brands. Brand equity, sometimes measured by the excess of a firm's market capitalization over its net worth, represents a long-term investment in market share, wallet share, and heart share. And as the legendary bands featured in this book show, the greater the heart share or emotional connection between fan and brand, the more likely that brand is to be adopted into consumers' lives.

The ultimate cheese-and-cracker combo was born in the merger of Kraft and Nabisco to reign as the largest branded food and beverage company in North America, with revenues of nearly $30 billion. Kraft brought the world's number-one brand of cheese, along with leading brands of salad dressings, packaged dinners, barbecue sauce, and other products to the table, while Nabisco brought with it the world's leading cookie and cracker brands. The marriage, which is expected to result in cost savings of $600 million a year by 2004, transcends languages, permeates cultures, and sells in 150 nations around the globe.

PROMOTING INDIVIDUAL IDENTITIES: MARKETING ONE COLLECTIVE BRAND

Many brands featured in this book are *single* brands, firms whose corporate identity is closely tied to one brand. Unlike JetBlue, Wal-Mart, and Madonna, however, Kraft is a *family* of brands that holds the number-one share position in 21 of 25 product categories in the United States and internationally. The company owns over 150 brands that, according to Nielson data, are so culturally relevant that at least one can be found in 99 percent of U.S. households at any given time.

Reading like the *Forty Licks* greatest hits CD, Kraft brands include Tang, DiGiorno, Tombstone, Knudsen, Cracker Barrel, Bakers, Calumet, Shake 'n Bake, Grey Poupon, Cream of Wheat, Milk-Bone, Jell-O, Balance and Oasis Bars, Sure-Jell, Claussen, Minute Maid, Good Seasons, Seven Seas, A-1, Chips Ahoy!, Ritz, SnackWell's, Triscuits, Zwieback, Corn Nuts, Altoids, Toblerone, Life Savers—and we *could* go on, but won't! Kraft follows the branding strategies from the classic rock era in which each member of the band projected a unique identity. When Mick Jagger, Keith Richards, Ronnie Wood, and Charlie Watts walk on stage together, they are the Rolling Stones, but each draws screams from fans because of his individual personality. For instance, some people are huge Watts fans because they have an affinity for him greater than the connection they feel toward Jagger. Today's contemporary bands usually promote the name of the band, passing up the marketing effort required to promote individual personalities. Like the Rolling Stones, each Kraft brand has its own identity, any one of which may connect with consumers better than another family brand.

FUNCTION + FUN = FOCUSED BRANDS

In their recent *Face to Face* tour, Elton John and Billy Joel electrified audiences with an integrated display of piano genius and personality. Their endless string of combined hits kept concertgoers emotionally engaged for over three hours, but it was their unique synergy that kept fans on their feet a majority of the time. John and Joel blend just the right amounts of function and personality to pack a powerful entertainment punch to even the most discerning fans. Though each artist has tremendous skill and personality, it is their collective formula that allows them to work as a successful team; John adds more parts function (with more serious piano interludes and focused demeanor) and Joel more parts fun (laughing more and jumping around the stage).

Oscar Mayer—the leading hot dogs, cold cuts, and bacon brand in the United States—is Kraft's Elton John, Billy Joel duet. The brand consists of quality, good-tasting lunchmeat marinated in vats of personality. Just think of the Oscar Mayer Wienermobile. The giant hotdog on wheels hit the roads of America in 1936; today, a fleet of them travels the United States, Puerto Rico, and Spain, leaving a trail of people singing the infamous jingle, "Oh I wish I were an Oscar Mayer wiener. . . ." Admit it. You remembered it, didn't you?

LET FANS PARTICIPATE IN THE BRAND

Oscar Mayer also lets fans participate in the brand. An even more popular jingle than the wiener anthem is the bologna anthem. It is Kraft's Wal-Mart cheer—its "Rock and Roll All Night." The words, "My bologna has a first name, it's O-S-C-A-R . . . " still resonate through the minds of boomers and Generation Xers alike. Today, however, kids may not sing the bologna song in the cafeteria, but they do talk Kraft at lunch when they assemble and trade Lunch-ables. This modern-day brown-bag lunch is really a kit of snack-sized food that kids like to eat and can assemble and eat, such as pizza and taco Lunchables. Kids get to play with their food and trade among themselves, while parents don't have to take the time to make lunch for them.

Fan participation may also occur via web site, as Aerosmith has done well with its Notes from the Road section, chat room, and photo gallery. Similarly, Kraft spews out a slew of recipes and ideas about how to be creative with Velveeta, for example, and customers can enter contests and win up to $100,000.

DELIVER ON FANS' EXPECTATIONS

When fans attend a Rolling Stones or Eagles concert, they expect to hear a string of hits they can sing along with, performed with top-notch sound quality and delivered with high energy. Like these legendary bands, Kraft brands give customers what they expect. Kraft may not be gourmet food, but its fans don't expect it to be. They do, however, expect reliability, top-shelf quality, familiarity, and good value.

Firms must ask themselves, "Do our products really deliver the attributes consumers consider most important?" In a food company, those attributes might include taste, ease of preparation, consistency, reliability, and safety, all of which affect the overall perception of product quality. Distribution is the less observable attribute of great brands, just as road crews and staging may escape the attention of fans at a concert. But a focus on quality that customers expect has lead to a hit parade of number-one brands at Kraft, including Philadelphia, the number-one cream cheese in the world.

EVOLVE TO REMAIN RELEVANT WITHOUT ALIENATING CURRENT FANS

Many artists featured in this book are dedicated to innovation, often trying to incorporate the latest technology into their shows, musical sounds, and productions. Madonna sticks to her core brand, but innovates in terms of how she presents that brand to her fans. Neil Diamond, on the other hand, innovates by releasing new music but changing as little as possible, following more closely the adage, "If it ain't broken, don't fix it." Kraft follows a combination of the two.

A leader in the world of cheese, Kraft shows how to take an existing product and rework it a thousand ways to create new products. Building on its basic cheese formula, Kraft was the first to offer commercially packaged cheese slices in 1965. Philadelphia cream cheese now comes with pineapple, strawberries, or salmon already mixed in; Kraft sells over $1 billion annually in cream cheese alone. It put cheese in a spray can, called it Cheez Whiz (reaching a whole group of customers just dying to eat cheese from a can), and forever changed hors d'oeuvres at Middle America's dinner parties. It took fat out of Velveeta (Velveeta Lite), for calorie-conscious consumers in search of smaller waistlines, and put in jalapeños, for those wanting a little zing in their cheese loaf. Constantly innovating, Kraft now has bragging rights to a portfolio of 200 forms of cheese products—even Elton John doesn't have that many versions of "Candles in the Wind."

CREATE AN AUTHENTIC BRAND; CHOOSE AN ACCEPTED CONDUIT

Mooove over Elsie, there's a new cow in town—and she's purple. Kraft added Milka, one of Europe's leading brands of chocolate, to its vast array of brands sold in the United States. Founded by Phillippe Suchard in the mid-1800s in Neuchâtel, Switzerland, Milka transformed chocolate from a product available only to Europe's elite to a treat that could be enjoyed, and afforded, by all. Packaged in a lilac wrapper decorated with cows in a pasture, the brand is recognized around the world and reigns supreme throughout Europe as one of the most tender chocolates available. Through extensive advertising, Milka developed the personality of the lilac cow to the extent that when German schoolchildren are asked to draw a farm scene, they often color the cows purple.

As seen with Madonna, in order for a brand to be adopted by a culture, it needs to project authenticity, but Aerosmith's introduction of urban music into suburban markets also shows that acceptance in a new market often depends on how the product is introduced. Milka's long history as a leading manufacturer and popular brand of chocolate gave it authenticity among European consumers, which translated into brand authenticity among chocolate lovers in the United States. Consumer acceptance of the brand, however, was facilitated by Kraft—an established, accepted conduit through which to enter a new market. Today, you can find the lilac cow at your local Wal-Mart or Kroger.

KRAFT'S FRONT WOMAN

Kraft's brand and marketing strategies are built on six core values that serve as guiding principles or inner beliefs that define how the company operates. Some are similar to the values of other leading firms, including innovation, speed, trust, and teamwork. But two of Kraft's values pop out as different from those of the typical firm, and they parallel lessons to be learned from studying enduring rock bands. Those values are *passion* and *focus*. The company's brand includes the *promise* to bring a passion to win to everything it does, with a confidence to set high goals and an uncompromising drive to achieve them, and a focus on what matters most to consumers, and what's most important for building its people, brands, and business.

Kraft's corporate structure is unique in that it has co-CEOs—Betsy Holden and Roger Deromedi. Just as Mick Jagger and Keith Richards lead the band in different ways at different times, so do

Holden and Deromedi; it is Holden's personality, however, that makes her the Jagger of Kraft. She embodies both passion and focus in the way she energetically leads the company. A former fourth-grade schoolteacher, she entered the Kellogg School of Management at Northwestern University, where she energized case teams to excel. Before graduating, she led the fundraising campaign for a class gift, which normally raised a few thousand dollars—her class raised over $120,000.

Not surprisingly, she quickly rose in the ranks at Kraft, where today she is known for her nearly boundless energy and passion, constant contact with associates at every level throughout the company, and focus on maintaining Kraft's dominant brand positioning. People who work with Betsy report that she is still a teacher, showing *why* as well as *how* brands connect with customers so well that they become fans. Holden personifies the values of the corporation and the energy and passion of its brands with the same intensity as Jagger represents the Stones.

Kraft's overall branding strategy reads like a summary of the rock-and-roll lessons highlighted in this book. Among them: Provide consistent products of the highest quality that delight current fans, gradually change the product to remain relevant to changing lifestyles and cultures, and package products with a personality that connects with existing fans and attracts new ones. Whether for Kraft or Madonna or the Rolling Stones, it's a sound strategy that wins fans and influences profits.

STRATEGIES FOR GETTING INTO THE BRANDING HALL OF FAME

The greatest rock-and-roll bands of our time have been inducted into the Rock and Roll Hall of Fame, a contemporary masterpiece that rises above the shore of Lake Erie in downtown Cleveland. A trip to the museum is a must for music lovers—it ignites imagination, overwhelms the senses, stimulates creativity, and fills visitors with a sense of awe. The bands featured there are brands that are larger than life, representing the talent, ambition, guts, and marketing savvy that stardom requires. These bands' sagas teach what it takes for brands to become cultural icons. They also teach what it takes, at a personal level, to succeed in fulfilling dreams.

Several common themes, lessons if you will, rise from the close study of why some bands have remained successful decade after decade and why most have had a few hit songs and scurried off into oblivion. Though dozens of strategies leap from previous chapters of this book, some of the overriding principles learned from analyzing the careers of Elton John, KISS, the Rolling Stones, Aerosmith, Madonna and Neil Diamond are:

♫ Emotional connections turn customers into fans.

♫ Maintaining and adapting existing brands is more profitable than inventing new ones.

♫ Legendary brands evolve to stay culturally relevant.

♫ Passion and energy create brands people want to adopt.

♫ Being the best often evolves by borrowing from the best.

♫ Baby boomers rule much market demand.

Marketers looking to create legendary brands—those that capture a place in the fabric of mainstream culture—take note. Famous rock stars have succeeded in ways that few brands have. Here are some of the ways they've done it.

EMOTIONAL CONNECTIONS TURN CUSTOMERS INTO FANS

Studying the success stories of legendary rock bands reveals that customers buy a product, but fans invest in a relationship. When fans buy the latest Red Hot Chili Peppers CD, they invest time, money, attention, and emotion in furthering their connection to the band. Buying a concert ticket not only lets fans reinforce their ties to the Chili Peppers, but lets them add another experience to their memory scrapbooks. For fans, purchasing products and experiences is an investment in a healthy relationship they enjoy.

There are several ways legendary rock bands forge and foster emotional connections with their fans, including:

♪ *Practice reverse customer intimacy.* While much of corporate America is focused on CRM programs that help companies understand their customers better, many bands find ways to let fans get to know them more intimately. The better fans know a band through special information and personal experiences, the more likely they are to maintain a relationship with it. Aerosmith allows customers to get to know the band more intimately with remote staging and backstage tour packages, helping fans feel that they have a special relationship to the band. When the affective (emotional) components of attitudes toward a brand are firmly anchored in the cognitive (knowledge) components of an attitude, they are highly resistant to change or competitive encroachment.

♪ *Keep angel fans engaged.* Angel fans discover bands before they become stars, investing time, money and emotion in the success of the band. They take pride in the ultimate success of the band and are rewarded with bragging rights for picking a winning brand. John Mayer, 2003 Grammy winner, tells his angel fans to take tape recorders to his concerts and tape his music, which keeps them engaged in the concert experience and helps them create memories. This actually increases the likelihood that fans will buy the CD, because they will want a good-quality version of what they heard live. Whether it's the KISS Army or the Talking Heads intellectual crowd, harnessing the support of angel fans is key to the adoption of new products ranging from Google to JetBlue.

♪ *Involve customers in the brand experience.* There is a magical moment in Billy Joel and Elton John's *Face to Face* concert in which the stars stop singing and let the audience take over. Thousands of people sing the lyrics to "Piano Man" in one collective voice—it is total fan involvement in the John and Joel brands. Similarly, Harley-Davidson fans experience total brand involvement when they tour on their hogs and congregate for weekends with other enthusiasts. Though the company organizes the experiences, it mostly enjoys the ride that goes hand-in-hand with owning a brand that becomes a lifestyle.

♫ *Develop information and emotional exchanges with customers.* Brands and customers exchange information. Descriptions of product features and care and usage instructions flow from the brand to the consumer, while feedback on product performance flows from the customer back to the brand. But brands and fans go one step further and exchange emotions, from feelings of nostalgia to outright elation, that fans receive from the brand, relay back to it, and convey to others. Whereas many brands convey emotions to customers through brand attributes—from the music that is used in advertisements to product design and color—those looking to connect emotionally need to provide a conduit for fans to express their emotions as well. Web sites are becoming increasingly important in this area. Whether it's Amazon.com or Madonna.com, fans are more likely to become and remain engaged with a brand when they can communicate with it.

Each band featured in this book has connected with its fans by delivering an exceptional brand experience—not just good music on a CD, but an experience people live and remember. KISS is the king of concert experiences. To this day, fans flock to see the gruesome bunch strut around stage in makeup, costumes, and eight-inch heels, singing rock anthems of yesteryear, and setting the stage ablaze. But fans don't sit idly and watch the mayhem from their seats. They wear the makeup and costumes of their favorite band members, commune with other zealots, and live the entire concert experience.

Starbucks fans may be as close to KISS fans as you can get in the world of corporate branding. They parade down the street sipping from their Starbucks cups. They spew out orders the way KISS fans shout the words to "Rock and Roll All Night," sharing a special language that includes such words as *venti, nonfat cap, skinny, grande,* and *Frappucino.* And although attending your first Starbucks concert—er, ordering at a Starbucks for the first time—can be intimidating, new fans quickly become part of the community of other Starbucks zealots, often while surfing on their Wi-Fi enabled laptops.

How do Starbucks and KISS do it? With the right combination of product, atmospherics, and cast interaction. In addition to selling a functionally excellent product, Starbucks makes people feel part of a community or culture with an in-store experience providing individualized attention, service, options, and recognition.

MAINTAIN AND ADAPT GREAT BRANDS: IT'S MORE PROFITABLE THAN INVENTING NEW ONES

One critically important truth rises from analyzing legendary rock bands—maintaining, adapting, and improving a band's existing "product" is usually more rewarding than inventing a completely new one. Many recording labels have forgotten this lesson. In the early days they invested time and patience in the brands of their new stars, accepting a gradual rise to stardom. Today, if success isn't meteoric and if that success level isn't maintained, bands move to their label's second-class-citizen list or are dropped altogether. The label then looks for and markets the next new thing, forgoing a long-term view of the impact of the brand on the market. Individual artists have learned this lesson, however. Just as KISS's success diminished after it abandoned its full-makeup product, Prince lost a substantial portion of his following when he strayed too far from his core sound. Famed rocker Rod Stewart, although commercially successful in the 1970s, lost some of his credibility among rock-and-roll fans when he pulled on spandex tights and unleashed a string of disco hits. It took several years and a return to his bluesy version of rock to regain his position as a classic rock artist and legendary success.

No band exemplifies the principle of maintaining and improving the core product better, however, than the most successful rock-and-roll brand of all time—the Rolling Stones. The *Forty Licks* world tour was a masterful extension of the brand to new areas of the globe with new promotions and new merchandise. Fundamentally, though, it was mostly the same songs that were hits 40 years ago, borrowed from the best of Muddy Waters and other blues pioneers. Although the Stones produced several albums most years, usually they were recombinations of core songs with just enough new ones to enlist new listeners and justify the album purchase to existing fans. The bedrock of rock-and-roll product development is a greatest hits album or a new album salted heavily with tracks fans already know and love.

New products are very risky because 80 percent or more fail, simply because consumers generally don't change products with which they are satisfied. This principle stands out when studying rock music—fans continue to support the bands they like, the ones that reside on their personal all-time favorites lists. Just as new, unknown songs played at concerts, even by legends such as Paul McCartney or Elton John, are likely to be "restroom music" for lots of fans, companies also experience difficulty in getting consumers to accept something new, especially when they stray too far from their core product strength. Volkswagen, after its Aerosmith-like resurgence with the Beetle and other midmarket models, entered the luxury car market with the Phaeton—a $70,000 spectacular array of new features including a solar-powered sunroof and sensors that control both the temperature and humidity in the car, competing with Mercedes, Lexus, and Cadillac. Instead of maintaining and extending its successful Jetta or Passat brands with a SUV or other adaptations, the Phaeton was supposed to lead Volkswagen out of its middle-of-the road image into the premium market. By the end of its first year, sales totaled just 3,009 Phaetons, only a quarter of company projections. Rock legends, however, offer tips on how companies can adapt their brands and become accepted by consumers:

♫ *Evolve but remain true to your core sound or strength.* Bands that stray too far from their core sound often alienate the fans they took so long to acquire. Aerosmith's remake of "Walk This Way" spurred a brand reinvention with the perfect balance of familiarity and newness. Evolution is required if a brand is to stay relevant in the culture, but radical changes in look, feel, brand promise or personality may make the brand so different from what fans expect that it breaks the emotional ties between fan and brand.

♫ *Evolve the brand within the parameters of the brand promise.* At first blush, Madonna's brand promise seems to focus primarily on sex; however, further examination reveals it is really about challenging conventional thinking, setting trends, and zigging when everyone expects her to zag. With this definition, it is clear that her evolution from material girl to sex diva to modern mom to spiritual girl fits what her fans expect from her. Similarly, Porsche promises high-performance driving and high design, but its perceived promise among fans is to help make the person driving it more attractive to members of the opposite sex.

♪ *Alter offerings to accommodate different customer segments.* During its *Forty Licks* tour, the Rolling Stones offered three different concert experiences to fans willing and able to pay varying amounts of cash. Ticket prices ranged from $75 to $350 depending on the degree of intimacy fans wanted to experience with the band. Performing to sold-out arenas added to the iconic positioning of the band, while performing to exclusive crowds in small venues added to the aura of rarity and specialness. What people bought for upwards of $350 were special memories and an experience few will ever have.

Finding the balance between maintaining the old and introducing the new is one of the most difficult tightwires to walk for bands or brands—a balancing act in which it is easy to fall by launching radical new products or changing the brand too rapidly. When successful bands and brands don't innovate, however, they run the risk of gradually fading away like Elsie the cow, former top bovine in the once-strong portfolio of Borden brands. Radical innovations that force consumers to throw out the old in the name of the new often reach results similar to those of Pets.com, Webvan, or any other dot-bomb of the 1990s. Unlike the short-term success of these and other one-hit wonders of the e-world, eBay, in contrast, simply took a business format consumers had experienced for decades—the auctions—and migrated it to the Internet, with its enormous geographic reach compared to local auctions and flea markets. It has never strayed far from its core product, but has added technology and protection features to the point that eBay now dominates the auction business as the most profitable firm on the Internet today.

CREATE CULTURALLY RELEVANT BRANDS

Brands are often rejected if people feel they are not culturally relevant. If a product doesn't match their lifestyles, values, belief systems, or basic needs, consumers forego a new offering and stick with what they know. Innovations, whether they be new technologies or new styles, are more likely to receive mass acceptance when they are introduced through an accepted channel.

Perhaps the most poignant example of this is the migration of rhythm and blues from black culture to white culture. Elvis transformed minority music, then known as R&B, into majority music, known today as rock and roll. If it were not for the post–World War II prosperity and the economic and social environment of the massive numbers of teenagers—today's baby boomers—the transformation would have been much different, if it happened at all. To achieve cultural adoption, brands need to reflect and influence the market.

♫ *Fan retention depends on brand relevance.* Famed songwriter and performer Bob Dylan had always played folk music at the acoustic level, but as the Byrds, the Rolling Stones, and the Beatles changed the landscape of music, he ran the risk of being evolved right out of the market. Subsequently, he took folk music electric and contemporized himself. The songs were the same, the words were the same, but the delivery was altered and the relevance enhanced. Fans stuck with Dylan because he evolved to reflect changes that fans seemed to follow among other musicians.

♫ *Embrace technology, but understand how to use it best.* The Rolling Stones tried to relate to its audience's interest in the Internet by incorporating a computer interface that showed which songs audience members voted to hear. Though its execution was poor and it was quickly pulled from the show, the attempt caught the attention of the media, which credited the Stones with trying to be relevant in the new, technology-oriented marketplace. Releasing its most recent single on AOL did connect with fans, however, and positioned the band as technologically up to date.

♫ *Highlight the aspects of a brand that redefine a norm or standard.* The bands featured in this book are standouts in terms of redefining cultural norms. Mick Jagger puts a new twist on age, dispelling the notion that once you reach 60, you are doomed to a world of elastic waistbands and orthopedic shoes. Rather, he gains people's respect with his endless energy, spry body, nonstop dancing, and phenomenal performances at a lifestage at which many people have retired from far less hectic professions. Similarly, Tina Turner and Cher have redefined sexiness—proving that women over the age of 50 (and in the case of Turner, 60) can not only outperform their twenty-something counterparts, but that they can be every bit as sexy as well. Just as Jagger highlights his nonstop energy and Turner her nonstop legs, JetBlue highlights its value prices, clean interiors, efficient check-ins, and fun attitude in its brand, helping it to redefine the norm of airline travel and position it as a leader in that arena.

♩ *Predict the future with pop music.*   Music predicts the future, as probably do many of the creative arts. Sociological research journals have published studies by academicians on this topic for years, generally concluding that musicians from Mozart to Jay-Z reflect incipient trends in a culture. A half-century ago, Tennessee Ernie Ford dominated the pop charts with his hit "Sixteen Tons," foreshadowing a general awakening of public and corporate concern for the economic and physical afflictions—such as black-lung disease—and other maladies of the coal-mining industry. Fast-forward to 2003, and you may interpret the meteoric rise and success of more traditional musicians such as John Mayer, Norah Jones, and Vanessa Carlton as a desire to turn toward conservatism.

The music industry, like most others today, is dependent on perceived cultural relevance or the degree to which a brand is up to date. Few people want to be associated with a brand, style, fashion, or attitude that isn't current—it doesn't have to be the latest fad, but it has to be relevant to them to maintain favored status. Though rock and roll can be an effective crystal ball, cultural relevance is tricky for any brand, including bands, because musicians and other artisans often start as the outcasts of society and stay closely tuned to the perimeter of culture even after they attain success. In medieval Europe and England, it was the task of traveling minstrels to pick up gossip, unrest, and social concerns from the campfires of the countryside and taverns of the city and bring them into mainstream culture. In the Elizabethan days of Shakespeare, "fools" took the truth to the king or queen—hence the name of one of the best-known newspaper columns and web sites, Motley Fool, claiming to tell the truth about investing to help readers laugh their way to the bank.

What can corporate America do with the idea of listening to the fringe? In the late 1960s and early 1970s, Ron Castel, vice president of marketing at BankOne, spoke to national assemblies of bankers, recommending they attend protests (in jeans), listen to rock musicians, and visit campuses (where they would smell an aroma different from that of conventional tobacco products). It was controversial advice for the normally white-shirted, blue-suited bankers. Those who did break out of their suited environments and listened to the fringe went on to invent the automatic teller machine (ATM), point-of-sale processing of credit cards, electronic funds transfer, and a host of other innovations in banking products that eventually penetrated the majority culture.

PASSION AND ENERGY CREATE BRANDS PEOPLE WANT TO ADOPT

Jagger struts; Madonna vogues; Tyler twirls; Diamond radiates; Simmons stomps; John pounds his keys. Attend a concert by any of these superstars and you'll surmise that *the* commonality uniting them is the extraordinary degree of passion and energy they project. Night after night, city after city, these professionals take the stage and take charge of the tens of thousands of fans standing before them. They win their attention with the quality of the music they play; they captivate them, however, with the energy they emote. They never stop moving while on stage, leaving fans exhausted at the end of their two- to three-hour concerts. Leaving the venue, you'll undoubtedly hear people talk about how energetic they are. Fans respect sweat.

Brands project energy and passion as well—some just project more than others. Victoria's Secret emits an intimate form of passion, while Nike projects passion for exercise and life. Starbucks CEO Howard Schultz is passionate about coffee. Wal-Mart is passionate about consumers and giving them the best possible value. When cost savings are achieved in most firms, the savings often flow to the bottom line as higher profit margins. When Wal-Mart works with vendors to lower their costs—something it does with a passion—or works passionately to lower its own expenses, it returns those savings to consumers in the form of lower prices. In the long run, its passion for prices results in more consumers buying more items more of the time—one reason why Wal-Mart's revenues are now over one-quarter *trillion* dollars. Some firms rely on high margins, but market dominance is often achieved with velocity or rapid asset turnover. Firms with a passion for returning cost savings to consumers as lower prices master the financial magic of making a little on a lot. Though most of Wal-Mart's fans may not give much thought to the complexities of inventory turns and expense control, they connect emotionally with low prices and friendly service. Like rock and roll, they just know they like it—and they evangelize others to "attend the concert."

Energy and passion play the greatest role, perhaps, in personal branding. If you had to describe the brand called *You*, what would you say? How would other people describe you? Do you project energy and passion, or do you suck it out of others? Whether you explore these questions for personal or professional reasons, your brand affects whether people want to spend time with you or work with you. Ask yourself, who would you rather hang around—someone who mopes all day, feels sorry for themselves, is lethargic and just generally negative, or someone who smiles, gives off positive energy, and seems to enjoy life? Though the answer seems obvious, it's surprising how many people choose to settle for a personal brand that focuses on the former characteristics rather than the latter.

During the rehearsal of the 2003 Rock and Roll Hall of Fame induction ceremonies, crew, staff, and musicians alike gathered to go over lines and practice their sets. After reading through the script of the speech Steven Tyler would give that night as he inducted AC/DC into the hall of fame, he didn't leave the room like most performers. He moved off stage and into the audience area to watch the Police rehearse. Moving to different seats during the 30-minute session and occasionally singing along with Sting, Tyler watched intently as if he were making mental notes. Perhaps he was; or perhaps he was just enjoying the scene. Either way, his passion and commitment to his art was apparent. When asked later why he still does what he does, what keeps him going, he simply replied, "Passion, man, it's all about passion." He pointed to his left wrist and proudly showed a diamond bracelet that spelled the word passion.

Some people talk about wearing their emotions on their sleeves; Tyler one-ups the sentiment.

BORROW FROM THE BEST

The most obvious example of borrowing from the best lies in the evolution of rock and roll itself, which borrowed heavily from rhythm and blues, deeply rooted in black culture. Some even say rock pioneers stole the soul of African-American music, which emerged from a culture of suffering and survival to become America's most unique and globally dominating art form. Elvis was a key innovator who combined soul and gospel, the sounds that surrounded him in his youth, to create a new sound that mainstream culture gobbled up. The massification of his roots, which stemmed from exposure to black culture and music, divided pop-music culture into two eras— "B.E." and "A.E."—which not only changed contemporary music but changed cultural values around the world as well.

The transition of blues and soul to rock and roll was not limited to Elvis and Bill Haley; some first movers within minority markets, such as Louis Armstrong, Nat "King" Cole, and Chuck Berry, achieved substantial mass-market success. Following a trickle-up approach, they broke through the traditional race-based market barriers to reach and dazzle mainstream markets. But even rural blues stars like B.B. King achieved greater success because of the massification of his product by the likes of the Rolling Stones and Eric Clapton. In fact, today, his records sell to more white consumers than African-American fans.

Two white singers who helped pave the way for mainstream adoption of B.B. King were Bobby Hatfield and Bill Medley. Like Elvis, they listened to black singers such as Charlie & Ray and Jessie and Marvin, duplicating their soul-based, close-harmony songs so well that they were booked at black-oriented clubs. During one of their appearances, one fan yelled to them on stage, "That's righteous, brothers." You know how the story goes from here. Millions of records and scads of sold-out concerts later, it was clear that fans of all colors had embraced rock-and-roll sounds derived from the African-American culture. Hatfield and Medley were honored as the Righteous Brothers at the 2003 Rock and Roll Hall of Fame induction ceremonies for their "blue-eyed soul" music. At that same 2003 induction ceremony, Elton John acknowledged the debt rock and rollers owe to the blues musicians who developed the art form that led to rock and roll's dominance among global music and culture.

The principle of "Borrow from the best" lives deeply inside the walls of many stellar corporations, well illustrated by two of the most dominant brands in the world—Microsoft and Wal-Mart. DOS was the operating system licensed by Microsoft for IBM personal computers, but Bill Gates didn't write that program—it was purchased from someone else. Microsoft took an existing idea and made it a dominant product, diffusing personal computers to the masses. At Wal-Mart, Sam Walton was famed for plucking ideas from employees, competitors, and books and rolling them out fast. When a reporter asked him about borrowing ideas, he acknowledged the importance of this practice, but he added, "I always try to improve on them." The way great brands roll over everyone else is by incessant borrowing from the best—perfecting wheels, not inventing them.

BABY BOOMERS RULE!

It's a simple statement with profound ramifications for marketers. Just ask the Rolling Stones, Elton John, and Bruce Springsteen, all of whom have achieved market success in part because of their connection to the largest demographic segment in the United States. Once popular with this nostalgic, massive, and lucrative market, bands that evolve to stay relevant and remain top-shelf performers can ride the boomer wave to sustained profitability. Brands, such as Coke, have done the same.

Not only do baby boomers dominate the demographics of industrialized economies, they sit poised at the driver's seat of financial demand. In defiance of the Rolling Stones' admonition, baby boomers get satisfaction because of their freedom to spend on things they want. However, since they already have enough housing, cars, and clothing to satisfy what they need, they possess the power to withhold spending until brands deliver precisely on what they want as customers—a far cry from a decade ago when they were still paying for homes, cars, and educations. Today, the purchasing power of this group makes brand managers salivate because the likelihood of converting *interest* or *preference* into *sale* is higher among boomers than any other demographic segment.

Boomers significantly influence the consumption preferences of many products; hence, the recent resurgence of classic rock and bands such as Led Zeppelin and the Eagles. Just as music migrates as boomers move through different life stages, so also have other products followed this trend, with automobiles providing perhaps the most observable example. The 1980s were all about minivans; their personality defined baby boomers' needs for maximum capacity and flexibility to transport a cargo of kids. In the 1990s, however, cargo demands diminished and road dominance increased, leaving the SUV as the product of preference for baby boomers. In the 2000s, the personality of the auto industry reflects boomers' need for fewer seats but more experience—and sporty convertibles fit the bill well. Baby boomers will affect demand for products and services and provide growth opportunities for manufacturers, retailers, and service providers that understand the types of projected changes highlighted in Box 8.1.

The market power of baby boomers is undeniable. The strategies and nuances that have translated into bands' long-term dominance focus on staying in tune with baby boomers, who today represent an increasing proportion of music industry sales. Their most effective musical spokespersons are themselves baby boomers, and since these bands are part of this segment, relating to them is easier than for younger bands. Staying connected to them is challenging, but here are some of the ways they do it.

♪ *Relate to the desires and lifestyles of baby boomers.* Bruce Springsteen relates to sentiments representing the boomer generation, including his most recent hit, "The Rising." He touched an

BOX 8.1
What Will Baby Boomers Buy in the Next 10 Years?

Changing lifestyles and purchasing power of today's baby boomers will change their buying behavior and wants. Strategic planning of manufacturers, retailers, and service providers will be affected by these trends.

Maintenance and Parts   The old adage, "If I'd known I was going to live so long, I'd have taken better care of myself," might become the official motto of today's baby boomers. Consumers want to take care of their, skin, joints, bones, and body parts, looking beyond doctors to retailers and manufacturers for help on how to do it. Sears and Wal-Mart already sell eyeglasses, hearing aids, and prescriptions—are knees, hips, and hair far behind?

Crowded Closets   In a focus group about shopping, one consumer said nothing comes into the house unless something goes out. Hoarding unnecessary junk like our grandparents from the Depression did is out, and so is buying things to fill up an empty house like the 25- to 34-year-olds of the past. That's good news for marketers who sell stuff that people want *more* than what they already have and bad news for those who just sell stuff they hope consumers will add to the stuff they already own.

Creative Arts   As people increase the number of years they have as empty nesters, they will likely look to activities such as crafts, cooking, and foreign language or arts courses to keep them fulfilled. It's good news for retailers such as Michael's and JoAnn's and also community colleges, the University of Phoenix, executive MBA programs, and schools offering adult education.

Style over Fashion   Young consumers need the safety in numbers of fashion apparel. Muppies (mature urban professionals)

choose styles of clothing that give them comfort and good fit, having overcome the need to look like their peers and don the latest fashion craze. Consumers will be loyal to the brands and retailers, like Chico's, that provide quality, stylish, comfortable clothing they can count on.

Services Galore   As consumers age and need fewer things, the demand for services will increase. In addition to financial and travel services, consumers will want to buy more daily chore home services and life-management planning services (including career and family advice).

Home Reconfiguration   In addition to beautifying their homes with nicer furniture and decor, consumers will likely begin changing their homes to adapt to their changing lifestyles. Many will look to stay in their homes longer, opting for first-floor master suites and laundry rooms and handicap-accessible doorways and bathrooms. And those with financial freedom may buy second homes.

The bottom line is that firms need to monitor these types of trends to anticipate how aging baby boomers are likely to change their wants and buying behavior.

emotional chord in all of us with his tribute to the September 11 tragedy, but he represented well the emotions of boomers. The Rolling Stones relate to the desires of boomers to be active, energetic, and young at heart, as Aerosmith connects with the lifestyle and desires of fans who want to be young again, not defined by the traditional chronological definitions of age.

Even with the desire to be young again, boomers can't escape the realities of aging, including natural weight gain. In fact, most women in the United States today wear size 14 or higher. Lane Bryant, a 100-year-old brand in the $32-billion plus-size market, celebrates curves and uses rock and roll to help position its brand as hip and upbeat. Its 2003 fashion show featured Roseanne Barr as emcee, singer Kelly Osbourne, who endorses Lane Bryant fashions, and model Mia Tyler—daughter of Aerosmith's Steven Tyler. Lane Bryant's 2002 runway show featured KISS, singing the opening words "You show us everything you got," from "Rock and Roll All Night" as the lingerie-clad women strutted their stuff on the runway. Jennifer Peterson, director of brand development at Lane Bryant, says, "The brand is empowering women by making them feel better about themselves and their bodies." By focusing on sexy plus-size fashions with rock-and-roll stars, sales in the 18 to 34 group of women also have increased by 30 percent without losing any of the older age groups.

♫ *Use music to connect to boomers.* Whether it is Elton John's "Rocket Man" in an AT&T commercial about a father who travels a lot for work and misses his family, or Steppenwolf's "Born to be Wild" in a recent Valvoline ad, classic rock connects with boomers. Some evoke a tear; some cause even the most staid executive to play a little air guitar; all bring attention to the brand being advertised. "Using a rock song that boomers already love in an ad allows products to piggyback on established emotional connections and connect with customers," says Eric Steinhauser, vice president of J. Walter Thompson. "Breaking through the clutter is easier when they not only recognize the music but relate to it and become actively involved with it."

The power of music is massive. It enters the minds of consumers peripherally, without the filter of thinking about direct claims featured in the advertisement. Classic rock songs serve as extrasensory connectors between memories and associations stored in consumers' minds, relating the connections to new products or ads. This makes acceptance of an ad's message more likely, writing the brand indelibly into the minds of consumers, to be retrieved as they drive by stores or choose brands within the stores.

♫ *Use transgenerational appeal.* The best of rockers reach across the ages with a transgenerational appeal. You see it most vividly in the appeal of Elton John, Aerosmith, and the Stones, but it is omnipresent in the bands described in this book. They've found the sounds and emotional appeals that transcend cultural values and ages. That's what boomers want. Whether they are dining, traveling, or shopping, they like to be able to do it with their children and their parents and sometimes both. This is changing the way winning firms configure stores and advertise products.

If classic rock were a restaurant, it might well be Max & Erma's. This middle-American restaurant has achieved growth and profitability with several strategies found in these pages including transgenerational appeal. Described in food books as the inventor of the gourmet hamburger, Max & Erma's goal is to serve the best gourmet hamburgers in America and help guests enjoy their dining experience so much they can't wait to come back. The functional element of the brand—its outstanding hamburgers and other great food items—is complemented by its personality of being "the Hometown Favorite."

Breaking through any negative images chain restaurants might carry with them, Max & Erma's decorates each store differently, featuring local artwork and pictures of local sports and community heroes, and in some stores local menu favorites. The personality of the firm, however, is derived from innovative local promotions directed by Bonnie Brannigan, vice president of marketing for Max & Erma's. Some stores open to the fanfare of the local high school band marching through the streets, sometimes stopping traffic, on its way to the store's ribbon-cutting ceremony—generating television and newspaper coverage more effectively and less expensively than through media advertising.

What happens inside the store makes Max & Erma's a favorite among boomers. The music, a boomer-friendly selection, plays throughout, but at levels over which people can talk rather than yell. It also offers an eclectic food selection—one that cuts across tastes and themes—that allows children, teens, parents, and grandparents to find something they like. Because the food doesn't fall under the category of just Italian or Mexican, for example, people can eat there more often, which explains why Max & Erma's boasts twice as many frequent customers as its competitors, with lower advertising expenses. Just like the Rolling Stones, Max & Erma's figured out that it's more profitable to serve existing customers more frequently than to acquire new ones. In fact, it calculates that the lifetime value of a customer reaches over $25,000. (Unfortunately, we don't know the lifetime value of the typical Rolling Stones fan.) Whether they're soccer moms with minivans full of eager athletes, students on a date, or baby boomers who dine out frequently in a causal atmosphere, Max & Erma's creates Elton John–type fans—those that transcend a multitude of generations.

STANDING OVATIONS LEAD TO ENCORES

At first glance bands and brands may seem worlds apart, but after close consideration it's clear that they differ by little more than a letter. Both strive to create fans, going beyond what it takes to capture customer attention and delving into the realm of loyalty. Brands that maintain top-shelf positioning in consumer's minds and win market share and wallet share connect with people at a much deeper level than their competitors.

So next time the Rolling Stones, KISS, Elton John, Aerosmith, Madonna, Neil Diamond, or any other legendary band invades your town, go to the concert. Experience firsthand the emotions you and the thousands of people around you feel, and think about how to capture some of that in your brand, whether that brand is a product or yourself. These bands prove that forging emotional connections with fans and fortifying them over time leads to long-term revenue streams. That requires getting under their skin, into their souls, and connecting to something even fans have a difficult time describing.

But they feel it; they know it's there.

It's what happens when girlfriends get together and dance around to "Holiday" by Madonna. Or when guys get together and play air guitar to AC/DC's "You Shook Me All Night Long." The emotions are different, the intensity the same. The combination of emotion and intensity creates within people a devotion to the music they love and the bands that create it. It's what keeps classic rockers performing night after night, city after city. It's what keeps people buying new releases of old favorites. It's what brings audiences to their feet, screaming for another encore when the band has already played three.

It's what turns customers into fans.

Rock on.

NOTES

CHAPTER 2

1. Jon Pareles, "Eminem Becomes a Franchise," *New York Times,* June 2, 2002.
2. Marty Racine, "The Sounds of Selling: Advertisers Discover Rock 'n' Roll Can Make Them Cash," *Houston Chronicle,* August 5, 1990.

CHAPTER 3

1. Elizabeth Rosenthal, *His Song: The Musical Journey of Elton John* (New York: Billboard Books, 2001), 8.
2. Rosenthal, *His Song,* 11.
3. If you want to deepen your understanding of why people buy, we refer you to R. Blackwell, P. Miniard, and J. Engel, *Consumer Behavior,* 9th ed. (Fort Worth, Tex.: Harcourt, 2001), a reference used by corporations and universities around the world.

CHAPTER 4

1. Gene Simmons, *KISS and Makeup* (New York: Crown, 2001), 27.
2. Simmons, *KISS and Makeup,* 38.

CHAPTER 5

1. Andy Serwer, "Inside the Rolling Stones Inc.," *Fortune,* September 30, 2002, 63.
2. Interview by Ed Bradley, "The Rolling Stones: Ed Bradley Goes on Tour with the Rolling Stones," *60 Minutes* (CBS), December 18, 2002.
3. Serwer, "Inside the Rolling Stones Inc.," 64.
4. David Welch and Gerry Khermouch, "Can GM Save an Icon?" *BusinessWeek,* April 8, 2002, 60–67.

CHAPTER 6

1. Aerosmith and Stephen Davies, *Walk This Way: The Autobiography of Aerosmith,* (New York: Avon, 1997), 180.
2. Aerosmith and Davies, *Walk This Way,* 134.
3. Jon Swartz, "eBay Faithful Expect Loyalty in Return," *USA Today,* July 1, 2002, B1.
4. *Rolling Stone,* February 22, 1979, quoted in Aerosmith and Davies, *Walk This Way.*
5. David Kiley, *Getting the Bugs Out* (New York: John Wiley & Sons, Inc., 2002), 101.
6. Kiley, *Getting the Bugs Out,* 152.

CHAPTER 7

1. "Madonna's Real Life," *People,* April 2003, 84.
2. Interview by Larry King, *Larry King Live* (CNN), 2003.

INDEX